D0178197

1039
12/06

CVs
FOR
DUMMIES®

by Steve Shipside and Joyce Lain Kennedy

JOHN WILEY & SONS, LTD

CVs For Dummies®

Published by
John Wiley & Sons, Ltd
The Atrium
Southern Gate
Chichester

West Sussex

PO19 8SQ

England

089565   658 · 311 SHI

Email (for orders and customer service enquires): cs-books@wiley.co.uk

Visit our Home Page on www.wileyeurope.com or www.wiley.com

Copyright © 2004 by John Wiley & Sons, Ltd, Chichester, West Sussex, England.

Copyright © 2004 by Joyce Lain Kennedy

All Rights Reserved. No part of this publication may be reproduced, stored in a retrieval system or trans-
mitted in any form or by any means, electronic, mechanical, photocopying, recording, scanning or otherwise, except under the terms of the Copyright, Designs and Patents Act 1988 or under the terms of a
licence issued by the Copyright Licensing Agency Ltd, 90 Tottenham Court Road, London, W1T 4LP, UK,
without the permission in writing of the Publisher. Requests to the Publisher for permission should be
addressed to the Legal Department, Wiley Publishing, Inc., 10475 Crosspoint Blvd., Indianapolis, Indiana,
46256, United States, 317-572-3447, fax 317-572-4447, or e-mail permcoordinator@wiley.com

Trademarks: Wiley, the Wiley Publishing logo, For Dummies, the Dummies Man logo, A Reference for the
Rest of Us!, The Dummies Way, Dummies Daily, The Fun and Easy Way, Dummies.com and related trade
dress are trademarks or registered trademarks of John Wiley & Sons, Inc., and/or its affiliates, in the
United States and other countries, and may not be used without written permission. All other trademarks
are the property of their respective owners. John Wiley & Sons, Ltd, is not associated with any product or
vendor mentioned in this book.

LIMIT OF LIABILITY/DISCLAIMER OF WARRANTY: WHILE THE PUBLISHER AND AUTHOR HAVE USED
THEIR BEST EFFORTS IN PREPARING THIS BOOK, THEY MAKE NO REPRESENTATIONS OR WAR-
RANTIES WITH RESPECT TO THE ACCURACY OR COMPLETENESS OF THE CONTENTS OF THIS BOOK
AND SPECIFICALLY DISCLAIM ANY IMPLIED WARRANTIES OF MERCHANTABILITY OR FITNESS FOR A
PARTICULAR PURPOSE. NO WARRANTY MAY BE CREATED OR EXTENDED BY SALES REPRESENTA-
TIVES OR WRITTEN SALES MATERIALS. THE ADVICE AND STRATEGIES CONTAINED HEREIN MAY NOT
BE SUITABLE FOR YOUR SITUATION. YOU SHOULD CONSULT WITH A PROFESSIONAL WHERE APPRO-
PRIATE. NEITHER THE PUBLISHER NOR AUTHOR SHALL BE LIABLE FOR ANY LOSS OF PROFIT OR
ANY OTHER COMMERCIAL DAMAGES, INCLUDING BUT NOT LIMITED TO SPECIAL, INCIDENTAL, CON-
SEQUENTIAL, OR OTHER DAMAGES.

Wiley also publishes its books in a variety of electronic formats. Some content that appears in print may
not be available in electronic books.

British Library Cataloguing in Publication Data

A catalogue record for this book is available from the British Library

ISBN:0-7645-7017-X

Printed and bound in Great Britain by Biddles Ltd, King's Lynn, Norfolk

10 9 8 7 6 5 4 3

WILEY   is a trademark of Wiley Publishing, Inc.

About the Authors

Steve Shipside: is old enough to remember when "Give us a job" entered the language and became a business journalist not so very long after. Since then he has written for newspapers including *The Guardian*, *The Daily Telegraph* and *The Times*. He has written for a large number of business and technology magazines, including *The New Statesman*, *The Director*, *Management Today*, *Personnel Today*, *Campaign*, *Revolution*, *Wired*, *Business 2.0*, *MacUser* and the BBC's web sites. He also survived a three-year stint appearing as the "IT Industry Commentator" on Sky TV.

He is the author of half a dozen books including *Remote and Virtual Working*, *Travel,* and *e-Marketing*, all three being books from the Capstone/Wiley Express Exec series, as well as co-authoring books ranging from *100 Musts in Paris* to *The 100 Best IT companies in the UK*.

Joyce Lain Kennedy: is the author of the Tribune Media Service's twice-weekly column CAREERS NOW, in its 35th year and appearing in more than 100 newspapers and web sites.

Joyce has received more than three million reader letters. In her column, she has answered in excess of 4,800 queries from readers.

She is the author or senior author of seven career books, including *Joyce Lain Kennedy's Career Book* (McGraw-Hill), and *Electronic Job Search Revolution*, *Electronic Resume Revolution*, and *Hook Up, Get Hired! The Internet Job Search Revolution* (the last three published by John Wiley & Sons). *Resumes For Dummies* is one of a trio of job market books published under Wiley's widely popular *For Dummies* imprint. The others are *Cover Letters For Dummies* and *Job Interviews For Dummies*.

Contact Joyce at jlk@sunfeatures.com

Publisher's Acknowledgments

We're proud of this book; please send us your comments through our Dummies online registration form located at www.dummies.com/register/.

Some of the people who helped bring this book to market include the following:

Publishers Acknowledgement

Tracy Barr, Editorial Consultant

Acquisitions, Editorial, and Media Development

Executive Editor: Jason Dunne

Project Editor: Daniel Mersey

Technical Reviewers: Angela Poulter and Wendy Burns

Editorial Assistant: Samantha Clapp

Cover Photos: (c) Brand X Pictures/Cadmium

Cartoons: Ed McLachlan

Production

Project Coordinator: Regina Snyder

Layout and Graphics: Barry Offringa, Heather Ryan, Jacque Schneider, Julie Trippetti, Shae Lynn Wilson, Erin Zeltner

Proofreaders: Susan Moritz, Brian H. Walls

Indexer: TECHBOOKS Production Services

Publishing and Editorial for Consumer Dummies

Diane Graves Steele, Vice President and Publisher, Consumer Dummies

Joyce Pepple, Acquisitions Director, Consumer Dummies

Kristin A. Cocks, Product Development Director, Consumer Dummies

Michael Spring, Vice President and Publisher, Travel

Brice Gosnell, Publishing Director, Travel

Suzanne Jannetta, Editorial Director, Travel

Publishing for Technology Dummies

Andy Cummings, Vice President and Publisher, Dummies Technology/General User

Composition Services

Gerry Fahey, Vice President of Production Services

Debbie Stailey, Director of Composition Services

Contents at a Glance

Table of Contents

Introduction

Shades of déjà vu. While preparing this book, we often felt like time travellers pulled back to the first half of the last decade, trying to explain to a reading audience what an electronic CV is when they'd never heard of *keywords* or *scannable CVs* or *optical character recognition software*.

At other times, we relived the struggles of the second half of the last decade, when scannable self-marketing documents were less popular and CVs began their frenzied foray across the Internet, where, to assure safe arrival, they came dressed in the pedestrian garb of *plain text* (ASCII) embodied within e-mail. Coming up with attractive sample plain text CVs that didn't look like a telephone book without boldface type was a challenge neither we nor anyone else mastered.

But now, change is upon us once again! Big, spectacular change. Software designers in the recruitment industry have been working overtime – 24 hours a day, 7 days a week. (And if any software designers are reading this, then how about taking a break, chaps? Some of us are flat out trying to keep up!)

This book reports on the third big dramatic technological wave in the recruiting industry:

- ✔ **First wave:** Scannable CVs.
- ✔ **Second wave:** Internet plain text CVs.
- ✔ **Third wave:** The return of the handsome CV made portable and the emergence of online screening quizzes that determine whether your CV is accepted by recruiters and employers or buried at the bottom of the pile.

Chapter 1 has the intriguing details. And for good measure, this book still tells you how to deal with first- and second-wave technologies.

About This Book

Odds are that you are holding this book because you feel a need to discover what works and what doesn't work in representing yourself with a CV. This need is true whether you are:

- ✔ A new graduate starting out, a person in the the midst of their career, or a seasoned ace
- ✔ A downsized job searcher, an individual writing a CV to support a career change, a transitioning military member, or a displaced information technology professional
- ✔ A novice CV writer or a well-experienced professional CV writer

No matter what your experience, set of circumstances, or familiarity with CV writing, you've hit the bullseye with *CVs For Dummies*.

In these pages, the updated technical information – gathered from a wide variety of recruiting professionals – paired with classic strategies and smooth moves we've learned in three decades of career reporting, show you how to develop and distribute a state-of-the-art CV that says you're too superior to ignore.

It's a different job market out there: this book is the CV-writing tool that you need to stand out.

Technology Transition and Your CV

Our world is bigger and more diverse than when the employment market-place began to move from print to electronics about 20 years ago. People have more specific needs and opportunities – and deeper pitfalls to avoid.

Take just one aspect of the recruitment practice as an example: CV processing and applicant management. That activity is becoming ever more structured. Unless you are an A-list candidate – one employers fall all over themselves to hire – you may be better advised to avoid the rigid e-structures entirely or to use online resources in limited, specific ways described throughout this book.

Our mission here is to help you master change in your written word, whether you're an A-list candidate or not. The tool you'll use is a StandOut CV.

What Is a StandOut CV?

A StandOut CV is

- ✔ Carefully constructed to compete, compel, and capture attention
- ✔ Filled with skills too-rich to overlook

> ✔ Targeted to the job, showing that you can and will do the work
>
> ✔ Looks as good online as it is on paper

What You're Not to Read

The point of this book is to get you up and running (which in this case means happily employed) as soon as possible. To help you jump to the information you need and skip the bits that are optional for you we've broken the information down into bite sized chunks. Some of that will be essential for you, some of it is just nice to know and we've tried to make the difference between these sections as clear as possible. Where you see icons such as Technical Stuff then you know that it's information on how things work – interesting for some, but definitely not a must-read. Likewise any items that are boxed out from the main text are examples and asides and you may want to skip over them if you are in a hurry to get to the hardcore how-to magic.

Foolish Assumptions

You certainly don't have to be a dummy to learn from *CVs For Dummies*. In this book, we explain the way CVs work in today's high-tech world without ever blinding you with science. It is as much about the job-hunting virgin struggling with a blank CV as it is about the grizzled veteran rethinking a full CV in order to side-step ageism. Whichever you are – or if you're somewhere in between – we'll tell you everything you need to know to have a StandOut CV.

How This Book Is Organised

This book is divided into six distinct parts, and each part is divided into chapters. Here's the drill on what each part covers.

Part 1: CVs in the Changing Job Search Environment

This part covers the big picture trends and developments, and what you should do to get your CV in the right hands to be hired.

Part II: StandOut CVs for Affinity Groups

In this part, special attention is paid to recognisable groups of people – those who have been laid off, are feeling the bias of ageism, are information technology professionals who are not being hired, are leaving the military and reinventing themselves in the civilian job world, or are newly graduated and jobless.

Part III: The Making of a StandOut CV

The elements of presenting yourself as a StandOut candidate appear in this part. It explains which format to choose, offers worksheets to help you organise your information, suggests essential content material to include (and omit), describes the most powerful words to use, and explains how to think your way through deadly CV dilemmas.

Part IV: StandOut CVs Online

The three chapters in this part take you into the dimension of e-CVs, give you a script to use to determine which technology your target employer is using, point out how atypical e-CVs can work, and review the rules for scannable and plain text CVs for use in older systems.

Part V: Samples of StandOut CVs

This part presents examples of annotated StandOut CVs, arranged by career fields. Special needs CVs are included.

Part VI: The Part of Tens

For Dummies readers know that The Part of Tens is a collection of single-subject chapters that cut to the chase in a ten-point format.

In these lists of ten, we offer ways to back up your CV claims, identify actions that drive recruiters to mayhem, suggest simple adjustments to quickly improve your CV, give tips on choosing a professional CV writer, and give you a CV checklist to rate your work.

Icons Used in This Book

For Dummies signature icons are those little round pictures you see in the margins of the book. We use them to rivet your attention on key bits of information. Here's a list of the icons you find in this book and what they mean.

This icon directs your undivided attention to CV techniques that make you stand out from the crowd.

Differences of opinion are found throughout recruitment and CV writing. Nothing works 100 percent of the time for everyone in every walk of life. This icon reminds you to try to make the best choice for your situation.

Some of the points in this book are so basic or important that you'll want to commit them to memory. This icon alerts you to those points.

This icon flags information that can make a difference in the outcome of your job search.

The dinosaur icon points out outsize job-killing gaffs. Ignore these warnings, and you'll be history.

Where to Go from Here

If you're writing your first CV, the chapters in Part III offer worksheets, StandOut words, and formats to help you get it right the first time. These chapters are also a good place to get reacquainted with the world of CVs if you've been out of the job market or are unexpectedly job hunting after a layoff.

To be in tune with current standards and practices, you must check out Chapters 1 and 2 and then go to Part IV for the latest on e-CVs.

Otherwise, jump in where the topic and samples look inviting and applicable – we've done our best to make it all outstanding.

Part I
CVs in the Changing Job Search Environment

"It happens every time I start on my C.V."

In this part . . .

You find trends and developments impacting your CV that you absolutely, positively must know about to remain competitive in the whirling landscape that is recruitment today. Starting with the return of the handsome CV and the growing adoption of online screening, this part presents easy understanding of the best CV moves in an era of technology transition.

Chapter 1

New Realities: Big Changes in the World of CVs

*L*ook out everyone! Here comes the third big technological wave that's sweeping across the employment landscape. A word to the wise right from the start – getting to grips with the recruitment revolution is more critical to your job-hunting hopes than you may imagine.

Historically speaking, we raced through the first two waves in record time. In the ten years of the 1990s, job hunters learned to write (1) scannable CVs and (2) ASCII plain text CVs. The third wave is with us now, and this book describes this new technology – technology that's the basis for rethinking how you prepare your CV.

Formatted e-CVs and *online screening* are the two most dramatic developments turning up in large- and medium-sized companies in developed nations across the globe. We tell you about these two big changes in some detail and how they impact your CV. Then, in the remainder of this chapter, we give an overview of other big changes coming your way. You can find out about the rest of these changes in the rest of this book.

Below, you can read about the current state of the recruiting industry, which can help you to better understand what's happening now and what will happen next to your CV as it makes its way through the workplace steeplechase.

Unintended Consequences from a Seismic Shift in CVs

In our networked employment world of online CVs, e-mail, and applicant management systems, some of the vaunted technologies of the 1990s that were created to save recruiters' time and effort have measured up. But other technologies have produced unintended consequences brought about by staggering numbers of online CVs. The glut of CVs overloads recruiters, who are struggling to separate qualified from unqualified applicants for the jobs they're trying to fill.

These CVs are plucked from cyberspace by many elements of online recruiting that include the following: search engines, Web-savvy recruiters, job Web sites, corporate Web sites with career portals, CV distribution services, and newsgroups. But where are all these CVs coming from?

As one recruiter complained to colleagues in a recent online discussion:

> *Most job searchers no longer read job descriptions. Job ads have become a lot like horoscopes: every applicant thinks a job description describes him or her perfectly. Or if there isn't a fit at all, many job seekers reason that if they're not right for this position, maybe there's something else within the company that they're good for. Armed with an Internet connection, a list of job boards, and a CV, a job searcher can crank out about 100 applications in less than four hours.*

Job searchers aren't solely responsible for the high CV volume in cyberspace. Corporate human resources (HR) departments contribute to the nearly unmanageable workload when they fail to develop clear job requirements or use puzzling company jargon. These deficiencies force job searchers to work blindfolded, attempting to decipher inadequate postings of who or what a company is seeking.

Sometimes, the company is vague or purposely paints a rosier cast on a job than reality supports. A number of my newspaper column readers have written to me complaining that the positions they accepted are very different from their job descriptions; a single example is an undisclosed requirement to travel frequently and wear a beeper 24 hours a day.

The end result is that because of job seekers who apply for virtually every published job they come across – regardless of qualifications – and employers who write fuzzy job descriptions, the recruiting system is awash in CVs. Recruiters say most of them are unusable. Consider these examples:

✔ A recruiter working a career fair complains that, of 8,000 CVs left at his company's stand, about 60 made it back to the company's HR office. The others failed to meet the requirements of the open positions.

✔ Another recruiter reports a recent experience in which her agency posted a position for a project manager on major job boards and other free job-related sites. Some 654 applicants responded, of which 6 percent met 80 percent or more of the job's requirements and 11 percent met 51–79 percent of the job's requirements. But 82 percent failed to meet more than half of the job's requirements, and it took the recruiter two days to review the CVs to determine which ones were useful.

From the recruiter's viewpoint, taking the time to filter out about eight of ten applicants who weren't at all qualified for the job means that much less time can be spent doing in-depth assessments and negotiating and closing offers to the right candidates.

Meet the recruiting tribe

The term *recruiter* in this book is used to indicate any professional who plays a role in bringing candidates to a hiring manager's attention. The recruiter *screens* candidates, and the hiring manager *selects* candidates. The presumption is that candidates brought to a hiring manager have been checked out and possess the qualifications to do the job being filled. All recruiters read CVs.

✔ **Internal recruiters** employed by a company are also called *in-house recruiters, or corporate recruiters.* They are salaried and eligible for bonuses based on meeting targets.

✔ **External recruiters,** commonly called *headhunters* or *executive search consultants,* may also be called *third-party recruiters,* (recruiting) *agency recruiters,* or *independent recruiters.* They recruit for a variety of companies and are further divided by the way they are paid for their services:

• **Retained recruiters** are paid fees whether or not a search produces the candidate hired for the job. Retained recruiters may work on yearly retainer contracts and, like outside solicitors, are called upon when their help is needed.

• **Contingency recruiters** are paid on the transactional model — they get their money only when they deliver a candidate who is hired by their client.

Contingency recruiters vastly outnumber retained recruiters. Until the mid-management level, contingency recruiters may produce better results for your career advancement, but retained recruiters may offer the best opportunities at upper-management levels.

Hooray! The Return of the Handsome CV

The vast number of e-CVs are spun in plain text. They may read cleanly and easily for a computer, but for a human, they are eye-wateringly dull and likely to lead to sagging chins and glazing eyes amongst recruiters. Fortunately, help is here through better technology.

Do you remember – or perhaps you're too young to remember – those handsome CVs with the compelling embellishments: attractive formatting, appealing typefaces and fonts, boldfaced headings, italics, bullets, and underlining? Embellishments that were refreshing to read until technology all but killed them off a decade ago in favour of the electronically-correct but tearfully tiresome online ASCII plain text CV? (See Chapter 15 for more details on these.)

Well, the wonders of the Web will never cease, and smart technology is bringing back those good-looking specimens we grudgingly gave up in the 1990s to make sure our CVs arrived intact over the Internet. The handsome CV is making a welcome return for those CV readers who grow bleary-eyed looking at pure text day in, day out.

The new technology gang

The thrust for updated technology permitting handsome CVs to flourish comes from vendors selling technology known as *applicant tracking systems* (ATS) and *applicant management systems* (AMS). An ATS is any system, whether in software form or paper, that manages both a company's job posting and its data collection (of CVs and applications) to efficiently match prospective candidates to appropriate job openings. An AMS includes features of ATSs plus other functions, such as automated online screening.

Goodbye plain text, farewell scanning

As CV management technology evolves at breakneck speed, the end approaches not only for ASCII plain text CVs but also for scanning CVs into a system. This allows you to attach your fully formatted, word-processed, handsome CV directly into the applicant system from a Web portal. Submitting your CV through a Web portal eliminates the labour-intensive, error-plagued scanning process and allows line (department) managers who make hiring decisions to view an aesthetically pleasing formatted CV in its full glory complete with bold text, underlining, and pleasing fonts.

A portal is an entryway. A Web portal for CV submission is either a company Web site's career portal; a job site, such as Fish4Jobs or Monster; or another Web site, such as one operated by a college career centre or professional society.

How the systems work

In older applicant tracking systems, CVs are routed to managers by e-mail. A paper CV can be scanned and converted to a text file in order to do this, but the result is often an eyesore, full of errors introduced through the optical scanning process (optical scanners don't always recognise letters correctly).

Many reviewing managers see an error-studded CV and either assume that the applicant is not a detail-oriented person or that HR did a slovenly job in screening. Another feature of older systems is managerial overload. A manager could easily receive more than 20 e-mailed CVs daily in addition to all her other e-mail.

Newer systems send the manager only one e-mail: "Check your portal. You have new CVs to review." When the manager opens the portal, all the CVs are listed with a hot link to either the MS Word document or an HTML (*Hypertext Markup Language;* see Chapter 16 for more info on HTML CVs) version of the Word document. If the system includes an online screening component, the manager may choose not to look at all the CVs, but reduce their number by looking for certain specific requirements.

When the manager finishes reviewing the CVs, the appropriate recruiter in HR is automatically advised of the manager's interview choices. This streamlined process improves the staffing workflow and shortens the time it takes to bring a new employee onboard.

The rush to get onboard

New software releases by the major vendors of applicant management systems allow you to take advantage of the handsome CV option. Smaller vendors are expected to follow suit quickly or be placed at a competitive disadvantage. All major software programs accommodate these functions:

- ✔ Take in fully formatted, word-processed (MS Word, WordPerfect, for instance) CVs as an attachment
- ✔ Inventory the CVs in the original format (most often MS Word)
- ✔ Send CVs downstream to hiring managers in their original formats

The fact remains that plenty of older systems that cannot handle the format-ted handsome CV are still in use. These older systems continue to put new CVs into plain text database storage.

If your CV is already in a database at a company that has recently upgraded its applicant management system technology, your CV will remain in plain text. If you hope to work for a particular employer that already has your plain text CV in its database, should you bother to send in a handsome CV? We would.

See Chapter 14 for suggestions on how to find out whether a prospective employer uses technology that accommodates handsome CVs and, if not, what you can do about it.

Online Screening Comes of Age

Traditionally, employers checked out candidates' qualifications for a position during or after a job interview. Today's emerging technology allows automated selections to take place before the interviews are held. The online screening technology is a direct response to the congested CV marketplace. Online screening has an enormous effect on your CV's acceptance and, if you don't make it through online screening, the technology can banish your CV to the database basement.

Online screening is known by various terms – *pre-screening* and *pre-employment screening,* to mention two. By any name, the purpose of online screening is to verify that you are, in fact, a good fit for the position and that you haven't lied about your background. Employers use online screening tools (tests, assess-ment instruments, questionnaires, and so forth) to reduce and sort applicants against criteria and competencies that are important to their organisations. Sounds a touch futuristic for these shores? Don't you believe it; a survey of 500 UK companies revealed online screening of job applicants rose from 12 percent in 2000 to 54 percent by 2001.

Alastair Cartwright, the Commercial Director of recruitment consultancy Enhance Media, explains why:

> *What we've seen in online recruitment is a surge going back five years now that created a lot of response and generated a lot of CVs. The problem was that companies didn't have the technology to sift through them so that instead of saving money they ended up having to take on extra staff to deal with the response. That defeated the object, so they have since developed a number of ways to deal with that. The likes of Royal Bank of Scotland and*

Abbey National have now completely done away with the CV for their graduate programmes – instead using online personality tests. Another approach is that of United Biscuits where they start off with ten "killer" questions which have to be answered before a candidate can be considered.

The kind of questions you're likely to encounter in online screening include:

- ✔ Do you have a valid work permit?

- ✔ Are you willing to relocate?

- ✔ Do you have two or more years' experience managing a corporate communications department?

- ✔ Is your salary requirement between £25,000 and £40,000/year? (Of course, the salary figures inserted here will change from job to job.)

Answering "no" to any of these questions disqualifies you for the listed position, an automated decision that helps the recruiters thin the herd of CVs more quickly, but that could be a distinct disadvantage to you, the job searcher. Why? Well, without human interaction, you may not show enough of the stated qualifications, but you may actually have compensatory qualifications that a machine won't allow you to communicate.

On the other hand, professionals in shortage categories benefit by a quick response, such as nursing. For example: *Are you a Registered Nurse?* If the answer is "yes," the immediate response, according to a recruiter's joke, is "When can you start?"

Online screening can be described as an automated process of creating a blueprint of known requirements for a given job and then collecting information from each applicant in a standardised manner to see whether the applicant matches the blueprint. The outcomes are sent to recruiters and hiring managers.

Sample components of online screening

The following examples of online screening are not exhaustive, but they are illustrations of the most commonly encountered upfront filtering techniques:

- ✔ **Basic evaluation:** The system automatically evaluates the match between a CV's content and a job's requirement and ranks the most qualified CVs at the top.

- ✔ **Skills and knowledge testing:** The system uses tests that require applicants to prove their knowledge and skills in a specific area of expertise.

Online skills and knowledge testing is especially prevalent in information technology jobs where dealing with given computer programs is basic to job performance. Like the old-time typing tests in an HR office, there's nothing subjective about this type of quiz: You know the answers, or you don't.

✔ **Personality assessment:** The attempt to measure work-related personality traits to predict job success is one of the more controversial types of online testing. Dr Wendell Williams, a leading testing expert, says that personality tests expressly designed for hiring are in a totally different league than tests designed to measure things like communication style or personality type: "Job-related personality testing is highly job specific and tends to change with both task and job," he says. "If you are taking a generic personality test, a good rule is to either pick answers that fall in the middle of the scale or ones you think best fit the job description. This is not deception. Employers rarely conduct studies of personality test scores versus job performance and so, it really does not make much difference."

✔ **Behavioural assessment:** The system asks questions aimed at uncovering your past experience applying core competencies that the organisation requires (such as fostering teamwork, managing change) and position specific competencies (such as persuasion for sales, attention to detail for accountants). Chapter 10 further describes competencies.

✔ **Managerial assessments:** The system presents applicants with typical managerial scenarios and asks them to react. Proponents say that managerial assessments are effective for predicting performance on competencies, such as interpersonal skills, business acumen, and decision making. Dr Williams identifies the many forms these assessments can take:

- **In-tray exercises** where the applicant is given an in-tray full of problems and told to solve them

- **Analysis case studies** where the applicant is asked to read a problem and recommend a solution

- **Planning case studies** where the applicant is asked to read about a problem and recommend a step-by-step solution

- **Interaction simulations** where the applicant is asked to work out a problem with a skilled role player

- **Presentation exercises** where the applicant is asked to prepare, deliver, and defend a presentation

- **Team assessments** where the applicant is asked to work with other candidates to solve a problem or make a presentation

- **Integrity tests** where the system attempts to measure your honesty with a series of questions. You can probably spot the best answers without too much trouble.

Pros and cons

From your viewpoint, here's a snapshot of the advantages and disadvantages of online screening:

- ✔ **Advantages:** (A) In theory, a perfect online screening is totally job-based and fair to all people with equal skills. Your CV would survive the first cut based only on your ability to do well in the job. (B) You are screened out of consideration for any job you may not be able to do, saving yourself stress and keeping your track record free of false starts. (C) If you're judged a close match, you're halfway through the hiring door.

- ✔ **Disadvantages:** (A) The creation of an online process is vulnerable to human misjudgement; I'm still looking for an example of the perfect online screening system. (B) You have no chance to "make up" missing competencies or skills. (An analogy: You can read music but you don't know how to play a specific song. You can learn it quickly, but there's no space to write "quick learner.") (C) Tests may lead to test faking – not you, but job searchers who do find ways to cheat put you at a disadvantage. (D) You may be screened out of contention by impersonal software because you aren't Web savvy, but with a little computer coaching, you could do very well in the job.

Level playing field for salaries

When employers demand your salary requirements before they'll schedule an interview, you are at a disadvantage in negotiating strength. But with hundreds of Web sites giving out salary information (try Workthing – www.workthing.com), the tables are turning.

You can, with a few clicks, get a ballpark estimate of your market worth. For an additional sum, you can get a detailed report on your market value. With this information, you become a more informed and more equal partner in the negotiation. If your market rate is £45,000/year and you answer the question earlier in this section, "Is your salary requirement between £25,000 and £30,000 per year?" you can answer "no" and keep looking.

Background checks

Background checks are another component of online screening. They're booming in this era of ongoing security concerns. With your permission, employers can dig into your personal and employment history. Since employers are liable if they hire someone who doesn't have the right to work in the

UK, they can claim, quite fairly, that they have to do a certain amount of checking. Bear in mind, however, that equal opportunities legislation means that they must run exactly the same checks on everyone. Any company that asks for background information about one applicant, without doing the same for another, risks falling foul of discrimination laws.

So that you will be very careful about the accuracy of the information you convey during an online screening, here is a list of the information that an employer can legitimately look into:

- ✔ **Work status:** Since the onus is now on the employer to check that you've got correct immigration status, they can ask for a National Insurance number, birth certificate, or passport as proof that you are entitled to work in the UK.

- ✔ **References:** References are a tricky issue in the UK, as employment lawyer Colina Greenway of Klegal explains: "You can't ask for a copy of your reference from the person who gave it, but you can ask for it from the person who receives it. Even then it is subject to questions of breach of confidence. No one is obliged to give a reference, but if you give one, it must be accurate and complete. If it is misleading, then the referee could be liable. As a result a lot of employers give a very standard reference mentioning no more than dates of employment, the job title and perhaps the salary." As companies seek to protect themselves from liability, these bland references are increasingly common. That means you shouldn't necessarily worry if that's what your company gives you, nor does it necessarily ring alarm bells with prospective employers.

- ✔ **Positive vetting:** Detailed background checks are rare in the UK, and while there are exceptions, such as the security services, employers are normally careful to ensure that they have specific consent from any job applicant.

- ✔ **Medical records:** A company has to demonstrate that a) it requests the same information from all applicants and b) that this information is necessary to fulfilling the job. On the issue of HIV tests, a company can ask for one, but it has to treat everyone equally. Bearing in mind that by the end of 2003, sexual orientation will join sex, race, and ability as unlawful grounds to discriminate on, there will be an even heavier onus on companies to prove that required medical information is both relevant and non-discriminatory.

- ✔ **Credit history:** There are financially sensitive jobs that may require credit history, but remember that, under the UK's strict Data Protection laws, companies can't get access to any information that you can't. You have the right to request a copy of your own credit history. Credit histories are collected and stored by two companies, Equifax (www.equifax.co.uk) and Experian (www.experian.co.uk).

✔ **Criminal record:** Companies don't generally request your criminal record – instead you should apply for and supply a copy in a process known as *disclosure.* The body responsible for this is the Criminal Record Bureau Disclosure service (the CRB). Some employers may request your criminal record from the CRB themselves, but can only do so with your permission. More information is available at www. disclosure.gov.uk. There are different degrees of disclosure, ranging from the basic (which does not include "spent" or outdated offences) to the fully detailed.

Bear in mind that certain employers – for example schools and care organisations – have a particular duty to protect the vulnerable. These employers don't accept the simple disclosure and expect a fully detailed record.

When online screening questions ask for specific details such as your National Insurance number, think twice before supplying it. You can't be sure who is reading the information you're sending. A National Insurance number and a CV are all the data a crook needs to steal your identity. Substitute a series of "9"s in the space where the NI number is a required field. Give your NI number only when you're confident that the data is going to the right place.

Your rights in background checks

Finding derogatory information about you is not necessarily sufficient to officially disqualify you from employment. Deficiencies must be shown to be job-related, and any screening must be done equally for all.

To ensure that you are being treated fairly in a background check, remember the following:

✔ You must give signed permission for background screening to take place.

✔ You must apply for your own criminal record to be disclosed.

✔ You have the right to request a copy of any and all data about you that is held on a computer.

✔ You can insist that inaccurate information be corrected or deleted and that outdated information be stripped from your record.

To find out more about your rights, including Data Protection and employment legislation, take a look at the Department of Trade and Industry's site at www.dti.gov.uk, or try the Advisory, Conciliation and Arbitration Service's site at www.acas.org.uk.

Watch your back in screening rejection

The first thing to do to get your CV on the favoured short list of candidates: Be sure that you don't get knocked out by online screening simply because you don't know enough about the topic. Spend enough time cruising job sites and company Web site career portals to get a feel for the kinds of online screening that are apt to come your way. Take a few tests on company career portals where you really don't want to work to gain experience and increase your comfort level.

What about the online free psychology tests that aren't job specific? Don't bother with these baseless pop psychology instruments for this purpose – unless you feel you just need to get some practice interacting with online tests.

As for background checks, what can you do to protect your career against harm? Before you sign releases permitting the screening to take place, make sure your records in credit bureaus are correct. You can order a credit report from one of the national credit bureaus – Equifax or Experian – to correct errors. You can also order a credit report from each of the bureaus (they may have differing information about you) from their Web sites (`www.equifax.co.uk` and `www.experian.co.uk`).

Can your CV be turned away?

What if you get low grades on answering the screening questions – can the employer's system tell you to take your CV and get lost? In fact, companies don't "bin" a CV for the simple reason that they have to keep them to defend themselves in the event of accusations of discrimination. It's only natural, however, that if a company sets criteria and you don't measure up, you're not doing yourself any favours. As Joe Slavin, MD of Monster UK puts it:

> For a company that's dealing with the digital tsunami of CVs, the sensible thing is to look at the vacancy and come up with five questions that a candidate has to ask to get in the inbox – key questions like the number of years of experience. That's what we recommend to our clients, and we practice what we preach so, for example, there's a position right now in our organisation for a business development person. The only way into my inbox is to answer those five questions right because my Nirvana, like everyone else's, is to have just a handful of CVs left to look at – all of them good.

The bottom line is, if you don't score well in screening questions, your CV will be exiled to an electronic no-hire zone even if it isn't physically turned away.

TIP

Jumping through hoops

Job seekers complain that recruiters expect you to do far too much work before giving you an inkling that you're a contender for a position. When you post your CV, you may be instructed to also fill out a lengthy job application, breaking down your CV item by item, and filling out a long skills summary. You may be asked to do all this task online or through autoresponder e-mail.

When these demands are made, turn to your completed worksheets (that you can find out about in Chapter 13) for a quick tool.

The future of online screening

If all the online screening technology is beginning to feel like Big Brother, unfortunately, you can do little to avoid it entirely if you submit e-CVs through the portals specified by job ads.

But take heart: the vast majority of employers do not use the online screening technologies yet. And when, as demographers predict, the job market again becomes employee-driven, the rush to do online screening may slow down.

Employers who haven't adopted online screening say they forego the technology for a number of reasons. The two big ones: a lack of knowledge of online screening and scepticism about the results that its advocates claim.

More Big Changes on the Workplace Horizon

In addition to the handsome CV and online screening trends, other developments also influence how effectively your CV travels. Employers and job seekers alike are making great use of the Internet so having both a paper and an electronic CV has become more important than ever.

Job sites

Surveys report that the big general employment sites (such as Monster, WorkThing, and TotalJobs) aren't always the ones responsible for high numbers of job offers. In part, the reason is due to the growth of specialist sites and company Web career portals. Chapter 2 tells you more about these sites.

Company Web career portals

Almost all big corporations now operate company Web sites with career portals. This makes it easy to directly apply to the companies that you'd most like to work for.

Employee referral programs

The practice of employers asking their own workforce, "Do you know anyone who might be good for this job?" has blossomed into widely used formal employee referral programs in which bonuses are paid for each candidate hired. A strongly referred candidate is usually seen as preferable to someone off the street. In tempo with advertising, employee referral programs rise when too few unemployed look for work and slow down when too many unemployed look for work.

Profile-based systems

Profile-based systems are designed to bypass keyword searches entirely by standardising data fields on which the recruiter can search. (The e-forms described in Chapter 15 are also short forms, but profiles contain far more structured details.)

Basically, you dissect small pieces of your overall self-marketing information into specific data fields (boxes), which are filed in a company or job site database. You may use the site's automated CV-builder, answer lengthy questionnaires, cut-and-paste data from your plain text CV – or, in some systems, you may be asked to build a profile of yourself online.

Profiles often require that you express your preferences by naming your desired salary range, work location, job function, travel, work schedule, and so forth (a version of online screening).

Some companies, such as Predict Success.com and HR Technologies specialise in helping employers develop online competency questions (see Chapter 10) used to develop the applicant's profile. The profile is measured against a position model to predict whether a person has the skill set to succeed in a position.

Creating a standardised format that compares apples to apples is done for the convenience of recruiters. If you have superb qualifications, profiles can lift you above the competition. But, because the vast majority of job seekers don't fall in that category, profiling can work against you. In profiling, you are negotiating 100 percent on the employer's terms without the opportunity to express unique skills, an uncommon experience mix, or compensatory characteristics if certain requirements of data fields are missing in your background. The image of "robo-CV" comes to mind when I think of profiles!

XML technology

A decade ago everyone thought that *Hypertext Markup Language* (HTML) CVs would be the next big thing, but the technology never really took off. Most employers tell me that they receive less than 1 percent of their CVs in HTML.

XML *(eXtensible Markup Language)* is the new technology that allows staffing systems and payroll systems to talk to each other. An independent, non-profit worldwide consortium of companies, HR-XML, is attempting to develop standards for exchanging workforce staffing and management information between HR specialists.

HTML is a series of tags that are hidden (embedded) in a Web document and that point out how to mark up the text and pictures. HTML tags include layout descriptions to say, for example, that this text is in bold, or double size, or should be in a box in the top left-hand corner. XML is an extension of HTML that adds new tags so that the document not only "knows" that this line of text is in bold, but that it is also the name of the job applicant. Similarly XML tags can say that not only is this text in a box, but also that it is a list of previous jobs or an address field. The idea is that, if properly tagged, any CV laid out with XML would be readable by recruiter databases without any further modification.

The advantages are clear to recruiting insiders, but with so many other technologies to digest at once, the chances are that XML will remain one to watch, rather than one to worry about, for the time being.

Volatile job market

Economists say the *human capital marketplace* (latest buzzword for job market) should expect endless cycles of hiring/layoff at the same company. This prediction seems reasonable if the past decade is a clue, suggesting you keep your CV current, register with online job agents, maintain a network of employment contacts, remain visible in professional organisations, and follow tips for handling temporary jobs on your CV (see Chapters 4 and 12 for more details).

Human networking

If you are a job seeker with doubts about your job qualifications, age, or employability and fear you may run into a brick wall on the Web, stick with human-based job search. A survey of UK companies by TotalJobs showed that 60 percent of organisations considered themselves "still at an early stage" in terms of Internet recruitment, and the majority of small businesses don't use electronic methods at all. You can find tips on finding employment the old-fashioned way throughout this book.

But don't throw out your Paper CV

Despite the growing use of technology, your paper CV still has its place. Professionals in the e-recruiting industry have been trying to exterminate paper CVs for a half-dozen years, proclaiming them all but dead. But paper CVs are alive and well and will survive for use in local or regional job markets during the next decade – perhaps even longer. Among reasons why paper survives:

- **Paper to have and to hold:** Hiring managers, as well as recruiters, may like a tangible paper to feel, view, and save.

- **Job fairs:** Using e-CVs at some brick-and-mortar job fairs is possible, but paper CVs are the norm because they're easy to distribute.

- **Advertising mail address:** Job ads that include postal addresses keep the paper alternative in place.

- **Employee referral programs:** Companies that haven't converted employee referrals to Web processes often retain a form that instructs referring workers to clip a paper CV to the form before submitting a name to the HR department.

Chapter 2

Get Your CV Out There

In This Chapter

▶ Succeeding with a ten-step placement plan

▶ Using personal job agents

▶ Unravelling the real deal about job sites

▶ Safeguarding your privacy and credentials online

▶ Networking inside and outside companies

▶ Following up in professional style

*T*his chapter puts the cart before the horse. The water skier before the boat. The train before the engine. You get the point?

Suggestions on how to distribute your StandOut CVs before you've written a word come up front in this book because so much has changed during the past couple of years that knowing how you'll *use* your CV could help you do a better job of *writing* your CV.

Ready? Try on these ideas for size.

Marketing Your CV in Ten Steps

No matter how good your CV, it needs to get read to be appreciated. Follow these steps to get your CV to the right place:

1. **Target your job market.**

2. **Make a master list of job leads.**

3. **Take care of housekeeping chores.**

4. **Draft your CV(s).**

   5. **Draft back-up self-marketing CV content.**

   6. **Draft your cover letters and cover notes.**

   7. **Review today's submission technology.**

   8. **Save your CVs and cover letters in useful formats.**

   9. **Determine your online CV Strategy.**

   10. **Keep track of your progress.**

The following sections explain these steps in detail.

Step 1: Target your job market

You may not know precisely what you want, but having one to three choices can shorten your search. Choose an occupation, industry, company size, and location you think you'd like. For example, you may want a job, using your education in electrical engineering, in a medium-sized company in Sheffield or the Thames Valley. Or you may want to work in a non-profit organisation as an event planner in Westminster. In both cases, you'd want to check out specialist sites for your occupation.

You can be flexible and change directions if opportunity strikes.

Step 2: Make a master list of job leads

Identify and research potential employers that may be a good fit. At each company, try to uncover the name of the individual who is responsible for hiring people for the position you want. Here are resources for your list:

- ✔ **Job sites:** Big super sites like WorkThing, TotalJobs, and Monster, and specialist sites that relate to your occupation and job title, industry, and geographical location.

- ✔ **Newspapers:** Classified and larger display job ads, plus business page articles.

- ✔ **Business directories, trade publications, and other sources of company information:** The Financial Times (www.ft.com), Hoover's Online (www.hoovers.com/uk), and PR Newswire (wwww.prnewswire.co.uk), are three examples.

- ✔ **Networking groups:** Both local and functional; both online and offline.

- ✔ **Recruiting firms:** Independent, third-party.

- ✔ **Professional organisations:** In your career field.

✔ **College or university:** Glean contact details of your friends and peers from school or college from Friends Reunited (`www.friendsreunited.com`); school ties can sometimes help you out (unless you were the school bully!).

✔ **People:** Family, friends, neighbours, former co-workers, bankers, social organisation members, job club members, former professors.

✔ **Referrals:** Acquaintances and friends who work at companies you admire, and referrals from people you contact who don't know of a job opening but can give you more names to contact.

Step 3: Take care of housekeeping chores

There are many "little extras" that can help get your foot in the door. Some of the better ideas include:

✔ **Get a free e-mail address:** You can get a free e-mail address from Hotmail (`hotmail.com`) or Yahoo! (`yahoomail.com`). Be sure to check each and every one of your e-mailboxes every day. And while you're at it, why not rent a post office (PO) box and install a phone with an answering machine if you intend to add that layer of privacy to your search.

If you're a student, definitely get another e-mail address. Most college students get a free e-mail address on campus that ends with the extension.ac.uk – a dead give-away for student status. Many employers, who really want from one to three years' experience, won't consider CVs with .ac.uk in the e-mail address. Get another address for job hunting so that you can at least make the first cut.

✔ **Consider using split personalities:** Suppose you want to present yourself as a candidate in two occupations or career fields in the same database. You're looking for a job as a convention planner or a market representative. Or as a controller or internal auditor. Most databases are programmed to replace CV number one with CV number two, under the assumption that CV number two is an update.

If you want to be considered for two types of jobs, consideration may come automatically as a job computer searches the CV database for keywords. But if you want to double up to be sure, use your full name on CV number one. On CV number two, cut back your first and middle names to initials and change telephone numbers and e-mail addresses.

✔ **Self-send first:** Before sending out your CV, send it to yourself and a friend to compare and correct. It's surprising what you can miss the first time around.

✔ **Double-check your Web page:** Before making your Web CV address public by putting it on other types of CVs, review your site for links that you may have forgotten you added in a more carefree period. Stories of links to employment-killing naked lady pictures and bawdy jokes continue to circulate. And don't provide links to your school class or professional society; employers may slip out and find better candidates than you. Finally, if confidentiality is important, don't forget to password-protect your Web page. When employers call, give them the password. If you don't know how to password-protect your site, ask your Web site host or Internet service provider for instructions. You can read more about setting up Web CVs in Chapter 16.

✔ **Practice online testing:** Some employers, weary of having their databases crammed with candidates who don't meet their skill standards, are requiring that jobs seekers take a screening test before their CVs are allowed inside (see Chapter 1 for more about pre-screening).

✔ **Be mindful of legal issues:** Remember that CV banks must obey equal opportunities laws: Don't reveal any potentially discriminatory information (age, race, gender, religion, sexual orientation) by e-mail to a representative of a CV bank or job site that you would not reveal in a telephone call or during an in-person job interview. Assume the information will be passed on to employers.

✔ **Bookmark favourite job sites and search tools:** Add your favourite sites to your Internet Bookmarks and, on a regular basis, make a focused search by job title, industry, or geographical location. You could, for example, ask a site to show a list of all open jobs for emergency medical technicians in Glasgow.

Step 4: Draft your CV(s)

Create more than one CV if possible (see Chapter 8). Shape several different CVs: one general version plus several others that address the finer points of functions you want to do – for example, accountant, internal auditor, tax specialist.

Make sure your CV contains the relevant keywords (see Chapter 11) because, in a word-matching keyword search, your CV will be stuck to the bottom of a database if it lacks the required words.

Step 5: Draft back-up self-marketing CV content

Create mix-and-match text blocks for a fast tune-up of your CVs and cover letters. Write a variety of paragraphs and store them on your computer. Need ideas of what to say in the paragraphs? Read over CVs of others in your field and be inspired. Then, when you must quickly put together a CV targeted to a specific job – and none of your full-blown CV versions are perfect – your inventory of text blocks gives you a running start.

Step 6: Draft your cover letters and cover notes

Draft several cover letters and the shorter version, cover notes. *Cover Letters For Dummies* (Wiley) offers state-of-the-art tips on writing dynamic statements.

Step 7: Review today's submission technology

The handsome CV is making a comeback (we're really glad about this – see Chapter 1). But until the new technology completely drives out the old, telephone an employer about any job that's very important to you and enquire about that specific company's technology (see Chapter 14). When in doubt, paste your ASCII text cover letter and CV in the body of the e-mail message and attach a formatted Word or WordPerfect CV. The ASCII CV is backup in case the employer is using an old system and can't or doesn't download your formatted CV.

Step 8: Save your CVs and cover letters in useful formats

Ready your CV packages for battle by saving them on your hard drive and a floppy disk if you transmit CVs from more than one location. If you move around a lot, you may want to have a password-protected copy stored on your ISP's server. That way you (and only you) can access it, edit it, and send it wherever you have web access. Most ISPs allow plenty of storage space for this. Wherever you choose to save your CV, one version should be in MS Word or WordPerfect and the other in ASCII plain text. See Chapter 14 for specifics.

Making sure that the right people get it

If you send your CV to a hiring manager (good idea), send a duplicate to the human resource department. Note this effort in your cover letter to the hiring manager, which means that not only is the human resource professional not treated disrespectfully, but the hiring manager gets to keep your CV as a constant reminder of you instead of having to send it down to HR.

Making 100 per cent sure that you have the right names for both of these individuals shows that you have a flair for accuracy and that you care enough about the company to do your home-work properly. A quick phone call to a com-pany's reception desk usually equips you with the right people's names.

Step 9: Determine your online CV strategy

If privacy issues are of concern to you, you may choose any of several strategies:

- **Conservatively confidential:** No online posting of your CV, except as a response to specific job listings or to a targeted mailing list of potential employers. You take care to protect your identity. You plan to work with one or more recruiters (you understand that third-party recruiters are paid for finding the best candidates and will likely ignore you if you are spread all over the Net and can be hired for free).

- **Moderate exposure:** In addition to the conservative exposure just men-tioned, you are highly selective about the CV databases and personal job agents you submit your CV to. You may or may not cloak your iden-tity. You understand the privacy policy of the job sites you select.

- **Full visibility:** You are unemployed and need a job quickly. You post to every logical job site you can find. You want immediate action and are pulling out all the stops. You have read this chapter and know the pros and cons of such a move.

Step 10: Keep track of your progress

Don't let important aspects of your online activity get away from you. Keep records of where you submitted your CV, which personal job search agents are alerting you to the best job posts, and which source of job listings are proving to hold the most potential for you. Make mid-course corrections when needed.

When should your CV arrive? Mondays are busy days, and Fridays are practically the weekend. Try for arrival on Tuesday, Wednesday, or Thursday.

Sending Your CV the Right Way to the Right Places

Deciding whether to post your CV at a big job site or stick with the traditional paper CV is a decision deserving some thought. The following sections explore the options.

The good and bad of big online job sites

Even Net-savvy job searchers write to us saying they're becoming disenchanted with big online job sites:

> *I keep sending CVs for jobs to big job boards (generalised super sites), however I never hear anything back from them. As yet, I have never been contacted. I fill out the CV and make it specific to the job advertised. What am I doing wrong?*

> *I have sent out my CV to a number of positions posted on sites like (big job board), and I have noticed that a number of these positions stay posted for weeks on end. What is the average response to jobs posted on the Web? Are people actually hired from these sites?*

Back in 1995, a time when dinosaurs ruled the earth in terms of the Internet, advisers, including us, urged job seekers to get aboard the Web wagon or be left behind. The message was received around the world. Nearly a decade later, the online novelty has vanished as millions of job seekers found out how easy it is to pop a CV online and have done so.

As an unintended consequence, the CV cascade has overwhelmed the hiring managers. The online job sites are delivering virtual bodies but not many job offers and acceptances, according to recent studies. A study by employment consultancy Enhanced Media in 2003 suggests that 39 percent of jobseekers visited a generic recruitment site because they found it through a search engine or link, compared to 13 percent who were attracted by the advertising and only 7 percent who thought the site had the best selection of jobs. That doesn't mean that general sites have had their day. Monster UK, for example, aims to have a million online CVs by the end of 2003. It currently claims 600,000 CVs and 1.5 million employers looking at them, but there's no doubt that in some fields, specialist sites or company-specific web portals are a better bet.

Warning: Watch out for the black hole at major job boards

Recruiter Mary Nurrenbrock doesn't sugar-coat it when describing her view of the practice of responding to jobs advertised on the major job boards:

"When you respond to openings directly through job boards, your CV usually ends up in a black hole, a passive database. If you are responding right from the board, it's going to HR. Bad move. These guys are up to their eyeballs and usually don't even really know what the hiring manager is looking for. That is, if the HR person even sees the CV in the passive database.

"You need to get to the hiring manager, not HR. How? When you visit a job board and see a job that looks like it's a fit (you notice I didn't say that it looks interesting), go to that company's Web site and get a name. Most of the corporate sites have profiles. Get the name of the VP Marketing, CEO, CMO – whoever the open position is likely to report to.

"Figuring out the address isn't hard. Look under the press releases where you'll usually find a company contact e-mail address. Use the same format – joe_bloggs@, joe.bloggs@, jbloggs@ – to send your CV. If it bounces back, try a different format. If that doesn't work, try to get the address from the company receptionist. If all else fails, snail mail it.

"What usually happens next is that the hiring manager sends your CV to HR. But we are trying to avoid that, right? No, we are trying to avoid the black hole. Now the HR person is looking at a CV that came to her from an internal source. Big difference!"

The giant job boards do offer several advantages when you're floating your CV:

- ✔ Excellent for entry-level jobs with big corporations like Microsoft and Proctor & Gamble.

- ✔ Excellent for job searchers with broadly applicable skills, such as sales and marketing.

- ✔ Excellent for a number of fancy tools, such as job title converters that help job seekers figure out what their job title would be in other companies or career fields.

- ✔ More focused sections or channels (like healthcare and legal jobs) are being added to emulate the appeal of the niche job sites.

You shouldn't decide that, because of the low rate of hires, you're never going to speak to the Web again and that's that. As unsatisfying as the Web can be for the actual hook-up of people and jobs at the moment, the clock won't be turned back. Consider online searching as merely one more option in your tool kit.

Our recommendation? Use one or two major job boards, and devote the rest of your online time to the specialist sites and the corporate sites.

Specialist Web sites: Why smaller may be better

The super-generalised job sites – TotalJobs, Monster, and WorkThing – have been compared to broadcast TV, appealing to a very wide, diverse audience. Specialist sites, by contrast, operate a narrowcast model more like cable networks where channels like UK Gold and MTV are targeted to very specific groups of viewers.

The future of online job searching: Specialist and specificity

Generic broad-based Web recruiting is giving way to narrowly focused recruiting. And as go the recruiting sites, so go your CVs. I don't even want to guess how many specialist sites sit on the Net waiting to welcome computer-loveable CVs, but there are more than you could shake your CV at. Every profession, locality, industry, and lifestyle is joined by networking hubs and entrepreneurial watering holes catering to the select Web communities they target.

Guides to online resources

The comings and goings of dot.coms/dot gones means that finding reliable advice online is a bit of a moving target. That said, a few organisations can help make sense of the range of sites on offer in the UK. Support4Learning (www.support4learning.org.uk) is a general site aimed at students and those in the education sector but if you go to its Jobsearch section (wwww.support4learning.org.uk/jobsearch), you'll find a guide to using UK online recruitment agencies and an updated list of who's who and what's what in the job market. Although this site is intended for students and teachers, it's a pretty good guide to the scene for anyone looking for work online.

The Chartered Management Institute (www.inst-mgt.org.uk) also has links to listings pages lurking under the slightly misleading title of 'Managing Yourself' (www.inst-mgt.org.uk/external/manskill/self.html). Here you can find a list not only of job hunting sites but also of careers portals, advice centres, career development advice, and such things as stress management and emotional support sites.

UK Recruiter (www.ukrecruiter.co.uk), intended for use by the recruitment industry itself, also provides a lot of helpful advice and links. You don't have to hanker after a career in headhunting to benefit from UK Recruiter's inside information and horse's mouth advice on job hunting and current online recruitment sites.

Job seeker connects through specialist site

An acquaintance of ours, David, a consultant, spent more than 30 minutes building his CV on a super job site, filling out multiple screens of information and tick boxes. David wasn't a happy bunny because he already had a CV he liked, but he went along with the drill. Nothing happened.

David finally tried a local job board, a community site. Happily, this site let David cut and paste his own CV. Within a day, David got two calls for interviews that fit his requirements while his mandated super job site CV slept the sleep of the dead.

Specialist sites, by their nature, are more liable to appear and then melt away than their big generalist brothers. To get an idea of what's out there, try looking at directories that list the specialist sites, rather than trying to find each and every one individually. Some sample directories of specialist recruiters include the listings at Support4Learning (`www.support4learning.org.uk/jobsearch/jobs_special.htm`) or the UK Jobs Guide (`www.ukjobsguide.co.uk`), which has a handy listing of specialist recruitment sites.

When specialist sites shine

The reasons to customise your job hunt by posting your CV on small sites are the following:

- ✔ More focused job listings for your purposes.

- ✔ Fewer cumbersome procedures to post a CV.

- ✔ More control over what your CV looks like. Big general job boards tend to insist on a chronological job history format when using a project-oriented or functional approach may be more to your advantage. (See profiles of these different CVs in Chapter 16.)

- ✔ May limit listings by headhunters, which make up a heavy percentage of ads on super sites. Headhunters often don't name the potential employer, which could be a problem if it's your own company.

- ✔ Appear to have a higher percentage of mid- and upper-management jobs than the general super sites.

- ✔ Many job seekers say they like the smaller specialist sites' manageable size, better quality listings, and community feel.

Hail the corporate Web site

In the days before computers and the Internet, when you went directly to companies to apply for a job – without knowing whether any openings were available – the job search method was called "direct application". Today, you can still use the direct application method, but you do it online at corporate Web sites that recruit through their *career portals* (gateways).

A joint study by the Cranfield School of Management and the *Daily Telegraph* showed that, by end of 2002, the number of UK companies using the Internet for recruitment had reached over 50 percent (up from just 17 percent in 1999). Over the same period, however, the study suggested that while 40 percent of organisations used super sites for job ads back in 1999, that figure had fallen to 25 percent in 2002. The loss is put down to the number that have taken to advertising on their own corporate sites – some 43 percent of organisations now advertise via their own sites. This trend is sure to spread because it means companies can limit the fees they pay to third-party recruiters while building their own database of potential candidates for jobs. As software tools are marketed to help manage that process, companies also have an answer to the deluge of digital CVs and can safely encourage more without drowning their HR departments.

The following sections offer some things to bear in mind when submitting your CV to a corporate Web site.

Target your search

Although major commercial job sites, such as Monster.com, are centralised, the universe of corporate Web sites is decentralised. Exploring that universe is time consuming. You can easily spend two hours taking the measure of just one or two corporate career portals, picking up details of what you should know to maximise opportunity.

Begin by compiling a list of prospective employers. To prioritise the list, you can use company briefings on Hoovers (www.hoovers.com/uk) and other online company directories mentioned in Chapter 8, as well as information from newspapers and business magazines.

Another way to compile your list is to search large job sites – job boards, such as WorkThing or TotalJobs – to sort opportunities by location, by job function, or by industry. Verify appealing job ads on the corporate Web site.

Notice company interests

As you scan a corporate career portal, back up to the company home page and click to press releases, annual report, and general areas for any edge you can use to enhance your application when you move to the careers area.

Understand procedure

About the only standard advice for sending your CV to corporate Web sites is to submit information in a digital version only. Skip postal mail and fax (see the sidebar "Why two-for-one doesn't add up" for why).

Why two-for-one doesn't add up

To make doubly sure that your CV is in a database for a job you really want, should you postal mail a duplicate hard copy as a backup in case a clerk messes up the electronic file?

No. When the company's career page directs you to e-mail your CV or to submit it via the company's online CV builder, do not send in a hard copy to the HR department because the hard copy would more than likely be scanned, found to be a duplicate, and deleted. This unnecessary extra work causes a scowl on the poor scanning operator's face and doesn't get you anywhere. The only time to send in a hard copy is to a hiring manager.

If company managers wanted duplicates to clog their files with paper, they wouldn't have installed the more efficient electronic recruiting systems.

As technical reviewer Jim Lemke says, "With any system, once you submit your CV, you are in the pond. There is no need to send another CV through the system at the same time."

Pay attention to specific instructions on each corporation's site. Some corporate Web sites ask you to attach your CV. Others require that you cut and paste it into a standard form, or use the site's CV builder.

If you attach your formatted CV (my preference if it's an option) and can't decide whether to kick off with an objective and or skills summary (see Chapter 10), try both, like this.

> *Objective: Position at (name or type of company) in (general location) requiring a stand-out performer with the following skills and characteristics: (insert your keyword profile, as discussed in Chapters 9 and 10).*

Additionally, don't be surprised if you're asked to take online employment tests. Be ready to provide good information on your skills and interests.

Some corporate sites won't accept anonymous candidates who cloak their identity.

Use paper CVs to rescue your career

Remember that the Web is just one more pebble on the employment beach. A big pebble to be sure, but, let's face it, some job hunters are never going to get past the E-Gatekeeping Godzilla (Internet recruiting systems) because they are too old, too young, have the wrong skills, or whatever.

Evaluate why your online search isn't working

Is your online job search in trouble? Review this checklist and see which reason(s) could be at fault. Some job hunters:

☐ Strike out in e-job search because they refuse to invest the effort to learn the ropes.

☐ Come up with zero online because they just don't get this Internet thing, never did, never will and no longer care.

☐ Never lift off with their searches because their CVs lack the right keywords and accomplishment content.

☐ Bump into a wall of silence because their skills are not in demand and possibly are obsolete.

☐ Are ignored in today's youth culture because they're older ("overqualified") than the people employers want to hire.

☐ Are shut out because they're on the other end of the age discrimination spectrum – too young. Employers say they want a minimum of several years of current experience.

☐ Don't make it past the online screening programs because they lack the knowledge, competencies, skills, or ability to respond correctly to programmed questions.

☐ Never hear back because employers just aren't on a hiring spree.

Could this be you? Before cursing the darkness of a failed job search, decide whether you want to (A) improve your online search techniques or (B) decide the computer is rotting your mind and ditch the whole digital thing.

Go back to finding jobs the classic way

If you have reason to think you belong in the Internet expatriate class and your chances of finding a job by e-efforts (even if the "e" stands for excellence) are nil, my best suggestion is head back to job hunting the way it was before the Web arrived and wasted your time.

Use your paper CV as your marketing tool of choice when you turn to newspapers and trade publications to find out who's hiring. Use your paper CV as your calling card while networking person to person and finding employment thanks to human intervention. Use your paper CV as your ace when cold-calling hiring managers, many of whom dislike reading computer screens and like the feel of a piece of paper in their hands.

As we often say, when the machines seem to be beating you, use people to beat the machines. Some good opportunities will always be captured the old-fashioned way.

E-mail, post, or fax

A reader's letter to us: "A very simple, but important question: If you are asked to e-mail, fax, or post a CV to a prospective employer, what is the best way to send it?"

When a delivery mode preference isn't specified, we'd suggest e-mail because it's easier to inventory in a database and send downstream to hiring managers. Next choice, we'd send it by post (making sure it is scannable, see Chapter 15) and, as a last resort, fax.

Taking Online Issues into Account

As you submit your CVs electronically here, there, and everywhere, you need to be aware that there are tricks and tips specific to using the Web. These sections address those related to sharing your CV.

Respecting the difference between CV posting and CV blasting

Which do you do? Not sure? Well, CV posters understand the difference between quality and quantity and chose to place their CVs only on a few select sites. By contrast, CV blasters indiscriminately chuck out CVs like confetti all over the Internet.

CV posting

CV posting should be an exercise in thoughtful placement. If you do it yourself, you exercise 95 percent control. The other 5 percent is a wild card – despite privacy statements, job sites, and corporate Web sites have been known to "migrate" CVs to databases you don't know about. (Read about privacy protection issues later in this chapter.)

If you decide to post to a limited number of sites, heed these tips:

- ✔ Choose sites where you need not register first to search for jobs.
- ✔ Determine the control you have over your CV. On a case-by-case basis, what you want is the ability to choose when to release your CV to an employer listing a job you may want. The ability to say "yes" or "no" really shouldn't be negotiable if you want to control your own information.

✔ Determine the access you have to your CV. You want to be able to edit it (adding new facts or targeting it each time you apply for a different job), delete it entirely, and if your CV is expunged after a certain time period, you want to be able to easily renew it.

If you do want to post with caution but also want to save hours and hours, consider a CV-posting service that allows you to choose which sites receive your CV, give login information for each site, and allow you to apply directly to each site. Posting services allow you to select industry categories to apply to and so leave the job of finding industry specific recruiters to someone else. The service is usually free – take a look, for example, at CV Poster (www.cvposter.com).

Ed's attachment etiquette

"If you are attaching something, consider the following guidelines when doing so", says Ed Struzik, president of BEKS Data Services, Inc. (beks@beksdata.com). Struzik speaks from a dozen-years' vantage point in providing out-sourced CV processing services and applicant tracking system consulting to numerous Fortune 100 companies.

Do Not attach EXE files. An EXEcutable file could contain a virus, and no one will chance having the hard drive or network infected.

Do Not attach ZIP files. Who's to say the ZIP file doesn't contain an infected EXEcutable. And besides, can your CV be so large that you have to ZIP it?

Do Not attach password-protected documents. How would you expect someone or something to open it without the password?

Do Not attach documents with contact info in headers or footers. This one seems innocent enough. But the fact is, doing a "Select All" to copy/paste your CV may not capture your name, address, etc. if they are in header or footer data.

Do Not attach documents with text boxes. Another seemingly innocent situation. But again, doing a "Select All" to copy/paste your CV may not get the text box.

Do Not attach forwarded messages. In most mail systems, you have the option to "attach" a forwarded message or "include" the text of a forwarded message. For a number of reasons, choose "include" the text.

Remember that many company firewalls (the software that protects their system from unwanted intruders) may be set to simply strip-out any pictures or attachments. Even HTML may be switched off in the email reader at the other end, meaning that your beautifully embellished CV or cover letter is trimmed down to lowest-common denominator text without your knowing. If in doubt about what file formats will work, go for the simplest you can, and if you want to send attachments and other stuff, then take the trouble to ask whether they can get through.

CV blasting

You may already have received an e-mail pitch urging you to reach thousands of search, recruitment, and placement firms. At least a half-dozen CV distribution services ask you to let their companies carpet-bomb the Web with your CV.

At first glance, that kind of CV blasting may seem like a smashing idea, an easy way to get your CV out there and in front of every face that matters. But after you think it through, you'll probably change your mind – there's a big difference between getting your face noticed where it counts and putting yourself right in the face of those that count.

Indiscriminate posting of your personal information can trigger a wave of career failures and personal problems, which are intertwined with privacy issues. See the "CV confidential: Protect your privacy" section later in this chapter to find out how these disasters can happen.

One irate hiring manager of a CV blaster for IT (information technology) who began bombarding her with forwarded and unsolicited CVs even though she didn't have open jobs at that time. When the CV load proved to be too burdensome to comply with the company policy on replying to each job seeker, the hiring manager told the CV distribution service to stop. The hiring manager was frustrated not only because a large number of the forwarded CVs lacked contact or name information but also because she felt sorry for the job searchers who'd paid money for the CV blasting services and were actively on the market looking for work.

The hiring manager's parting comment: "These job seekers should know that (A) they are paying to reach recruiters without jobs or (B) to have their CVs forwarded in a way that cannot be responded to. They should use their money for something else".

As About.com's Allison Doyle points out, however, "Some CV blasting services will let you target only recruiters who asked to be put on a list to receive CVs in specific industries and geographic regions and will send you a list of the recruiters your CV was sent to".

There are other reasons to avoid services that send out a tornado of CVs, which are covered in the following sections.

We do not recommend CV blasting for a number of reasons, including the following:

- Negative perceptions of CV "spamming" (junk mail)
- Recruiter distaste for shop-worn CVs
- Loss of control over your own CV

TIP

What to do when you're all alone by the telephone

No matter how picky you were about the job sites where you posted your CV – including big national job boards and small specialist sites alike – if you're getting no action after a month to six weeks, whisk back your CVs from their current locations and post them elsewhere.

What about corporate Web sites you haven't heard from? Leave your CV in these databases.

Consider them lifers unless you decide they need refreshing or the company's policy requires deletion of unused CVs after a specified time period – usually six months to a year.

By the way, repeated postings of the same CV won't make a positive difference, and may, in fact, make you look like a loser.

Gerry Crispin and Mark Mehler (CareerXroads consultants and experts on the recruiting industry) agree that CV blasting is ill-advised:

We are absolutely not in favour of sites that promise to distribute job seekers' CVs to "hundreds of subscribing recruiters and employers". Most charge a fee, and it's a waste of money. Privacy and disclosure is too important, and while you may not care today, you certainly will tomorrow.

Realising that CVs live forever

After your CV leaves earth to live in the stratospheric reaches of the Web, you can't control it. It may turn up anywhere, anytime – including on your boss's desk.

But what if you've been cagey – wink, nudge, say no more – and only listed events prior to your current job? Can't you just tell your boss that the CV is old, posted before you took your present position, and you have no idea how or why it's still alive? Sure you can, but the missing information describing your present employment is probably your best selling strength if you're on the market.

Moreover, employers are realising that as soon as your CV is up in Web lights, you'll continually be contacted if you seem to have what's wanted somewhere. And if you're having a bad day, you might just be tempted to say, "I'm gone."

Marked for life

Individuals who put their CVs on the big national job boards two years ago are still hearing from recruiters and companies even though they have accepted other employment. Not only do the CVs live on eternally, but they may also find their way to unintended databases.

Even job seekers who report that they deactivated their CVs on the boards where they originally posted them hear from places they never knew received their CVs. "Marked for life" is the way one job seeker put it.

The chances that your CV will escape from its designated space are multiplying.

CV scraping

Job ads have long been openly "scraped" – a term for what happens when robots/spiders scour the Web looking for job listings and collect them on a second and unrelated site.

Now, CVs are being scraped, too. Ethical scrapers send you an e-mail and ask if you'd like to be included in the second database and are guided by your response. But most scrapers treat CVs like a commodity, don't get your permission, and take your CV to places unknown. When you don't know where your CV is, how can you call it back to make changes? Or withdraw it entirely?

Remember, online CVs may never die. They just blow like tumbleweed through the wastelands of the Web.

Recruiters keep their distance

One more reason not to spread your CV all over the map: When you're targeting the fast track to the best jobs, nothing beats being brought to an employer's notice by an important third person – and an independent recruiter qualifies as an important third person.

We've already seen how employers are becoming resistant to paying independent recruiters big fees to search the Web when they theoretically can save money by hiring in-house corporate recruiters to do it. That's why recruiting agencies need fresh inventory that employers can't find elsewhere. If you want a third-party recruiter to present you, think carefully before pinning cyber wings on your CV.

T-REX

Be stingy with your CV

In addition to losing control of your CV, its wide availability can cause squabbles among contingency recruiters over who should be paid for finding you. An employer caught in the conflict of receiving a CV from multiple sources, including internal CV databases, will often pass over a potential employee rather than become involved in deciding which source, if any, should be paid.

CV confidential: Protect your privacy

Identity theft may be the worst-case scenario, but it isn't the only life-altering problem that can arise when you put your business on e-street.

You can lose your current job, if you have one. "Many employers do search for their employees' CVs in job site CV databases and search engines", explains Susan Joyce, CEO of Job-Hunt.org, who tracks the privacy issue. "When employees' CVs are found grazing in someone else's pasture before noon", says CareerXroads' Mark Mehler, who consults with countless company managers, "they may be on the street by the end of that same day".

A recent survey by the Cranford School of Management and a BT working group showed that of UK SME's (Small and Medium-sized Enterprises), just under three quarters had the facility to monitor employees e-mail. By UK law, a company can't just listen in to your mail for the fun of it, but it is allowed to monitor your mail to establish a number of things, including whether or not those communications are relevant to the business. Any system that uses keywords will have little trouble spotting employees who are sending CVs. Companies are encouraged to have clear policies that explain to their staff just what kind of e-mail monitoring they indulge in. But many don't. Because all companies have the right to dip into mail to ensure that the business you're minding is theirs, a little discretion goes a long way.

Who can you trust?

People in the UK benefit from one of the most protective approaches to data. Both UK and European legislation are very strict about what information you can store about someone and just who you can pass it to. Despite this, there can't be many of us who have never received junk mail or spam from someone who has clearly begged, borrowed, or stolen our details.

A CV and an NI number are perfect building blocks for identity theft or harassment. Be wary of who you give them out to. Any reputable job site will guarantee confidentiality, but mistakes happen, and software "scraping" programs (explained in the section "CV scraping") snap up details without permission. If confidentiality is key, then it may pay to keep mum.

You can decide whether you want to be a victim of your CV's lack of privacy protection. Just remember: Problems could happen tomorrow or years from now because online CVs live eternally on the Internet.

Safeguarding your identity

In some recruitment circles, job seekers who protect their identity are more desirable than those who don't, notes Susan Joyce (CEO of Job-Hunt.org). Employers assume you're employed and have an existing job you are protecting. The downside in cloaking your identity is that some recruiters and potential employers won't accept anonymous CVs.

What should you do? We suggest you take that chance. After all, privacy protection doesn't mean relying on assurances from job sites that they're protecting your privacy for you. Here's how to look out for yourself: *Transform all identifying information into generic information.* But won't going generic hurt your chances of being hired? Maybe. Maybe not. There's a trade-off.

Combining suggestions by job hunt authority Susan Joyce, career expert and author Martin Yate, recruiter Steven Gatz, and ourselves, here's a roundup of techniques to help you avoid colliding with your boss, identity thieves, criminals, and other problems on the information highway:

✔ **Your name:** Replace your true name with an e-mail alias. Use a serious e-mail name, such as MEngineer. Or make up a name followed parenthetically by the words "screen name" – Able Smith (Screen Name). Or refer to yourself as someone like "Confidential Candidate" or "Confidential Systems Analyst". Or, using a special e-mail address that you maintain for just this purpose, just enter seven nine's – 9999999 – for each field requiring name, address, and phone number. Even if the original site sends your CV on to other sites, your personal information is never revealed.

✔ **Your contact information:** After obtaining a free e-mail account with Yahoo!, Hotmail, or the like, train yourself to check it daily. Use this address as your chief point of contact. If you feel you need to flesh out your contact information, for a street address, rent a post office box and use an unlisted telephone connected to a message recorder. Again, check regularly.

Recruiters often search by area and postal codes, so you may want to use the real ones in those spots, followed by fake numbers – most postal codes come in two parts, often of three letters or numbers. The first part is good enough to narrow down your location for a recruiter – offering the last two or three digits will usually narrow it down to a couple of houses which may be more information than you want to give. Here's another good tip: under pain of torture, never use your business e-mail address as your CV contact point. You risk being flayed alive when your boss finds out.

✔ **Your current employer:** Omit the name and replace it with a generic, but accurate, description. Nuts n' Bolts Distributors, Inc becomes "small construction supplies distribution company". Microsoft becomes "multinational information technology company". For company location, Cadbury Schweppes in Manchester becomes "FTSE food and drink company in the Midlands". The flip side of that coin is that your current company may be your biggest selling point for your next. As Joe Slavin, MD of Monster UK points out, "Employers are searching on keywords so that if a candidate uploads a CV that says they are currently working for Pepsi, then Coke will see that and give them a call immediately."

✔ **Your job title:** If your job title is uncommon (like "head geek" – yes, these sorts of titles do exist!) or, in combination with other facts, would identify you, use a generic title. However, if the title you choose could be misleading in any way, indicate that you've switched it – Network Engineer (position-equivalent title). South-East regional gadget marketing director becomes "Home Counties marketing manager of gadget-class products". If your job title is generic, such as "Editor" or "Sales Representative", just go ahead and use it.

✔ **Prior employers:** You probably won't need to sanitise information about earlier employers unless you're in a small industry where everyone knows everyone else and can figure out who you are by your work history. In that case, continue to camouflage yourself with the use of generic terms for the past ten years. Instead of "Five years with Jackson Plastics as a research design engineer", substitute "respected plastics company" for Jackson Plastics.

Listing previous employers by name, title, and dates of employment (research design engineer, 1992@nd1997, Jackson Plastics) can strip you of stealth options. A suspicious boss can check personnel files for your old CV.

✔ **Education:** Use either your degree and institution (MA, Durham University) or your degree and date (MA, 1987). Using all three makes you identifiable through Old Boy's associations or Friends Reunited. A really determined, suspicious manager may even be able track you down if you use both your undergraduate and advanced degrees by cross-checking academic lists. Of course if you're living with that kind of suspicion, you may well be in a hurry to get out anyway.

If one or both of your degrees are from a prestigious institution, ride on those coat tails, leaving off dates. Or just list your advanced degree and decide whether the college or a recent graduation date is most important in qualifying you.

The age factor as a potential discriminator plays a role in deciding which identifiers to include; if you're over 40, consider sticking to institutions and degrees. On the other hand, if you're under 40 and using your youth as a marketing tool, include dates.

✔ **Accomplishments:** Veil defining accomplishments with generic language. No to "Lead design engineer on development of DayNight onboard navigation component – headed a team of eight design engineers with a project budget of £7 million". Yes to "Led a large task force in a multi-million pound automotive technology launch."

✔ **Certifications and licenses:** Showing national or local certification isn't high risk, but professional associations may publish their member lists, and licenses are often easy to track down. That's why you generally should not list the date or precise location certifying your professional designation or granting your license.

✔ **Memberships:** Be careful which organisations you include. Exclusive or unusual bodies may identify you more precisely than you think.

If taking all these precautions seems a little paranoid, choose only the stealth strategies you think you need to protect your privacy. Admittedly, too much of a masquerade-ball environment can be off-putting to recruiters and employers.

Targeting the best lists for your e-mail CV campaign

A targeted e-mail CV campaign is a sophisticated and often highly effective strategy for a job search campaign, and it's best used for senior-level jobs. The formula is simple: You use a commercial list of selected independent recruiters and companies that logically could hire you, and you contact them with e-mail – or a combination of e-mail and post.

Let me play mind-reader for a minute and answer the questions that I think you might have.

Q: But isn't a targeted mailing campaign just an updated version of the old broadcast letter that most experts say doesn't work and that they'd rather drink bleach than recommend?

A: They are both about reaching-out, but these methods have substantial differences between them. The broadcast letter typically is sent indiscriminately to all addresses on direct-mail lists. The targeted e-mail campaign depends on careful matching of potential employers to the requirements of the job seeker. The quality of the list is a make-or-break factor.

Q: Are these e-lists new?

A: They're not new, but the e-databases that create the lists became a stand-alone tool only within the past several years. E-databases have the power to customise a list of recruiters by specialisation – both by industry (energy companies) and functional field (quality control). The way they're being used is very different than the old lists of the last century.

Yesteryear's recruitment e-databases were like the original television show, "Charlie's Angels", featuring soft plots and good manners. Today's powerful e-databases are like the new hyper-action feature film of the same title that blows its heroines through skyscraper glass windows. The old e-databases were offered on disk or CD-ROM and updated periodically; new versions are on the Web, and the premier products are updated daily. Earlier versions were produced by information vendors and resold by outplacement, executive marketing, and CV writing firms as an optional service; today's renditions are directly accessible to individual consumers.

The best lists are not free, but they include a mail-merge feature allowing you to send your cover letter and CV yourself. You can hire it done if you're not comfortable with computers.

Q: Is a targeted e-mail campaign a good bet if you don't have a degree?

A: Yes, if you use a CV letter instead of a CV; a letter doesn't flag your missing degree and gives you a chance to explain if a recruiter or employer calls you.

Q: What else is needed to find a good job by a targeted mail campaign?

A: You need good credentials and employers that are hiring your bundle of skills. Additionally, the following factors make the difference:

- ✔ You must address your mail campaign to a hiring decision-maker by name, not "Marketing Manager" or "President".

- ✔ Excellent marketing materials help attract employer interest. If you lack writing skills, hire a specialist to prepare them. The mailing package can consist of your CV and cover letter or note – or a combination CV letter.

- ✔ In the best targeted mail campaigns, you or your agent follow up with telephone calls to recipients within a week of the transmission. Anyone can be your agent for this purpose, paid or unpaid.

Q: Which is best – e-mail CVs or post CVs?

A: The Internet recruiter Reed (`www.reed.co.uk`) recently ran a survey of over 400 UK recruiters to find out who they would choose if they were faced with two equal candidates, one with a paper CV and one with a digital CV. Seventy-eight percent of recruiters said they'd take the candidate with the e-CV. Furthermore, 63 percent said they would favour people with e-CVs when selecting for interviews. Reasons given included the fact that e-CVs are "faster and more efficient to deal with . . . whether they arrive by e-mail, through a company's own web site, or from an external Internet job site". On a more subjective note, a third of recruiters noted that they saw candidates with paper CVs as being likely to be computer-illiterate or simply "behind the times".

It's a pattern that varies around the country. According to Reed, the areas least likely to handle their CVs digitally are Yorkshire and the North-East. At the other end of the scale, London-based employers are the most likely to use electronic CVs with over 44 percent of employers in the capital receiving 90 percent or more of their CVs electronically.

E-mail is easy to inventory in databases and to forward CVs to clients. Send two e-mail versions – your formatted attachment and also an ASCII text within the body (see Chapter 15) of your e-mail.

Q: Can you give an example of a real-life successful targeted e-mail campaign?

A: There is an e-mail campaign story we especially like. This one involves a father in top management and his son in sales. The father's search cost £1,000; his son's £250.

The father, Craig (not his real name, we're just too nice to embarrass him!), is a 50-something senior telecommunications executive earning a six figure salary. In his previous position, Craig had turned a "fallen dot.com" into a positive cash-flow business. After the flood of red ink was cauterised, the owners of the business decided to step back in, and Craig was out.

On Craig's behalf, an e-mail campaigner focused on retained executive recruiters and on venture capital firms specialising in the telecommunications industry. More than 1,600 e-mails were sent with Craig's cover letter and CV.

After five days, Craig had four major hits for executive jobs through recruiting firms in various parts of the country. Delighted, Craig began to proactively work those four leads. Craig's job search continued for 12 weeks, during which he reached final-interview status for all four positions. Two didn't pan out. The third company put him through 12 interviews before selecting the other short-listed candidate. As this book went to press, the fourth and favourite opportunity remains viable.

At the same time, Craig's son David (also not his real name) was looking for a better sales job. David's e-mail campaign went to 400 selected potential employers. Results were quick, and David began his new and much superior job within six weeks of the campaign.

Q: If targeted e-mail campaigns are so powerful, why doesn't everyone use them?

A: Targeted e-mail campaigns can be pricey, and they don't always work. You should be earning in the £50,000 and up range if you want to pay for a full-on turnkey campaign. And they aren't for everyone. You can do them yourself at a substantial time cost until you learn the ropes. Or you can hire a specialist if you have the money to pay for services. E-mail CV campaigns work best when you are contacting executive recruiters and when companies are hiring in your field.

Branching Out to Make Use of All Your Job-Finding Options

Networking (read *human interaction that includes employee referrals*) is rated number one in hiring results. That said, putting the following tools to use will be a great help to you.

Seeking endorsement through employee referral programmes

If you want fast action and special interest in your candidacy for a job, book your CV for the *employee referral programme* (ERP) tour. That is, identify companies where you'd like to work. Start with ten and then move on to a second batch of ten. And so on.

At each target company, network your way to an employee. You may already know some of the people inside a few companies. When you don't know a soul, keep asking someone who knows someone who knows someone. After you identify a contact, enlist that employee's aid in forwarding your name for employment.

Building a corporate insiders network sounds like hard graft, and it is. But this is a gift to yourself that keeps on giving – your efforts could pay off big, not only for your next job but also for a number of ever more responsible positions in coming years.

Formal Employee Referral Programmes are still in their infancy in the UK, compared to the US, where they are now the number one source for new employees. ERPs are used by 74 percent of *Fortune* magazine's "100 Fastest Growing Companies". Nonetheless the ERP approach is likely to grow since experience suggests that candidates hired through employee referrals stay longer and settle in faster than those hired through other methods, including the Internet and headhunters.

Sometimes, employees cruise available openings and forward them to friends with the click of a mouse. But you can't sit back and wait for the call to come. To remain on the ERP tour, stay in touch with your employee contacts regularly. Formal ERP or not, networking pays dividends and "jobs for the boys (and girls!)" doesn't have to be a term of exclusion.

Shape of things to come? Taking a dip in talent pool programmes

Swimming in a company talent pool isn't the same as trying to capitalise on an employee referral programme, which is described in the previous section. Building a network of employees ready to refer you to their companies could result in a fast job hunt, at least theoretically, while managing to get yourself in company talent pools could stretch out your search or produce future jobs.

The talent pool concept is a new idea – except perhaps to professional sports teams where emerging talent pools are often called "schools of excellence". But just as a newcomer from the school of excellence isn't guaranteed a place on the bench, let alone the pitch, so a company talent pool member isn't guaranteed a job with that company.

What exactly is a company talent pool? Some recruiting industry consultants describe the talent pool function as a kind of customer service to woo potential future employees. Corporate use of online screening and communication tools (see Chapter 1) is used to identify well-qualified applicants who could fill a variety of positions in a given company. Once tapped for the talent team-in-waiting, recruiters and candidates are supposed to maintain two-way communication (chiefly e-mail and e-newsletters), staying in touch as needed. Others see the talent pool differently, instead using the term to mean a database of passive job hunters who aren't actively seeking a job at the company but whose faces might fit. Executives Direct (www.executives-direct.com) is one such example of the passive job hunter pool.

Talent pools are an idea from the US. As the pool idea takes off on the other side of the pond, it will surely wing its way over to this side, so keep an ear open. Just because you find yourself in the pool doesn't mean you can relax. Splash around, get noticed – or in this case make quite sure you continue to send interesting or pertinent (job change) messages to the recruiter who got you included in the pool in the first place.

Asking job agents to stand guard

Millions of people change jobs each year, voluntarily or involuntarily. Because of diminishing job security, increased ambition, and new technologies, many people are locked into a perpetual job search. Sounds like a grind, and it can be. A job agent could be what you need to lighten the load and let you know you when a job you want comes along.

089565

LIBRARY RESOURCE CENTRE
CANOLFAN ADNODDAU LLYFRGELL

The basics are, well, basic

The nitty-gritty of engaging a *personal job agent* is simple but varies slightly among job sites. Most personal job agents are free to job seekers, but some come with membership in fee-based sites. On the job sites of your choice, you fill out a template to produce a profile of the job you want: your desired occupation, job title, industry, location, and salary range. You may have to provide a profile or use the site's CV builder to provide a profile of your qualifications. You supply your e-mail address and go on with your life.

Now, for the part about the cyberservant who comes to tell you that "Employment is served": When a fresh job ad comes to a chosen career site that's a pretty good match for your profile, the site's personal job agent sends you a circumspect e-mailed message. The employer is identified in the message. If you're interested, you say "Yes, release my CV to this employer", and if not, "No, don't release my CV to this employer".

If you're mobile and have high-demand skills, personal job agents are the best thing since headhunters to add zest to your career management fortunes. Best of all, they do all the hard work so you don't have to.

Let the job come to you

You may have a way out of interminable job hunt pressure. If you're not in a hurry, you can post your career-move preferences on each of your chosen job sites and then sit back and wait for employers to find you – perhaps even being offered opportunities you would never have found on your own initiative.

We are witnessing the rise of what recruiters call "the passive job seeker" and the job search tools that serve them. A *passive job seeker* is employed and is not actively on the market, but is always interested in exploring the "right offer". It is good to be king, and it is good to be a passive job seeker. A passive job seeker isn't too easy to get, so he or she is valued above all others. After all, if a passive job seeker is employed doing a particular job, someone must think that person is good at it, right?

Are you a passive job seeker? Congratulations! You can use any of hundreds of personal job agents that will keep their ears tuned to the job market, and when a promising position you might like comes to their attention, they'll tip you off with an e-mail alert.

Just as the devil is usually found in details, the downside is in the ratios: Each personal job agent has tonnes more registered job seekers than job vacancies. Like 250,000 job hunters and 4,000 job openings. So don't count on personal job agents to come through if you need to get a job fast.

Following-Up – an Act of Job Finding

The vast majority of employers – as many as eight of ten according to some surveys – that use digital recruiting systems (applicant management systems) send out an automatic receipt of your application, commenting that if they want to talk to you, they'll make contact. The response rate of third-party recruiters is unclear, but if you are a potential candidate for a job opening they're trying to fill, you'll hear back fairly quickly; if not, you may get an auto response or none.

Even when an auto response is sent, job searchers say they're underwhelmed, with the boilerplate e-mails seeming next to meaningless. Whether or not you get an underwhelming Web response, you run the risk of sounding particularly needy if you then call to ask a transparent question, "Did you receive my CV?" Instead, try something a little more professional sounding – some version of:

> *I've had another job offer, which prompts me to ask if you had planned to contact me within the week.*

We suggest other ways to make contact later in this section.

Bear in mind, however, that in these transitional times, the majority of smaller employers still don't use a digital recruiting system. If you send a CV to a workplace without a digital system (you know because you called first to check), calling later to ask, "Did you get my CV?" *is* a good question.

Reaching out when you don't "have mail"

The reasons that employers ignore applicants who send their CVs are many. They range from too few staffers to handle the clerical response task to uncertainty about whether the position actually will be filled. No matter. For your purposes, you must take the offensive and follow up.

If you've had previous contact with the recipient of your CV, the nature of that experience (stranger, referral, friend, telephone call, personal meeting) will suggest whether your follow-up is a thank-you letter or some other kind of communication, such as carrying out the employer's direction: "At your suggestion, I forwarded my CV . . ."

If you've had no earlier contact with your CV's recipient, e-mail or telephone your follow-up. Which is best – e-mail or telephone? We recommend you use the medium that makes you feel most confident and comfortable.

If you've had an auto response and know your CV is in the database, you can ask what happened to it:

Was my CV a match for an open position? Was my CV passed onto a hiring manager? Can you tell me which manager?

After you know your CV has been routed to a hiring manager – or you have personally sent your CV to that hiring manager – don't call the human resource department because HR will automatically consider you for all open job requisitions.

Try to contact the hiring manager, who is the one who makes the decision to hire you or not hire you. If your CV was passed onto a departmental hiring manager and you can uncover the manager's name, try calling that manager early in the morning or late in the day. Lunch is not a good time.

Beating that frustrating voicemail

What should you do when you try to reach the manager but can't break through voicemail? Leave a short message showing upbeat interest, not desperation:

My name is Steve Shipside, and I'm calling you because I've successfully outgrown my job, and you have a reputation for running a progressive department. I think you have my CV. If you like what you see, we should talk – 01234 567 890. The best time to reach me today is between 2 and 6 pm. I look forward to hearing from you.

Pronounce your name clearly and say your telephone number at a moderate pace. Give the hiring manager a chance to write it down without replaying the message. Otherwise, the manager hears a "garbledrushofwords" and decides "Idon'thavetimeforthis" and moves on.

How often should you call? Some very smart experts suggest calling every ten days until you're threatened with arrest if you call again. But busy employers insist that – unless you're in sales or another field requiring a demonstration of persistence – after you're certain your CV was received, call two weeks later, and then no more than once every six weeks.

An excessive number of telephone calls brands you as a pest. Instead, send notes or e-mail with additional facts about your qualifications, ideas to solve a problem you know the company is facing, or just an expression of your continuing interest in working for the company and the manager.

Everyone agrees that, in this increasingly impersonal world, effectively following-up on the CVs you send out is becoming harder and harder. But the challenge of getting your CVs into the right hands means going beyond transmission to connection with as many recruiters and employers as you reasonably can manage.

Part II
StandOut CVs for Affinity Groups

"Well, for a start, it's your spelling....."

In this part . . .

You find special tips and targeted CV guidance to use if you're a bit older, an information technology professional, have been laid off, or are a new graduate. You also get tips for CVs when you want to change your career field or occupation.

Chapter 3

When You Lose Your Job and It's Not Your Fault

In This Chapter

▶ Looking at special problems for jobless job searchers

▶ Managing a job-hopper image

▶ Giving exit reasons at the appropriate time

▶ Considering a retainer CV

▶ Checking the transferable skills checklist

*I*f we lived in a world where each of us was automatically given a job, which we then kept for life unless proven by judge and jury to be as much use as a glass hammer then, and only then, it might be right to attach a stigma to redundancy. Take a look around you, however, and you'll see that this is a world of "flexible labour" markets in which jobs get cut, exported abroad, or just vanish, and people find themselves downsized, right-sized, and plain old fashioned let-go.

Sixty percent of FTSE 100 companies made redundancies in the nine months following September 11. Was that because the HR companies of the majority of Britain's brightest and best companies suddenly found they'd hired a sack of glass hammers? Of course not. Does that come as any consolation whatsoever to those who found themselves let go? No, not a bit. You can rationalise redundancy; you can see it as meaningless and assure others that it doesn't reflect badly on them, but as soon as it happens to you, you're plunged into the pit of self-doubt and glass hammerdom. It hardly feels like the time to write up a CV singing your own praises.

Which is exactly what you're about to do. Job loss is not the end of the story – it's the start of the fight back and the following chapter takes a hard look at what you're up against and the best weapons for your fight.

A bundle of emotions

Job loss, first felt as a combination of depression and anxiety, is seasoned with nervousness, anger, and a sense of betrayal, as these two statements illustrate:

- A laid-off person explains, "Words I normally think of will not cover the feeling. It's as if I am going crazy, or having a bad dream, and am unable to wake up. My attitude towards everything is negative."

- Another discarded individual elaborates on the feeling of betrayal: "You can accept it if a company has done everything possible and just isn't financially capable of keeping you on. But when it costs you your livelihood because someone high on the corporate ladder, who doesn't even know your name, was too slow to get new business, you feel angry, bitter, and empty."

Add to those feelings the rage provoked by early-twenty-first-century corporate abuse, and you quickly understand why a job loss that wasn't your fault can affect your physical and mental health.

No wonder writing a CV seems a dreary chore.

Facing Facts about Job Loss

Unless you were miserable in your lost job, there really isn't any good thing about losing it, so there's nothing to be gained from meaningless adages like "Worse things happen at sea" because you feel like the one who's been swept overboard and washed up as flotsam on the beach. But if there is one "least worst" factor about losing your job, it's that today you're far less likely to be viewed as a failed performer or as unable to get along with others and therefore unemployable – a far different perception from an earlier time when most employers tended to assume your joblessness was your fault. In this downsizing-happy era, you're far more likely to be presumed innocent, unless proven otherwise. So many people have worn the badge of joblessness that it has almost become a designer sportswear label.

Fighting back – starting NOW!

So you think the hurt is too raw, the sting too acid, and the anger too lingering. Today is not a good day for CV writing. You just don't feel like writing your CV, and you'll wait until you feel better.

That attitude is easily understood, but it's not in your best interests. When a job loss lays you out, the number one action for putting your troubles behind you and landing new employment is moving on! The first six months are critical; after that, the odds of your being hired at comparable or better pay begin to get longer.

Rethinking, retraining, and relocating

When large-scale layoffs occur, entire occupations and industries may be thinned out. Re-establishing yourself in the workplace may depend on becoming competent in another line of work or relocating to a more prosperous job market. A number of studies insist that flexibility in deciding what you'll accept, including a change of career, is the way to go when you've been P45'd.

But here's a time-honoured counter caveat: Don't go overboard on changing your line of work if you don't have to or if you don't want to. Remember: If you're laid-off, find a new job in your field is much easier than changing your career and starting over.

Two schools of thought surround another issue. Should you accept temporary work, related or unrelated to what you hope to be doing soon? I can argue that issue either way, depending on the circumstances:

- ✔ **School 1:** Stick to your career track. If you don't, your CV will lose focus and, to some degree, you'll lose rising-star quality. Recruiters will want to know why a promising professional seemingly lost his or her footing.

- ✔ **School 2:** Accept temp work when you've been jobless for a while and prospects are bleak. The money helps, and the good feelings of acceptance and the momentum you derive from the work are equally valuable. (When you explain the detours from your career track in future job interviews, say that you experienced and overcame a rough patch of life, but now you're again ready to fight dragons.)

Writing a Successful Layoff CV

Have you ever wondered why so much is written for the downsized job hunter about the wider issues of job search and survival, and so little about the narrower issue of CVs?

The reason is simple. With a few exceptions, the same basic CV guidelines apply for the employed and unemployed: **Don't use your CV to explain why you left a job; save explanations for job interviews.**

There are exceptions, outlined in the following sections.

Overcoming a job-hopping image

Even when it wasn't at your initiative, holding five or more jobs in ten years can brand you as a job hopper. The fact that you're out of work now underscores that impression. Even employers who are guilty of round after round of employee dismissals instinctively flinch at candidates they perceive to be hopping around.

Take pains to reverse that disapproval. When you draft your CV, post a list of negative perceptions on your desk; when you're finished writing, compare your CV with the list. Offer information that changes negative perceptions of you as a job hopper. The following table lists the perceptions employers often have of a job hopper and ways to counter them.

Perception	Counter
Is disloyal and self-focussed	Perfect attendance, volunteer office gift collector
Will scarper in a blink for a better offer and take company secrets along	Competition of projects
Doesn't know what he/she wants and is never satisfied	Diverse background that promoted impressive results

After checking for damage control, go back and review your CV for accomplishments that enhance your image as the following:

- **A fast learner:** Give examples of how your skills aren't company-specific and you rapidly adjust to new environments.

- **A high achiever:** Show favoured skills much courted by headhunters, and at end of each job mention, put "Recruited for advanced position."

- **A quick adapter:** Mention examples of agreeable flexibility in adjusting to new ideas, technology, and position requirements.

- **A relationship builder:** List praise from co-workers for commitment to team success.

If your current joblessness comes after a background that a quick-change artist would admire, use your CV to prepare the way to acceptance. Emphasise project completion and career progression, using years, not months. If you still have trouble landing interviews, use positive statements in your cover letter to tackle your history.

When a departure wasn't your fault, but you look like a job hopper if you don't explain, do reveal the reasons.

Giving focus to a patchwork career

When a laid-off job searcher says she has too much in her background, and her CV is a scenic tour of the world of work, the solution is CV *focus*. Every creative cell in your brain will be challenged, but give it a go. Here's a case in point:

A woman in her early 50s wants to make a career move that's back to the future. Her career brief is as follows: master's degree in education; MBA studies; educating for six years as a teacher and department head (left because pay was low); working in human resources for a major corporation for 20 years (downsized); operating a part-time fitness counselling and training centre for women for 10 years (still going); writing for an online dot.com for two years (dot.com went bust); and replacement teacher (now wants regular teaching position to improve cash flow).

What, she asks, should she call all her diversified experience – human resources, fitness, journalism?

Our answer: Build a *theme* (focus) and, in this instance, call everything *educational*. Relate the human resource experience to training and instructional experience, the fitness experience to guidance and knowledge-building, and the journalism to educational writing.

Although the educator in this example is older than many downsized job searchers, the same unifying technique works for much younger people with short tenures in various career fields.

Dealing with multiple layoffs

Hard to believe, but good workers sometimes experience one layoff after another. One of our readers wrote that he'd experienced four no-fault severances within seven years.

When you've been to the chopping block a few too many times, explain the circumstances after each listing of the company name:

> Carol Interiors (company closed doors) . . . Salamander Furnishings (multiple-rounds of downsizing) . . . Brandon Fine Furniture (company relocated out of town) . . . Kelly Fixture Co (plant sold and moved overseas).

Offering brief explanations takes the blame from your shoulders – but we suppose that a cynic could think that you're a jinx.

Explaining mergers and acquisitions

Another of our readers writes:

> *Upon graduating from college, I went to work for Company A. Several years later, Company A was acquired by Company B. More years passed, and Company B was acquired by Company C. Eventually, Company C merged with Company D, and as a result, after 10 years with the four companies, I was laid off.*
>
> *My question is how best to handle this work history on my CV? I worked for four different corporate entities, with four different names, without ever changing jobs. Do I list all four on my CV? Or just the last one?*

Always try to show an upward track record (that you acquired new knowledge and skills and just didn't just do the same thing over and over each year). And you don't want the reader to assume that you worked for only one company that laid you off after a decade.

Taking these two factors into consideration, can you show correlation between your job titles and responsibilities with the changes in ownership? If yes, identify all four owners:

> Job title, Company D (formerly Company C), years
>
> Job title, Company C (formerly Company B), years
>
> Job title, Company B (formerly Company A), years
>
> Job title, Company A, years

If no, you can't show an upward track record that correlates with changes in ownership, just use the current owner name with a short explanation:

> Job title, Company D, years
> (Through a series of mergers and acquisitions, the entities for which I have worked since college graduation were known as Company A, Company B, and Company C.)

The reason for naming every entity is perception. Background and credit checks will turn up those company names, and if your CV doesn't mention them, it sends up a red flag for your potential employer!

Rising through the ranks without a degree

Laid-off workers who rose through the ranks without a college degree and now can't find a comparable position in another large company have a problem. The educational shortfall can easily do them in.

Everyone knows about Bill Gates of Microsoft, a college dropout, and Virgin's Richard Branson, who dropped out of school to set up his first business. But that knowledge really doesn't help you much when you can't even get interviews because you lack a college degree.

What can help is using the CV letter (combination cover letter and CV) instead of a CV. In it, refer to your "experience-based" knowledge and "skills-building" experience. Emphasise that you enjoy learning and give examples. Mention that you've taken courses as you've found a need for them. And although you don't bring up the fact that you lack a degree, you do mention that you continue to be eager to get on with "real work," as opposed to theorising about it.

Target smaller companies because they may have fewer formal educational requirements and may be more willing to zero in on your knowledge and skills rather than where you acquired them.

Writing a Retainer CV

A *retainer CV* is an internal, self-marketing document that you give to new management when rumours of mergers and acquisitions surface. It can also be used to resell you to current management when rumours of layoffs spread through the grapevine in your company.

A retainer CV differs from an *internal CV,* which points out qualifications that fit you for a different job where you work. A retainer CV proclaims to the acquiring or dominant company management why you're an invaluable asset to the company and should be kept on when staffs are combined. To your existing management, it provides reasons why they should re-mortgage the house before letting you go.

When your company is bought out or merged, the new owners usually take an oath that they have no plans to make personnel changes. View those assurances with a healthy dose of scepticism. The mergers and acquisitions (M&A) market has never been known to burn the candour at both ends. While they're denying that cuts will be made, stacks of P45s are being spit out by a computer. M&A business guru Stanley Foster Reed, who has a half century of M&A experience, says layoffs will occur 70 percent of the time. Although being on a buyer's workforce is usually safer than being on a seller's, exceptions arise because of the tax posture of the merging entities.

Here's your best move, says Reed:

> *While you should never believe your job is safe just because you have a good track record, do the best you can to assay the company's productivity and your seniority, tempered by your cost and age before assuming you're history.*

> *Rarely do employees gird up their loins and confront the new owners or their representatives with a statement like this: "I love my job and I want to keep it. What can I do, or learn, that will make me more productive, more useful to the new combined companies?" Do it; then hand the owners a copy of your newly created retainer CV.*

Pack Up All Your Skills and Go!

Just when you thought getting laid off was *your* fault, you took a step back and remembered it was *their* inability to manage well that put you on the pavement.

To reinforce your inner pep talk, glance over the transferable skills checklist later in this chapter. This checklist is far from being comprehensive or scientifically organised. We offer it merely as an illustration of the skills that you can tuck into your CV and take with you to a new workplace. Add any other skills that you think are important. Try to identify 20 skills.

Skills versus competencies

Skills and competencies (see Chapter 10) are part of the same bolt of cloth. Skills have been discussed for many years, and that concept is better known than the relatively new *competencies*. Both address positive factors you bring to the employer.

The reason skills and competencies are presented separately in this book is because of wide recognition that everyone needs skills to work, but competencies as a concept hasn't hit the mainstream yet and is chiefly used in technology that screens applicants online (see Chapter 1 for more on the most current HR practices).

Transferable Skills Checklist

This checklist is a simple tool to use in highlighting skills that you can pack up and take with you to a new job or career field. Check your winners. Add any other skills you're good at that you want to use again.

Work Skills

supervising	problem solving
managing budget	meeting deadlines
public speaking	planning
scheduling	structuring
systematising	program designing

Organisational/Interpersonal Skills

reporting	generalising
managing	networking
leading	implementing
teaching	consulting
reviewing	assessing
time-managing	advising
organising	negotiating
conceptualising	interpreting
achieving	judging
delegating	extracting information
serving customers	administering

Dealing with Things Skills

assembling	building
constructing	operating
inspecting	purchasing
repairing	innovating
certifying	designing
delivering	selling
using tools	using complex equipment
lifting	remodelling

Dealing with People Skills

building relationships	showing cultural sensitivity
interviewing	role-playing
empathising	putting people at ease
coaching	motivating
co-operating	co-ordinating
promoting	listening
persuading	showing diversity awareness

Dealing with Words/Ideas Skills

outlining	creating
synthesising	programming
inventing	researching
articulating	visualising
remembering	calculating
reasoning	quantifying
recognising patterns	editing
deciphering	thinking critically
explaining	comparing
analysing	communicating

Behavioural Skills

diplomatic	flexible
loyal	versatile
warm	open
frank	co-operative
tenacious	discreet
initiator	efficient
diplomatic	orderly
expressive	enterprising
sophisticated	candid
adventuresome	decisive
responsible	self-confident
risk-taking	result-oriented

A Bevy of StandOut CV Tips

The following tips help you work up a StandOut CV at any time – jobless or employed:

- ✔ **Discuss teamwork in job descriptions, giving specific examples and results.** Employers love the word *teamwork.* They like *team building,* too. Talk about participating in tough tasks that help focus teams. Speak of trust as being essential to teamwork. Say that you were part of a team that succeeded in reaching a unified goal.

  The difficulty comes in making clear for which portion of the team's production you can take a bow. You must separate your contribution from the group's. If you don't, you risk being looked upon as one who falsely claims credit for work you didn't do. If you do find room for hobbies, be sure they're related to your job objective. Team-player sports such as football, hockey, and cricket are ideal for hobbies related to work in a group. (Building ships in bottles would better suit work as a lighthouse keeper.)

- ✔ **Give examples of leadership.** Even as organisational structures flatten by the hour, every team needs a leader – unless you're headed for a support job where leadership is a liability. In the same vein, vision and drive are desirable characteristics. What did you originate, initiate, spearhead, or propose? What have co-workers praised about you? What suggestions have employers accepted from you?

- ✔ **Discuss an upward track record.** Without mentioning specific amounts, paint yourself as a winner by mentioning that you received raises, promotions, and bonuses.

- ✔ **Answer the "So What?" question.** This question is hidden and lying in ambush in every employer's mind. Forget about sticking to the old name-your-previous-responsibilities routine. Every single time you mention a duty or achievement, pretend someone fires back: So what? Who cares? What does it all mean? Imagining these questions isn't really pretending – these are employer responses.

  Don't just relay what you did – spell out the consequences and implications. A medical technologist may say:

  - Organise daily work distribution for effective teamwork of 12 lab workers; absorb and solve workload issues from previous shift – backlog cut from three days to three hours.

  - Monitor quality control; identify problems, find solutions; lab insurance rates, related to mistakes, lowered this year by three percent.

  - Perform preventive maintenance on 14 machines on daily basis; reduced repair costs eight percent over previous year.

- ✔ **Showcase anything that you did in the top 5 percent of company performance ratings.** Employers are impressed with the cream of the crop.

- ✔ **Don't apologise on your CV for any weakness that you may observe in your professional self.** Until you can do something about it, like get additional education or experience, don't even think about your shortcomings, and they certainly don't belong on your CV.

- ✔ **Show how and whom you trained.** Employers appreciate the knowledge base suggested by the ability to teach. A smaller company in particular may be run by an entrepreneur whose nightmare is being forced to take time away from running the company to hire and train new people.

- ✔ **Don't try to explain a lifetime of disasters on a CV.** Save your explanations for an interview. Use your friends and acquaintances to help you obtain interviews. Make the CV as brief and as adversity-free as you legitimately can. At the interview, be prepared to justify your moves, without becoming defensive, and be sure to provide good references.

- ✔ **Ask a business-savvy friend to read your CV before you send it out.** Prepare a list of questions regarding the comprehensiveness of your CV's explanations and job victories for your friend to answer. Examples: Does this CV show my mastery of bookkeeping skills? Does this CV adequately emphasise the prestige of my awards and recognition for design skills? It's better to know sooner than later when you're rowing with only one oar.

Making a Comeback

Hold this thought: *I will recover from this setback and I will rise again.* There are plenty of comeback kings and queens to prove the point. John Travolta spent a decade as a byword for has-been disco kitsch until he came back as a cult film actor. At the end of the eighties Kylie Minogue was the pint-sized pop queen of the known world. Anyone remember what she was doing by the mid to late-nineties? Come the new millennium, however, and Kylie has moved on from bubble gum pop and sidekick roles in Van Damme films to become a clubland diva. George Davis, the man who founded high-street fashion chain Next was kicked out of the company in 1988 when it came close to collapse. He subsequently turned round the fashion fortunes of Asda with his George range of clothes and looks to have done the same for Marks and Sparks with the Per Una range of women's' wear.

Believe in yourself. This too shall pass. Bin your old CV and start fresh with the insights you're gaining.

And if you feel that you need to talk redundancy through with some people in the know, try contacting The Redundancy Advice Network, a charity whose aim is to help both individuals and employers facing change. Their Web site is http://www.ran-advice.co.uk.

Chapter 4

Fifty-somethings Fight Back

- -

In This Chapter

▶ Fight-back CV tactics

▶ Jack Chapman's special reports

▶ Career-change CV tips

▶ Stepping down to lower-level jobs

- -

*J*ohn Glenn first joined NASA in 1959 and took to space in the early sixties. When he returned to space in 1998, he became the world's oldest astronaut at age 77. More remarkable even than his personal achievement is the fact that he got the thumbs up from scientists and senior managers from one of the planet's most exclusive personnel selection processes – there's no reason why healthy older people can't fly in space. So if you can fly in space, what's to stop you getting another (perhaps less dangerous!) job, no matter how old you are?

Contrast that attitude towards age to letters we receive nearly every day, like these two:

> *I am a 59-year-old involuntarily "retired" electrical/electronic engineer with lots of varied experience. I was replaced by two recent graduates from my old college. I've been out of work before but never at age 59. How do I find a job that uses my experience, or must I, as some suggest, take a counter job at a DIY centre?*

> *I write concerning what to put and what not to put on a CV at age 48. I was laid-off four years ago and have not had a full-time permanent position since. I am feeling age discrimination – how does one tone down a CV for work I've done, just to get my foot in the door for an interview and hopefully find they are not discriminating against older adults?*

This chapter looks at ways to combat biases an older job hunter faces, including a new CV-alternative idea. It also raises points to consider if you're a fifty-something who may want to change careers. Don't worry though – we're not going to tell you that you have to become an astronaut.

Older but Not Golder

Age bias is shoving high numbers of fifty-somethings (and beyond) into unemployment and underemployment – picture professionals over 50 replaced with cheaper and younger talent, and PhDs working on computer help desks.

As if the normal wear-and-tear that an older worker racks up in the workplace weren't enough, recent looting and other criminal misdeeds by corporate officers have destroyed the retirement funds of many thousands of these workers. Now, like it or not, older workers and retirees are having to deal with the stress of remaining or returning to the workplace just to make ends meet.

Fight-back Tactics for Seasoned Aces

To forestall age discrimination, tailor your CV to make yourself look like a well-qualified candidate – not a well-preserved one – by using these tips:

- ✔ **Shorten your CV.** The general guideline is, "Go back no more than 15 years". But if that doesn't work for the job you seek, one answer is to create a functional CV where you blow up your relevant skills in detail toward the top of the CV and play down overly impressive titles by dropping them down to the bottom.

- ✔ **Focus your CV.** For emphasis, I'll repeat that: *Focus your CV.* Concentrate on highlighting your two most recent or most relevant jobs. Do not attempt to give equal attention to each of your past jobs. If your job experience has been diverse, your CV may look like a job-hopping tale of unrelated job after unrelated job.

✔ **Show that you are a tower of strength.** Give examples of how you solved problems, recovered expenses, and learned to compensate for weaknesses in your working environment. Emphasise how quickly such adjustments occurred. Grey heads who have survived a few fallen skies are valuable assets in difficult times.

✔ **Demonstrate political correctness.** This is especially important for positions that have contact with the public. Show that you are familiar with contemporary values by using politically correct terms wherever appropriate. Examples include *diversity, cross-cultural, mainstream, multiethnic,* and *people with disabilities* (never handicapped).

✔ **Try shipping your CV online.** You'll help dispel any ideas that you're over the hill. Surveys show that recruiters in some fields see a lack of an online CV as proof of being behind the times. Just don't give them the ammunition. See Part IV for more on digital CVs.

✔ **Annihilate ancient education dates.** Of course, the absence of dates sends a signal: *This is an old geezer who read a CV book.* But at least it shows that you have sufficient faculties left to play the game.

✔ **Trim your CV to fighting weight.** For very experienced professionals, sorting out the most powerful CV points can be difficult. It's like being a gifted child – so many choices, and you're good at them all! You know what they say, though: The longer the cruise, the older the passengers.

Jack Chapman's Special Reports: A Tool that Boosts CV Response

The *special report technique* is the creation of US-based career coach Jack Chapman (jkchapman@aol.com). It is primarily a networking tool. It says, "Notice me. Talk to me. Remember me".

Specifically, a *special report* is three to ten pages describing how to do a simple but essential task relevant to the job you're seeking. The CV is added as the back page to a special report, so special reports don' replace CVs. A special report can be distributed online or delivered by postal mail or courier.

Special reports are kindred to the e-newsletters described in Chapter 16, but they are one-shots rather than ongoing publications.

Chapman has used the report technique more than 70 times, pointing out that it almost always (nothing is bullet-proof) works better than a CV. We asked Chapman what "better" means, and here's his response:

> *Did your contact know who you were? Was your contact receptive to meeting with you? That's what I mean by "better." Special reports are remembered ten times as often as CVs.*

Ideal for fifty-somethings

Because you've been around for a while, you've got the know-how and the credibility to do a special report. (Exception: Don't use this CV tool if you're trying to change careers. If you were trying to change careers from teaching to sales, for example, issuing a special report called "Ten Top Sales Techniques" would be presumptuous.)

Describing the value of a special report, Chapman says:

> *As a fifty-something, whatever your profession, you have some wisdom about how to make things run smoother, better, easier, more profitably, and so forth. Your special report would contain practical tips and techniques that can be easily applied in the daily work life of the reader.*
>
> *You may recall the book, Seven Habits of Highly Successful People by Steven Covey. The book is powerful, but how much rocket science is required to tell people to (1) be proactive, (2) begin with the end in mind, (3) put first things first, (4) think win/win, (5) seek first to understand and then to be understood, (6) synergise, and (7) sharpen the saw. YOU could have written that book, couldn't you? The ideas in its pages are simple, and they are as old as Napoleon Hill's Think and Grow Rich. Yet this book was a multi-million-copies best-seller. That's the power of a special report – simple ideas that work.*

Examples of special report topics

Jack Chapman gives the following examples of special reports his clients have written:

54 Ways to Market Career Services (a college careers advisor illustrates methods of attracting more students to the campus career centre).

Ten Ways to Make Your Property Make Money (a residential property manager shows simple things to do to make renting apartments easier, retain more tenants, and reduce costly maintenance calls).

An International Trade Trend Opens Brief Window of Opportunity to Double Your Margins and Undercut Your Competition (a purchasing manager reveals how to source certain cast-iron parts from China at a ridiculously cheap price).

Six Money Tips for Self-Employed and Small Business Professionals (an accountant building a private practice gives tips on taking more tax deductions, protecting your business from an IRS audit, and managing your own expenses).

A Simple Low-Tech Manufacturing Solution that Saved Hundreds of Thousands of Dollars with No Increase in Staff or Overhead (an oil refinery plant manager gives seven examples of challenging 'TWWADI' – That's the Way We've Always Done It – and saving £200,000). Figure 4-1 shows excerpts from this report.

Why sample reports are effective

Chapman says a special report puts a routine CV in the shade because it:

- ✔ Speaks immediately of the contributions you can make, a good opening in a networking conversation in a company where no opening has been announced.

- ✔ Positions you as an expert by providing substance and depth to your competence.

- ✔ Provides interesting reading.

- ✔ Offers value to the reader. Special reports give money-making or time-saving information. They don't need to be highly original; they just need to offer good information.

You have enough information to start using special reports on your own. But if you want more coaching or examples, Jack Chapman has published a book titled *Ten Best: A Variety Pack of Special Reports*. You can get more information and order the book on Chapman's Web site salarynegotiations.com.

SPECIAL REPORT: A SIMPLE LOW-TECH MANUFACTURING SOLUTION THAT SAVED £863,000/YR WITH NO INCREASE IN STAFF OR OVERHEAD.

Most managers today look for high tech, computerised solutions to keep pace and stay competitive. While technology can produce savings, that's not the only place to look. My experience has shown that paying attention to one simple low-tech principle can save 10 times as much as the high-tech solution, and do it with virtually no increase in costs or staff.

I call this low-tech solution: Challenge the "TTWWADI" method of business. Here are ten examples of what I term "ANTI – TTWWADI" and the savings of each. TTWWADI stands for "That's The Way We've Always Done It." I illustrate each principle with a short story from plants I've worked in: but remember, my experience is not unique. Old solutions linger, even when the problems no longer exist. "That's The Way We've Always Done It" can keep them in place for a long time, sometimes imbedded in written SOPs, maybe even [horrors!] in your plant!

I hope you enjoy and profit from this report. As you ponder the question after each example, you may find some of my strategies will apply right now to your situation.

1) **Special Work Assignments**

Two mechanics were called out on overtime each weekend during the winter months to perform preventative maintenance inspection of a steam system. For safety and quality sake, they made sure no pipes were frozen.

I noticed the overtime on the payroll and questioned it. I asked "Why do we do it on days when the temperature is above 32 degrees?" The reply was, "That's the way we've always done it." (TTWWADI).

By limiting the call outs to days with below freezing weather, we saved over £16,000 in overtime costs and still made sure no freeze damage would occur.

QUESTION: Are there tasks still regularly done by employees that no longer serve a purpose?

2) **Let's Replace It with the Same Thing**

When it was time to replace a piece of malfunctioning equipment with something new, the first thing the engineering and maintenance people would consider was replacing it "like-kind," i.e. equipment essentially like the existing equipment.

Did they ask the question of "How well does the existing equipment work now?" No, they just planned to replace it like-kind.

When I asked the question, I uncovered a glaring waste of money. The plant loads liquids, and operations had paid demurrage throughout the years for delays in loading.
What was the cause of the delays? It was those pumps that were to be replaced like-kind. The pumps were undersized for our current loading needs. We had paid the demurrage for delaying trucks for many years. No one questioned it, because "That's the way we've always done it." (TTWWADI)

Figure 4-1: An abbreviated two-page illustration of a special report. Source: Jack Chapman.

By replacing the equipment with adequate equipment to get the job done on time, the demurrage was eliminated, saving over £50,000/year.

QUESTION: Is your plant engineering or maintenance personnel just replacing without investigating?

> *[Ed. Note: To give you the idea of the whole report, here are the titles of the next 8 TTWWADI lessons, and the cost savings Mark attributed to each. Note that the ideas here are not "rocket science," they're just things that demonstrate wisdom and experience on the job. Perfect for anyone experienced in his or her field.]*

3)	Double Work	£15,000
4)	Doing a Study and then Not Implementing the Recommendations	£30,000
5)	Waiting for Breakdowns to Maintain Equipment	£25,000
6)	Cleaning Up after Yourself	£50,000
7)	Cost of Renting Equipment	£12,000
8)	Not Meeting New Regulations	£200,000
9)	Costs of Not Calibrating Equipment	£400,000
10)	Spending More than You Make	£65,000

Total:£797,000/year

If you wish to discuss ways this report can be applied to your operation, please call Mark A. at 0207 555-4951. By the way, this report is not copyrighted. Feel free to pass it along to your friends – just keep my name and number on it.

Thanks, Mark.

Concepts for Career-Changing Fifty-somethings

Some 72 percent of out-of-work professionals change industries, with 16 percent starting their own businesses, says a survey of 14,000 people from 35 countries by DBM, a leading human resource consulting and outplacement firm.

DBM offers three salient points to bear in mind about how to use your CV in a career-change effort.

> ✔ **Forget about ads and search firms.** With the exception of entry-level positions, companies run ads to recruit prospects with specific experience. The same is true of search firms – they are paid to find highly experienced talent that matches the job description exactly.

✔ **Network, network, network.** Networking is especially the key in the case of career change to a successful outcome. The most effective way to transfer skills to a new field or career is by using your contacts. Companies are more willing to take risks on people who are referred to them by individuals who can attest to the candidates' abilities and potential.

✔ **Find a mentor.** Mentors provide guidance, facilitate introductions, and endorse your capabilities.

Additionally, we offer the following suggestions when new directions beckon.

Turning your life around with portable skills

Skills, not preferences, entitle you to be employed. (It's a sad fact that doing what you love is rarely the road to riches.)

The molecules of self-discovery are elusive. Self-discovery in a group setting is more fun than sitting alone scratching your head. Sign up for a career workshop and get help. The group dynamics are similar to those that motivate members in a weight-control organisation: "How many pounds did you lose?" translates to "How many skills did you come up with?"

Start trawling for transferable skills as you review abbreviated lists in Chapters 3 and 11. Plan to spend as many as 20 hours over the next few weeks in putting a name to each of your marketable skills.

What if you don't have the transferable skills you need to ply a new trade? Maybe you can use volunteerism as a stepping stone to a new career. Volunteer for a brief period of time through a volunteer referral service to make sure that you're legally working without pay.

Choosing your best format

Choose the functional format or its hybrid offspring. This class of formats emphasises the transferable skills in your pocket. Your presentation must help the employer see what you can do, not merely what you have done. A by-the-numbers reverse chronological format doesn't give you the flexibility to change your image.

Starting with pertinent skills

Place the skills relevant to your intended change up front in your CV. If you don't have any, start the analysis process again or get a night job to cover your bills while you gain relevant experience or education. Relevant skills are what employers must hit on immediately.

Acquiring more skills

Figure on two indispensable skills for most career changers:

- ✔ **Computer literacy.** You need to at least be able to use word processing and spreadsheet programs.
- ✔ **Internet literacy.** You need to at least be able to use e-mail and search engines.

If you didn't grow up digital, take seminars and find a tutor (think laterally – a neighbourhood teenager may be perfect), or sign up for community college courses or adult education classes. Possessing computer and Internet skills makes you seem not old and rigid, but young and flexible, which encourages employers to look at you and see reduced training costs along with a new source of technological support.

Matching your target job description

When you've firmly labelled your mobile marketable skills and found more than you expected, what's next? Here's a practical idea to begin your career shift: Find or write job descriptions of your target occupations. If you like your current field and are leaving involuntarily because it's disappearing from under your feet, start with job descriptions in closely related jobs. Compare requirements of related jobs with your transferable skills profile. If you don't like your current field, forget we mentioned it.

To identify occupations closely related to your current field, check the *Occupational Outlook Handbook*. It's published by the US Department of Labor but is still recommended by UK careers guides as a round up of available jobs (www.bls.gov/oco).

Show skills as they apply to new position

In a career change, as you list your skills, education, and experience, lead with the information relevant to the new position and then list the other data. You have to quickly convince the employer that you have the ability to handle the position.

Assume an engineer wants to move into sales. The CV should mention things like "client liaison", "preparing presentations for meetings", and "strong communications skills".

In an asset statement (see Chapter 13), you may begin by writing: "Used a strong technical background and excellent communications skills in a sales role". Then continue to speak of your ability to provide good technical advice in a business relationship. But writing that you "enjoy learning" is a coin with two sides; the employer may see you as flexible in your desire to further your education, or, conversely, make a negative judgement that you're saying you don't have the skills right now to hit the ground running.

Knowing the name of what you have to offer gets you up off your knees, out of the past, and into the future. You no longer have to say, "This is what I have done; can you use me?" Now you can write a CV that readers will respect, by saying, "This is what I can do for you that will add to your productivity, efficiency, or effectiveness. Not to mention a little bump on the bottom line".

Using appropriate headings

If you are using freelance, hobby, or volunteer experience, use the heading *Work Experience* and list it first, unless you have changed your focus through education. Then begin with the heading *Education.* To refine this heading, substitute target-job-related education, such as *Accounting Education* or *Healthcare Education.* Your employment history follows.

What do you do with all the experience that was great in your old job but means nothing where you want to go? Lump it together at the end of your CV under *Other Experience* or *Earlier Experience.* Shrink it to positions, titles, employers, and/or degrees and educational institutions. If extraneous experience is older than five years, give it the old heave-ho.

Taking a lower-level job

When you are willing to step down from your previous level of work, the first thing to know is don't try to do it with a CV. Do it by a personal first contact where you get a chance to paint yourself in the best light and to defuse intuitive rejection. You tell your story before recruiters and employers can say they don't want to hear it.

You are not a manager lowering yourself by looking for a much less responsible job. You are a career changer exploring new fields:

> *In the past decade, I've put in very long hours and exceeded expectations in jobs in the same industry. I realised I'm a doer who needs new mountains to climb. I have too much to give to the business world to ride on autopilot the rest of my life. I want to check out other ways I can make a contribution in a different career field, hopefully at your company.*

Go directly to the hiring manager and explain why and, from the manager's point of view, WIIFM (What's in it for me?):

> *What's in it for you? I have a great work attitude and excellent judgement. Show me a new task, and I get it right away. I understand, of course, that the trade-off in looking into your industry is less pay and responsibility.*

When you've opened the door, hand over your CV. Write a hybrid CV (detailed in Chapter 9) with heavy emphasis on the functional part. You need breathing room to shape your CV in a way that spotlights your transferable skills as they pertain to the job you seek, such as talent for working with numbers, reliability, and good attendance record, as well as fast-learning ability.

When you are a major seeking a minor position, emphasise that, sometimes, good people need new challenges.

And don't forget WIIFM. WIIFM may not prove to be the answer every time, but that's the way to bet.

Striking it rich by career changing

From the very first moment a reader sets eyes on your CV, the answers to these questions must be apparent:

- ✔ Why are you qualified for the position in my company?
- ✔ Why doesn't your last position relate to this one?

Answer these on your CV, and you're on your way to the career change you seek.

Gaffes Common to Seasoned Aces

When you've got a long job history behind you, you're more likely to need updates on the following issues. You're probably aware of the more obvious changes in the job market, like the growth of technology, and are keen to avoid appearing behind the times – but have you thought about the shifts in job focus? Or how you can present your experience so that it doesn't date you or stir up stereotypes about old dogs and new tricks?

Using old CV standards

Many fifty-somethings, still working on last decade's calendar, have an out-dated concept of what a CV should be. A client recently expressed surprise when we told him to leave out his personal information, which once was standard fare on CVs. "Oh, I thought personal information was supposed to humanise you", he said. Busy employers and job computers don't care that you are a par golfer or play tennis; this kind of personal bonding information comes out at the interview.

Revealing age negatively

Don't blurt out your age. Your mindset should be this: Start with ageless – you can always move to senior. Do not put old education first on your CV (unless you are a professional educator). Avoid listing jobs with dates older than 10 or 15 years. If you must include dusty jobs, tone down the dates or omit them. You can summarise old jobs under a heading of "Prior to 2003" (or whatever year) and avoid being too specific. Alternatively, you can include all jobs under functional headings. Try not to describe older jobs in detail.

Choosing the wrong focus

Choosing the wrong focus is a problem shared with new graduates who fail to elaborate on those jobs that best address the hoped-for next job.

Try this approach: Use the worksheets in Chapter 13 to draft an ency-clopaedic master CV. The number of pages doesn't matter – you'll never use it in its entirety. Each time that you're tailoring a CV for a specific job opening, review your master CV and choose those jobs most directly related to your new goal.

TIP

Presenting short-term work on your CV

Fifty-somethings may find that they're doing work for a specific company but are being paid through a temporary staffing firm or other intermediary. So how do they report the information on their CVs? Don't list the middle-man firm. Note only the companies for which the work was performed. Here's a brief template:

Company A, Company B, Company C 20xx to present

For **Company A,** Name of Department/Division

    As **job title,** performed:

✔ achievement

✔ achievement

✔ achievement

For **Company B,** Name of Department/Division

    As **job title,** implemented:

✔ achievement

✔ achievement

✔ achievement

For **Company C,** Name of Department/Division

    As **job title,** credited with:

✔ achievement

✔ achievement

✔ achievement

By the way, if your job titles are extreme – whether insignificant or overly exalted – don't put them in bold.

Lacking a summary

Because of the extensiveness of your experience, your CV may be unwieldy without a summary. Usually, using both an objective and a summary is superfluous, but exceptions occur. Suppose you're fed up living as a city slicker and want to move to a small town where agribusiness is dominant. Your objective may take only one line – "Wish to work as internal auditor in the farm equipment industry". Follow that statement with a one- or two-paragraph summary of why you are qualified. Think of a summary as a salesperson's hook. It describes some of your special skills, your familiarity with the target industry, and your top achievements. For examples of summaries, see Chapter 13.

T-REX

If your objective and summary are two ways of saying the same thing, dispense with one of them.

Appearing low-tech

Seasoned aces who do not have computers still type CVs; others with computers have old-fashioned dot matrix printers. Their CVs are often stopped at the door. Today's readers like crisp, attractive layouts that only a computer and laser printer can create. Trade a dinner for CV services from a friend, use a computer free at a library, rent a computer by the hour at a copy centre/Web café, or pay a professional to do your CV.

Not supplementing a school education

If your highest education attainment is at school level, don't forget to mention any continuing education, including seminars and workshops related to your work – if it applies to what you want to do next.

Smiling Beats Frowning

No one is silly enough to claim that for mature workers the rejection experience in job hunting is fun. But a smile a day helps keep your morale from sagging. Here's one to start you out: "Oh Lord, give me patience – and give it to me NOW!"

Chapter 5

Info Tech CVs: Write Them Right

In This Chapter

▶ Getting across your skills and experience

▶ Looking at your CV through recruiters' eyes

▶ Finding the right formula

*I*nformation technology (IT) professionals were the golden boys and girls of the job market until the downturn in the early twenty-first century. Now, they're the market's gladiators, battling for every job opening. If you're one of these tech-savvy job hunters, this chapter is for you.

Give Your Job Search Your Best Shot Right Now

If you've been laid off or you just want a better IT job, get cracking without delay. That's the word from experts who track IT careers. This isn't the time to kick back or take time off to go adventuring through a rain forest.

First, Janet Ruhl, CEO of RealRates.com, says:

> *Working is always better than not working. A couple of years ago, you might have been able to turn down a couple of jobs while you held out for £70 an hour, but in the current down market, you'd be wise to take any contract or job that keeps your skills current. A gap of more than six months on your CV may make it much harder to find any new position.*

Dr Norman Matloff, professor of computer science at the University of California, Davis and operator of the number-one mailing list for IT professionals (`matloff@cs.ucdavis.edu`) also has some advice. He says that you shouldn't let grass grow under your feet and warns against age discrimination fall-out:

If a programmer goes, say, more than a year without programming work, he or she is considered "out of the field" and is generally shunned by employers and headhunters. The programmer is told, "Sorry, the field is changing extremely rapidly, and you are just not up to date." Actually, the situation is somewhat similar to the one in which a programmer stays in a job that uses an old technology and then gets laid off and tries with poor luck to find other programming work. But the out-of-the-field people have it even worse. They are presumed to have even forgotten how to program altogether during that year of absence.

The glory days of Y2K compliance and Euro conversion work are but a fading memory, and large scale computing projects are fewer and further between. Competition, therefore, is fierce. IT jobs specialist CW Jobs (www.cwjobs.co.uk) points out that IT vacancies plummeted by 38 per cent in the last quarter of 2002. That said, the announcements of IT reviews for the NHS, along with the Inland Revenue's Aspire system mean that work is not about to completely dry up.

What does seem to have vanished is the demand for basic Web creation skills. CW Jobs keeps a regularly updated top ten list of IT skills. While tried and trusted basics like SQL, C++, and Unix have held their top spots for the last three years, relative newcomers like HTML have dropped out of the top ten in the wake of the dot.com downturn. The situation isn't exactly doom and gloom, but it's certainly no time to take your foot off the pedal. Reduced demand and increased competition don't mean you should turn to plumbing, but they do mean you need to strive to stand out from the CV crowd.

Components of a StandOut IT CV

No one can predict when the IT job market will re-ignite, so we won't even try. Instead, what we can do for you human technical powerhouses is describe the important fundamentals in making a StandOut IT CV (we also provide general advice throughout this book).

We talked with the recruiting manager for a well-known defence contractor, Adrian Barbour. Barbour says that he spends 90 percent of his time at a computer screen reading CVs. And how many does he review each year? "Thousands!" the very experienced CV reader replied.

We asked Barbour a series of questions. Here are his responses.

Us: Which is more important on a CV: technical or people skills?

AB: On the IT side, technical skills weigh more heavily than personality. On the management side, the reverse is true. People skills are an area in which techies are very, very weak.

Us: What kind of CV makes HR people warm to you?

AB: HR professionals like CVs that centre on a focus statement. A CV that says "I'm a networking administrator", for example, immediately clues HR professionals into what to look for. The HR person can say, "Does this person have enough years of experience? Okay, that's what we want". And we go from there. Contrast that direct connection with a CV that's all over the place. When job seekers have a multiplicity of skills, they need to split those up into different CVs. You'd be surprised how many people fail to spell out their skills and talents in relationship to the job they want. In effect, they're saying, "Do you think I can fit anything you do? Let me know". I don't have time to guess.

Us: So the main problem is a lack of specificity?

AB: That's correct. A CV that lacks a specific objective receives scant attention. Is it software? Is it engineering? I don't want to have to think for an applicant.

Us: Anything else that causes a CV to be passed over?

AB: A problem I see over and over is the failure to relate functions to the positions you've held. A CV will mention a long list of applications or operating systems, but they're never explained – never fleshed out – in the body of the positions held. It's a kind of disconnect. The CV claims abilities in Java, C++, and says in a cursory manner, "I programmed this and did a database" – but gives no details to back up the claims.

The IT CV Explained

This section contains two IT CVs from Adrian Barbour's electronic cellars. They illustrate both ends of the experience spectrum. Dates, job searcher names, and some company names are fictional on both. Figure 5-1 markets a senior candidate, and Figure 5-2 is a CV for a junior candidate.

Robin Churchouse

The Robin Churchouse CV in Figure 5-1 is heavily muscled, highlighting the candidate's seniority. Churchouse opens with a strong summary of qualifications, so the reader quickly gains an overview of his experience, skills, and abilities.

IT Executive

Robin Churchouse
MBA
robinc@ciomagazine.com

(0207) 543-3456 (home) ❖ 31 Talbot Road, Notting Hill, London W11 ❖ (0760) 555-8450 (mobile)

EXECUTIVE SUMMARY

A leader. A self-motivated, results-driven senior information technology (IT) professional with hands-on experience in company operations, and all aspects of IT. Have business background in manufacturing processes. Experienced with Lawson, JD Edwards One-World, and many other ERP software platforms.

Possess an in-depth understanding of emerging technologies. Seeking a position in a dynamic environment, with extensive experience developing, managing, analysing infrastructures with NT, Sun Solaris, SQL, JDE, VPN, TCP/IP, AS400, SAP, Oracle, PeopleSoft Financials, e-business, EDI, IP telephony designs, software development and customer service solutions.

Responsible for P/L's, multi-million pound network deployments and product launches, budgets, policies, business analysis, risk assessment, auditing and cross-functional operations, domestic, global and tactical planning. A seasoned professional with senior management planning, international and domestic business operations experience.

AREAS OF EXPERTISE

- SQL Server
- VOIP/Unified Messaging
- Software Programming
- Data/Internet Security
- JDE One-World
- HMTL, ASP
- Network System Engineering
- TDMA/CDMAWireless
- Web Development.
- Visual Basic
- Unix, AS400, Sun
- ASIC Design

- ERP/MRP/Globally
- MS NT Exchange/Citrix
- International Development
- Sales Order Processing
- Disaster Recovery Planning
- Supply Chain Management
- Data Warehousing
- Buying/Purchasing
- Financial Systems
- Product Management
- Risk Management
- Project Management

EDUCATION

- MBA, Barbour Center for International Business, University of California at Oceanside, CA, USA.
- BSC Degree, York University.

EMPLOYMENT HISTORY

10/02 - Present
PeopleVu International Corporation, Canary Wharf, London.
Executive Manager Information Technology
- Established goals, objectives, and policies. Developed and implemented programs to ensure attainment of business plan for growth, profit and branding. Implemented cost-savings, cost avoidance exceeding four hundred thousand within two months. Responsible for daily operations of IT department. Developed organisational structure, strategic growth plans and all operational policies and procedures. Created business processes and flows for revenue and initiated data/Internet security, auditing, implementing best practices.

Figure 5-1: CV of a senior professional.

- Managed and implemented Oracle platform, Unix, IBM AS400 IT-related projects to supply chain management and operations, including Lawson software and EDI Platform. Responsibilities include three WAN/LAN networks and a lab using management methodology for "IT", budget analysis, user requirements, and communication of project status, schedule development and tracking.

10/99 - 9/02
WonderWerks, Irvine, California, USA.
Chief Information Director of Operations
- Developed and implemented the JDE One-World experience technology for Star Trac and all operations in every department on a Unix platform. Implemented over five million pounds worth of cost savings, and cost-avoidance procedures within two years on several initiated programs. Initiated all IT budgets, manufacturing supply chain management, recruitment and P/L.

- Initiated and developed the disaster procedures and methodologies appropriate for the information infrastructure, EDI, SQL, web site and telephony system to mitigate risks. Successfully created and deployed the infrastructure utilising LAN/WAN globally for international and domestic projects, VPN solution, DHCP, SSL, Citrix, wireless solution and Microsoft globally. Developed and initiated data/Internet security, auditing, implementing best practices procedures. Initiated, designed the infrastructure and rollout for all desktop computers, NT processes.

- Successfully replaced the old "PBX phone system" and developed the new "IP telephone system" telecommunication from Cisco System VOIP unified messaging.

- Created a platform and published white papers for internal and external distribution.

- Led 11 project manager-teams globally on Cisco deployment remote access (RAS).

8/89 - 10/99
Lamb Enterprises, Reading, Berks.
IT Business Manager
- Implemented best practices on risk mitigation and emergency contingency with manufacturing, ERP, MRP processes, IS departments and all phases of operations and finance. Managed product development life cycle and communication platforms. Developed business processes and flow for revenue, platform with JDE. Implemented cost savings, cost avoidance over two million pounds.

- Extensive hands-on experience with MS Exchange, CICS, and IBM products, AS400, OS/390, RS/6000 and network server clustering. Initiated "San" backup solution technology in the event of a catastrophe and developed and implemented numerous disaster recovery designs, defining and documenting new processes and interdepartmental relationships with contingency plan. Successfully developed and implemented network designs, SAP, e-business platforms, ERP/MRP, IP phone systems processes, EDI and supply chain management. Created platform and published white papers for internal and external distribution. Conducted seminars on catastrophic and contingency plans for customer service. Effectively directed, influenced, developed and motivated subordinates, obtaining positive team solutions.

Notice that Churchouse's heading includes immediate credential identification. Additionally, it offers multiple means of contact to interested employers. This feature is very important because each hiring manager has a preference for contacting applicants: Some prefer e-mail, and others take the traditional approach of using the phone.

The "Areas of Expertise" section allows for easy scanning into databases, yet the CV maintains an attractive professional appearance. The style is conservative and tasteful. If the candidate wrote his own CV, a reader could ascribe these same characteristics to the candidate.

Short paragraphs and bullets in the "Employment History" section make Churchouse's CV easier to read and comprehend.

The general rule in CV construction is to lead with the most important, relevant, and impressive information. Churchouse has already done that with his powerful executive summary and areas of expertise. That's why Churchouse has placed his education section before a formal description of his experience. When educational attainment is a firm requirement with no possibility of exception, a recruiter wants to know quickly so that time isn't wasted reading through to the end only to find that the candidate has high achievement but a shortfall of educational credentials.

Note that Churchouse doesn't supply the years of his graduations. Although some employers still insist on knowing the year when a candidate graduated and received a degree, those details can easily lead to age discrimination. So Churchouse omits the years, wanting to be evaluated for the benefits he brings, not for the candles he blows out on his birthday cake.

Daniel Bessant

Daniel Bessant, a much younger and more junior candidate than Churchouse, also "gets it". He provides several forms of contact and clearly states his objective in Figure 5-2.

Bessant launches his self-marketing with a statement of what he has to sell. The skills list incorporates personal characteristic statements (such as "positive attitude," "dependable," "accountable," and "work under minimal supervision") as well as an itemising of his abilities. The certification information validates his claims of competence and is very important.

Bessant's work experience is scant, but he makes the most of it by listing functions and adding a statement about his self-employed moonlighting activities repairing computers, a clue that he truly enjoys technical work.

IT Technician	**Daniel Bessant**

25 The Pavement, Clapham Common, London SW4 9NG
Home: 0208 543-6789 ~ Mobile: 0760 111-2314 ~ E-mail: dandan@peoplevu.com

Objective

Computer Technician/Network Support

Skills

➤ Proficient in assembling, diagnosing, repairing, and rolling out new computer systems
➤ Effective helpdesk trouble-ticketing system and remote desktop connection experience
➤ Able to resolve network connectivity, security, e-mail, and protocol issues
➤ Experience with Novell, Linux, Windows 9x, XP, NT, 2000 server and workstation
➤ Knowledgeable in MS Word, Excel, Outlook, PowerPoint, and Access applications
➤ Qualified to create, update, and deploy Symantec Ghost System Images
➤ Able to fabricate, test, and install UTP or Fibre-optic cables
➤ Possess strong written and oral communications skills along with a positive attitude
➤ Reputation as dependable, accountable, and able to work under minimal supervision

Certifications

➤ **MCP** – Windows 2000 Professional
➤ **Network+, CompTIA** – Networking Technologies
➤ **A+, CompTIA** – Software and Hardware Technician
➤ **Network Architect/Telecom Cable Installation** – Network Design

Experience

Helpdesk I – Major Insurance, Canary Wharf – 2003 - Present
Successfully used a helpdesk trouble-ticket system to document event-calls and remotely connect to customer computers. Involved with Symantec Ghost System Imaging, transferring user preferences, data integrity, and insured domain user connectivity associated with a new computer rollout. Performed PC service calls to troubleshoot and replace hardware, install applications, and upgrade memory. Performed printer maintenance, upgrades, and resolved network connectivity issues.

PC Repair – Self Employed – 1997 - 2004
Repaired, upgraded, and built PC's.

Education

Miracosta College – 2003
➤ **MSC Computer Science Information Systems and LAN Support Specialist**
Emphasis in PC troubleshooting skills, network security, connectivity, structured cabling design, and Microsoft Office applications. Continually achieved highest academic performance of the year.

Figure 5-2: An IT CV that makes the most of limited experience.

The young technician's formal education rounds out a straightforward CV of a job searcher who's not yet able to report a history of measurable achievements similar to that of Robin Churchouse's CV but who clearly has the qualifications to work in a position a step or two above entry-level employment.

Security clearances help IT hiring

Security clearances are likely to be required in any defence-related industry.

A friend of ours recounts the story of a recent IT candidate who applied to a defence contractor for a position. The candidate later called the company to complain that he was not contacted for a job for which he was confident he was a match. Our friend looked at his CV and, indeed, he was a match – except that the candidate omitted the fact that he holds a secret clearance. Because the position he applied for required a clearance, he never came up in a search of the database.

With the UK government said to be preparing for a £5 billion, ten year overhaul of its IT system, now might seem like a great time to apply for military contract work. If you currently have or qualify for a clearance, add that fact to your CV. Here are a few tips about security clearances:

✔ The Professional Contractors Group (www. pcg.org.uk) points out that "many IT freelancers are finding themselves in a Catch 22 when applying for MOD contracts;

unable to get clearance until they have a contract, and unable to get a contract until they have clearance". To get a clearance from the Defence Vetting Agency, you need to have a *sponsor* – the company that contracts you for the work – but most jobs advertised require *current clearance*. In theory this means that, once you're in, you can swing from job to job, but breaking in can be a nightmare.

✔ Even then there's no guarantee that the clearance from one job will necessarily be transferable to the next without going through screening again.

✔ Instead of waiting for a job to be advertised and then losing it to someone with clearance, try thinking ahead and developing a relationship with those companies and agencies that regularly hire out contractors to the defence industry.

For more information on the types and processes of vetting take a look at the Defence Vetting Agency Web site at www.mod.uk/dva.

Chapter 6

Out of Uniform and into Civvy Street

. . . .

In This Chapter

▶ Civilianising your military experience

▶ Reviewing sample CVs for returning to Civvy Street

▶ Networking with other vets

. . . .

*T*he military recruiter told you that service in the Armed Forces – with its training programmes and real-life experience – would make the civilian world walk over hot coals to employ you when you finished serving your country. Now that the moment for leaving is near, you're wondering: Was that just marketing hype?

Okay, soldier . . . Okay, sailor . . . Okay, airman . . . you're about to find out the truth as you transition to a workplace where you no longer salute. In this chapter, we help you get your bearings and show how your military experience is transferable to a civilian job.

Turning Your CV into a Civilian Must-Read

Military veterans are highly trained, exceptionally skilled, and remarkably disciplined. They have a strong work ethic and try to get it right the first time. Many military members move ahead much faster than their civilian counterparts. The problem is that, in order for Civvy Street to understand your qualities, you first have to learn to speak in the language Civvy Street is used to hearing. The services are big on "doing" rather than "talking", which is great, but when it's time to sell yourself into a new career, you're not going to get a chance to show what you can do if you can't communicate your skills.

Take this example, from veteran Bill Gaul who is now himself in the recruiting business:

> *An Army colonel's CV we were recently sent read: "As commanding officer of a 500-person organisation, I was responsible for the health, morale, and welfare of all personnel." Health, morale and welfare? Just think of the incredible range of skills and experience completely overlooked in that Milspeak phrase. Far-reaching accomplishments and important responsibilities are whitewashed into non-effective boilerplate terms that mean nothing to a civilian hiring manager.*
>
> *For example, digging into "health, morale, and welfare", we found policy development, human resource management, budget planning and administration, process improvement, operations management, and staff development.*

The following sections highlight the areas where it is particularly beneficial to translate from military-speak to a language HR people can understand.

Making job titles reader friendly

One key area where military jargon whitewashes any real meaning is in job titles. Many military job titles are impenetrable to outsiders; others are dangerously ambiguous. Is a fire control officer someone who put out fires or someone who operates electronic weapons targeting systems? Give a thought to translating your job title into its civilian equivalent and break it down into the transferable skills that go into it.

To help do that, select a functional CV format (see Chapter 9) that emphasises skills first and lists work history and job titles last.

List your relative position in an organisation – "unit supervisor" instead of "platoon sergeant", for example. Titles like Petty Officer or NCO are meaningless to most civilians, so consider what you did and see whether alternative terms like "logistics/facility supervisor", or "trainer/manager" can help put your experience into focus for the civilian world.

Here's a CV tip for officers: If you intend to work with third-party recruiters, check with several to determine their CV format preferences. Many want a description of your responsibilities by job title, almost like a chronological format but without the years spent at individual posts. This format works well for any officer selling management experience because it highlights important assignments and allows you to select only those that support your objective.

Turning military responsibilities into civilian skills

Take nothing for granted. Explain, detail, describe. Suppose you're a technician; what specific technical aspects of your job are transferable to the civilian sector? Do you read blueprints, schematics, and technical drawings? Have you utilised specific diagnostic equipment? Your objective is to let an employer know just how much training she would *not* have to provide if she hired you.

If you're short on equivalency facts, research can mean the difference between a trip for your CV to the "No" pile and a trip to the interview room. (See Chapter 8 for ways to market yourself in the civilian workforce and Chapter 13 for worksheets you can fill out to uncover the skills you want to highlight.)

Quantifying training

To help CV reviewers understand the depth of your training, list the number of classroom hours you studied. To determine the number of hours, multiply the number of course days by 8, or the number of weeks by 40. If you completed the course within the last 10 years, list the completion date. If the course is older, leave off the date.

✔ Leadership and Management Training, 3/95 (160 hours)

or

✔ Leadership and Management Training (160 hours)

Sample CVs: Examples That Work

Take a look at the two examples shown in Figures 6-1 and 6-2. The first CV, Christopher Hart, shows through his experiences that he offers a great deal more competencies and skills than may be associated with an NCO (non-commissioned officer). He uses civilian equivalent job titles followed by his actual title in parenthesis and itemises his background to highlight his role in training, employee retention, and accountability for property. By defining his demonstrated skills, Hart increases his universe of potential employers. He has stayed away from the overused term "Responsible for" and instead used action verbs to do his talking.

MILITARY TRANSITION

Christopher Hart
24 Eden Gardens,
Victoria Park, Manchester
chris.hart1@earthlink.net

0161 987-6543

EDUCATION	**Open University** Master of Arts: March, 2002 in Human Resource Development	**University of Liverpool** Bachelor of Arts: January, 2001 in Business Management

EXPERIENCE

British Army

King's and Cheshire Regiment, Warrington

January 2000 –
March 2002

Senior Administrative Manager (Senior Military Clerk)

- Personally directed the organisation of a newly activated company consisting of 400 employees
- Improved the company's training program which greatly increased morale, discipline, and motivation
- Maintained prudent care of a £4 million facility housing a maximum of 672 employees
- Recognised as mastering the Army's complex personnel management system
- Cited as a Master Trainer for exceptional ability to motivate and train

British Army

King's and Cheshire Regiment, Liverpool

Nov 1997 –
Jan 2000

Senior Personnel Supervisor (Military Clerk, HR)

- Designed and developed automated tracking procedures for individual awards and outstanding personnel actions
- Conducted individual counselling and professional development programs for over 200 employees daily
- Provided training and supervision of employees on the proper operation and maintenance of the Army's personnel database
- Lead research initiatives designed to improve personnel services for remote employees
- Advised superiors on equal opportunity matters

British Army
Recruiting Centre Peter Street, Manchester

Apr 1991 –
Sep 1996

Personnel Specialist (Personnel Sergeant)

- Served as the personnel manager for a nation-wide organisation with extensive overseas offices
- Provided short- and long-range personnel requirements
- Co-ordinated hiring actions
- Provided training and professional mentorship to seven district personnel managers

SKILLS

Security clearance, facilitator and motivator, Microsoft Office, equal opportunity advisor, advanced leadership and management development courses

---

Figure 6-1: A military career translated into equivalent civilian job positions.

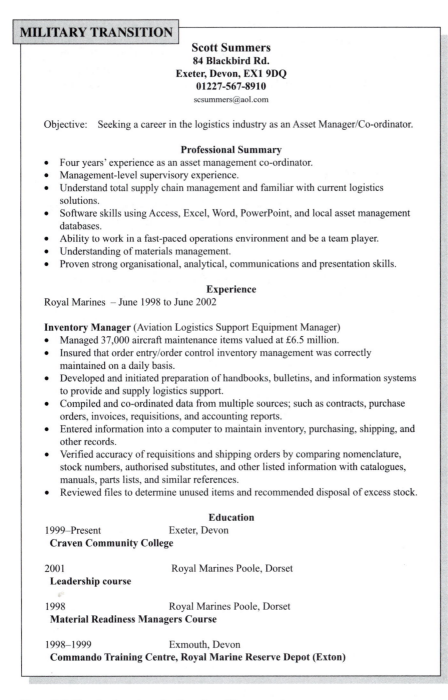

MILITARY TRANSITION

Scott Summers
84 Blackbird Rd.
Exeter, Devon, EX1 9DQ
01227-567-8910
scsummers@aol.com

Objective: Seeking a career in the logistics industry as an Asset Manager/Co-ordinator.

Professional Summary
- Four years' experience as an asset management co-ordinator.
- Management-level supervisory experience.
- Understand total supply chain management and familiar with current logistics solutions.
- Software skills using Access, Excel, Word, PowerPoint, and local asset management databases.
- Ability to work in a fast-paced operations environment and be a team player.
- Understanding of materials management.
- Proven strong organisational, analytical, communications and presentation skills.

Experience
Royal Marines – June 1998 to June 2002

Inventory Manager (Aviation Logistics Support Equipment Manager)
- Managed 37,000 aircraft maintenance items valued at £6.5 million.
- Insured that order entry/order control inventory management was correctly maintained on a daily basis.
- Developed and initiated preparation of handbooks, bulletins, and information systems to provide and supply logistics support.
- Compiled and co-ordinated data from multiple sources; such as contracts, purchase orders, invoices, requisitions, and accounting reports.
- Entered information into a computer to maintain inventory, purchasing, shipping, and other records.
- Verified accuracy of requisitions and shipping orders by comparing nomenclature, stock numbers, authorised substitutes, and other listed information with catalogues, manuals, parts lists, and similar references.
- Reviewed files to determine unused items and recommended disposal of excess stock.

Education
1999–Present   Exeter, Devon
  Craven Community College

2001   Royal Marines Poole, Dorset
  Leadership course

1998   Royal Marines Poole, Dorset
  Material Readiness Managers Course

1998–1999   Exmouth, Devon
  Commando Training Centre, Royal Marine Reserve Depot (Exton)

Figure 6-2: Showing broad applications for military experience.

The second CV, Scott Summers, also shows a good understanding of the need to write CVs in "civilianese," not Milspeak. Although Summers' military title, Aviation Logistics Support Equipment Manager, is impressive, it's more than a mouthful when applied to the type of managerial position he seeks. By using the civilian term, "Inventory Manager", an employer quickly sees that Summers is not limited to the aircraft or military sectors, but can be considered for any type of industry.

A Final Thought

Finally don't overlook the fact that the move to civilian life isn't always as smooth as people would like, so make the most of any contacts and introductions you can.

Whilst it is true that selling yourself in Civvy Street can seem a tough proposition, you do at least come with a support group of people who understand the importance of working together. The military is a family, and networking is natural among family members.

Chapter 7

Good Advice for Graduates

In This Chapter

▶ Implementing hot tips

▶ Knowing what to do when you have little or no experience

▶ Handling advanced degrees on CVs

▶ Avoiding self-defeating errors

*Y*our first job after graduation is a pivotal point in your life because it sets the stage for what follows. Whether you're writing your first CV in anticipation of putting work clothes on your bachelor's degree or updating your CV as a graduate who went back to college for an advanced degree, this chapter can help you master the CV-writing course.

Tips for New Graduates

If you're getting out of college in a year of plentiful jobs, congratulations, you lucky graduate. But if jobs are scarce and the going is tough, show that you know how to take a punch and come up swinging. Using the strategies scattered throughout this book can help you make a winner's case for jobs you want. And any recent graduate can benefit from using the CV tips in these sections.

Getting educated about CVs

The number one tip for new graduates: Attend CV and application workshops.

CV workshops are offered at your campus career centre or careers advisory office – look out for them in "Careers Week". A good workshop will give you an understanding of what has worked for others in your position including specific approaches for specific companies. It's also a chance to ask for advice on your own personal niggles or doubts. Whether you're an undergraduate, graduate student, or a fully-fledged graduate, nothing beats a classroom setting for focusing on the knowledge presented.

Seek advice from your school's careers advisors. They can help you understand the prerequisites individual recruiters look for in their specific career fields. Applying to company X may feel like a shot in the dark to you, but a careers advisor has probably helped others do the same and can help you turn that experience to your advantage when tailoring your CV.

Compensating for shortcomings

If you can't qualify for a hiring prerequisite, try to figure out a compensatory benefit you offer. For example, if your hard-earned 2:2 falls a little short of the 2:1 specified, use an opening summary that focuses on knowing the value of hard work – especially if you learned that value by holding a series of demanding student jobs while working your way through college. For information on writing your CV's summary, head to Chapter 10.

Beefing up a sales pitch

Thicken your work experience by including all unpaid positions – job-shadowing, special projects, and volunteer jobs. List them in chronological order in your Work Experience section. Statements like these are powerful agents on your CV:

Sales: Sold £1,200 worth of tickets for the college arts festival

Student Body activities: Advised 16 undergraduate students as Women's Group peer counsellor

Public Policy Co-ordination: Organiser for student petition to save rare marshland habitat from green-belt encroachment, gaining 2,000 signatures in 35 days

Highlight the work experience most relevant to your intended future. If you have more than two years of full-time professional experience, lead with that and emphasise it above your educational record.

Clarifying your aim

Make your objective clear if you use an objective statement. Don't resort to meaningless marketing jargon or lofty loopiness along the lines of this one:

I'm seeking a challenging position that will allow me to actualise my talents in saving the world, with good potential for professional growth and pay commensurate with my ability.

For more information on writing objectives – and why, as a recent graduate, you should – head to Chapter 10.

Including positive information

In your extracurricular activities or highlights section, list awards, honours, and achievements. Be sure to include items such as scholarships, appointments, elections, chairs, and the names of particular members or bodies of the university faculty who hold you in esteem. Use reverse chronological order.

Omitting unhelpful information

Recruiters and hiring managers don't have a lot of extra time on their hands, and they don't want to waste any of it trying to find your CV buried among a lot of other stuff that you've sent. Help them out a little – do not enclose your CV in a report cover, put it in a bulky package, or attach transcripts or letters of recommendation, unless they are requested.

Similarly, they'll want to get to the meat of your CV as quickly as possible. Include an activity only if it reveals skills, accomplishments, results, or the qualifications to support your intended job. Omit your school information unless you're sure it's bringing something to the party. So, for example faithfully recording your stints as School Librarian might be a plus point for a budding archivist, but it's a bit of a yawn for anything else.

What about the laundry list of your individual college sub-courses – do they earn their keep on your CV? No, unless the course work is unusual or you have little to say without them. Many graduates struggle to fill one page, so use the worksheets in Chapter 13 to get rolling. The quick reminder list in the "Data-Mine Your College Experience" section later in this chapter may nudge the memory banks.

When you graduate at the wrong time

If you find yourself graduating into in a tepid job market, make up your mind that your paste-click-send CV won't pull the interviews you need. Instead, research companies and rewrite your CV to address the companies' needs. Highlight your experience that most applies to the company you're interested in and get it to a hiring manager. Your competition is writing targeted CVs – should you do less?

Even when the job market is flying high, you can soar above the crowd by writing a targeted CV for each job you really want.

Being open-minded

When you're striking out in a slow job market, look for alternatives. For example, if private industry is ignoring you, take a look at opportunities in the public sector. Use a search engine to find an abundant site stash of public sector jobs. The likes of Monster.co.uk and Workthing.com have a large selection, or you can try the government Job Centre at www.jobcentreplus.gov.uk.

Other back-up plans students use include finding temporary jobs, joining VSO (see Chapter 6), relocating to another part of the country, and enrolling in further education.

Data-Mine Your College Experience

Consider the following factors in identifying the experience and skills you garnered in college and matching the information with the job you hope to land:

- **Work:** Job-shadowing, summer jobs, part-time jobs, campus jobs, entrepreneurial jobs, temporary work, volunteer work, and so on.

- **Sports:** Proven ability to achieve goals in a team environment.

- **Awards and honours:** Any academic or sporting recognition that shows that you stood out from your peers.

- **Research papers and projects:** If you did some formal research on a subject relevant to your desired job, whether or not you finished a doctorate, then you should stress that fact.

- **Campus leadership:** Did you take an active role in the student council, or help create and run societies or clubs?

- **Technical skills and software facility:** Did you pick up computer skills in the course of your learning? Have you created your own web pages or mastered a graphics design package?

Before you vault in and write, read the reminders in the rest of this chapter to be sure the results are StandOut style.

New graduate with laudable experience

The following three examples show the different approaches of three graduates, one with a solid background of experience to stress, one with less depth of experience, and so more careful emphasis on the high points, and one with little experience who makes up for it with emphasis on skills and talent.

Figure 7-1 shows the CV of a new graduate who has good experience. Knowing that he may face an apathetic job market armed only with a liberal arts degree, the graduate makes certain that he highlights his impressive work experience to beef up his self-marketing document.

New graduate with some experience

Work-experience and student jobs are the ticket to the job market. Many students are getting the work-experience message, as this question from a reader suggests:

> *My school's career centre is holding CV workshops for graduating students. I can't go because I'm doing as I was told – getting work experience. Do employers really believe that a student job produces valuable real-life experience?*

Absolutely yes. And a StandOut CV shows every shred of work experience, paid and unpaid, through internships, student jobs, co-op education, and extracurricular activities. Figure 7-2 presents a student with some experience.

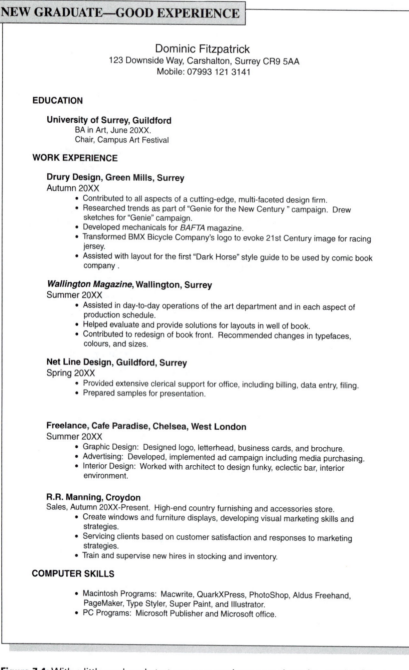

NEW GRADUATE—GOOD EXPERIENCE

Dominic Fitzpatrick
123 Downside Way, Carshalton, Surrey CR9 5AA
Mobile: 07993 121 3141

EDUCATION

University of Surrey, Guildford
BA in Art, June 20XX.
Chair, Campus Art Festival

WORK EXPERIENCE

Drury Design, Green Mills, Surrey
Autumn 20XX
- Contributed to all aspects of a cutting-edge, multi-faceted design firm.
- Researched trends as part of "Genie for the New Century " campaign. Drew sketches for "Genie" campaign.
- Developed mechanicals for *BAFTA* magazine.
- Transformed BMX Bicycle Company's logo to evoke 21st Century image for racing jersey.
- Assisted with layout for the first "Dark Horse" style guide to be used by comic book company .

***Wallington Magazine*, Wallington, Surrey**
Summer 20XX
- Assisted in day-to-day operations of the art department and in each aspect of production schedule.
- Helped evaluate and provide solutions for layouts in well of book.
- Contributed to redesign of book front. Recommended changes in typefaces, colours, and sizes.

Net Line Design, Guildford, Surrey
Spring 20XX
- Provided extensive clerical support for office, including billing, data entry, filing.
- Prepared samples for presentation.

Freelance, Cafe Paradise, Chelsea, West London
Summer 20XX
- Graphic Design: Designed logo, letterhead, business cards, and brochure.
- Advertising: Developed, implemented ad campaign including media purchasing.
- Interior Design: Worked with architect to design funky, eclectic bar, interior environment.

R.R. Manning, Croydon
Sales, Autumn 20XX-Present. High-end country furnishing and accessories store.
- Create windows and furniture displays, developing visual marketing skills and strategies.
- Servicing clients based on customer satisfaction and responses to marketing strategies.
- Train and supervise new hires in stocking and inventory.

COMPUTER SKILLS

- Macintosh Programs: Macwrite, QuarkXPress, PhotoShop, Aldus Freehand, PageMaker, Type Styler, Super Paint, and Illustrator.
- PC Programs: Microsoft Publisher and Microsoft office.

Figure 7-1: With a little work and strategy, new graduates can have impressive CVs, too.

NEW GRADUATE—SOME EXPERIENCE

MARTINA RABINOVICH
123 College Drive, Boston, Lincs, PE21 7JG Tel 01205 111-2233

OBJECTIVE
Position with environmentally and socially conscious public relations firm. Proven skills in public relations, research, and organisation; demonstrated leadership qualities throughout university activities and professional experience. Computer Skills.

HIGHLIGHTS OF PUBLIC RELATIONS EXPERIENCE

- **Nottingham County Council**, Summers 20XX-20XX
  Assisted Councilor Glamer to resolve constituents' issues. Communicated with legislative committees, researched legislation through the computer system, and attended town meetings. Accumulated invaluable public relations skills, using interpersonal abilities effectively in high-pressure, deadline-oriented situations. Major project: Veteran's Festival, 50th Anniversary.

- **Student Body Vice-President**, Lincoln University, 20XX-20XX
  Chaired Council Operations Committee. Conducted all student body elections, using strong leadership and public speaking skills to accrue 1,600 votes.

- **Medford Municipal Pool Lifeguard**, Medford, Lincs, Summers 20XX-20XX
  Began as snack bar employee, earned certificate, promoted to lifeguard, then to head lifeguard with managerial responsibilities. Supervised 11 employees.

- **OTHER PUBLIC RELATIONS ACTIVITIES:**
  Student advisor, tour guide, campus delegate, student ambassador for alumni, peer tutor for critical thinking.

RESEARCH EXPERIENCE

- **Labour Party Pollster**, Medford District, Medford, Lincs, May & Nov, 20XX
  Distributed more than 50,000 sample ballots. Tabulated results, using maths skills. Developed effective organisational skills, communicating with the general public and responding to their interests diplomatically.

- **Lincolnshire Historical Society**, Lincoln, Autumn 20XX
  Course-related work experience; using practiced research skills, researched and designed an exhibit focusing on elections of Progressive party candidates. Exhibit is on display at Lincolnshire Museum, visited by over 200 individuals a day.

ORGANISATIONAL SKILLS

- **Chairperson, Student's Women's Group**, Lincoln University, 20XX-20XX
  Chaired Assault-Risk Management meetings, 20XX-20XX. Organised events to minimise individual and group risks of physical assault on campus. Assistant Bursar, 20XX-20XX. Used strong prioritising and mathematical skills to assist Treasurer in distribution of funds.

Figure 7-2: Turning student work experience to good account.

One technique is to separate your jobs into fragments and explain them. For example, don't say that your job title was "office help" or "office clerk" and stop there. Divide the job into such functions as telephone reception, telephone sales, contract negotiations, purchasing, inventory, staff training, computer application training, public speaking, and written communications. Describe each one in terms of your accomplishments and their outcomes (see Chapter 10). Your inventory of worksheets (see Chapter 13) is invaluable to pump up your experience without fibbing about it.

Stretching your experience is the spin, although you can't get away with claiming that you spent your summers as vice president of Microsoft.

Don't rely on the function-inflation technique if you have other good information such as the lifeguard experience in Figure 7-2.

Too little or no experience

Need a job? Get experience! Need experience? Get a job! This predicament has frustrated new graduates since the continents broke apart.

A few graduates get the message almost too late. Frequently, a marginal new graduate not only drags along a less than glowing degree, but has also spent three or four years developing skills as a television watcher, shopper, or social butterfly. This new graduate not only has no career-related job-shadowing or work experience, but also didn't bother to get a job on restaurant row to fund such frivolities as beer and skiing. There were no extra-curricular projects (of the repeatable kind), no volunteer stints – nada, nothing, nought!! This reader writes with a challenging query:

> *I'm just a college brat – I have no experience, plus I didn't exactly distinguish myself with grades. How do I write a CV from thin air?*

Having nothing but education to work with makes for a difficult CV scenario. Only dedicated job research and customising each CV gives you a chance of producing a StandOut product. Perhaps you overlooked something; even baby-sitting or pet-sitting offers experience in accepting responsibility and demonstrates reliability.

If an exhaustive search of your hobbies, campus activities, or community service turns up nothing worth putting on your CV, your education must carry the entire weight of candidacy for employment. Milk it dry, as the example in Figure 7-3 suggests.

NEW GRADUATE—SOME EXPERIENCE

Fiona McNealy
Tel 0151 321 4567

123 Elgin Crescent, Birkenhead,
Merseyside BM1 3JT

Seek entry-level retail sales position. Offer more than three years' intensive study of public communication. Completed Bachelor's degree, developing strong research, language, interpersonal, computer and disciplinary skills. Proven interactive skills with groups and individuals. Energetic, adaptive, fast learner.

BACKGROUND & EDUCATION

• **Bachelor of Arts, Liverpool University, May, 20XX, Literature & Social Studies**

Self-Directed Studies   20XX - Present
Focusing on mainstream culture and trends, study merchandising and population demographics of individuals between the ages of 18 and 49. Browse media and advertising extensively, developing an in-depth understanding of material consumption in U.K. culture.

University Studies
1/8- 29/12, 20XX   Literary Philosophy, Graduate, Liverpool University
Accumulated skills in prioritising, self-management and discipline, accomplishing over 90 pages of commentary on the subject of philosophical thought.

23/1 - 25/5, 20XX   Social Text and Context, Liverpool University
Developed in-depth understanding of public consensus and modern value systems. Concentration: the relationship between ideals and historical and economic patterns.

23/1 - 25/5, 20XX   Critical Thinking, Liverpool University
60 hours of self-directed research and lecture attendance, studying essential elements of critical thought. Developed skills in argumentative dialogue, logic, analysis, and approaching perception from an educated and diverse perspective. Focus: anatomy of critical thought.

23/1 - 25/5, 20XX   Public Communication, Liverpool University
Intensive study of the psychological and social techniques of speech and communication. Developed comprehensive understanding of debate, physical language, formal and informal delivery, subliminal communication, and advertising. Focus: written and visual advertising techniques.

Other Experience   20XX - Present, **Liverpool University**
15th and 16th Century Rhetoric, French Poetry, Literature in Music, Women, Words & Wisdom, Film Theory, Shakespeare, British Fiction, U.S. Fiction, World Literature.

SKILLS
Computer: All word processing applications on Macintosh and IBM, Internet savvy.
Interpersonal: Experienced in working with groups, and individuals, using teamwork and collaboration, setting goals, delegating and communicating effectively.

Figure 7-3: The CV of a graduate with little experience but marketable skills.

Starting Over with a Master's Degree

An advanced degree represents another kind of "too-little experience" when you use it as a door-opener to a new career instead of continuing in your current field.

After career mishaps, many people see a master's degree as a born-again employment credential for a well-planned career change. And new beginnings often are the happy outcome. By contrast, if your goals are murky as a master's degree graduate, you're likely to be disappointed. You may be better educated, but you'll probably fail to get what you want. The CV takes the brunt of the blame, as this question from a reader suggests:

I am seeking a job with a new master's degree – obtained at age 47 – and experiencing a lot of difficulty. I have mailed out at least 500 CVs and received only one response – from a telephone company suggesting that I install telephone equipment. What is wrong with my CV?

The CV isn't the real problem here. If the reader sent the same CV to 500 potential employers, he's clearly not focused on what he's best fit to do. When it comes to CVs, one size does not fit all. This individual should learn a great deal more about job hunting and then write a career plan to be reviewed monthly. If your master's degree upgrades your credentials in the same field in which you now work, begin your CV by reporting your work experience. Follow up with the education section, leading off this section with your newly minted master's degree. Make use of a CV-ending section titled *Other Information* to say that you view learning as a life skill, as evidenced by the master's degree.

A PhD Can Be a Liability

A doctorate traditionally has been reserved for research or teaching, but those job prospects aren't living up to expectations. Doctorate-holding job hunters return home day after day with heads hung low because they are rejected for being "overqualified".

Although it's disheartening, unless you are certain that a PhD is required for the positions you seek, we suggest that you omit the Piled High and Deep degree from your CV. If asked in an interview, claim it but don't go out of your way to bring it up. As for the application form, when asked for "highest educational achievement", assume they mean as related to the job you seek. If your PhD is in a totally different field you may have to swallow your pride and accept that in the employer's eyes it belongs in the category of "hobbies and outside interests".

Gaffes Common to New Graduates

New graduates are more likely than experienced job seekers to make these mistakes:

- ✔ **Not meeting image standards:** If you present your CV personalised with little printing errors, such as off-centred or crooked placement, ink blotches, or flaws in the paper itself, you fail to make the grade.

- ✔ **Aiming too high too soon:** An imperfect understanding of the world off campus may cause you to indicate in a job objective that the job you're seeking is over your head. You'll be dismissed as naive if you write such aims as becoming "an operations manager in a well-established organisation". "Manager" isn't quite the word for an entry-level person, although graduates with several years of experience leading up to a managerial position could swing it. "Well-established organisation" may exile you not only from dynamic start-up companies but cause a perception that you expect a lot – perhaps more than an employer can deliver.

- ✔ **Overcompensating with gimmicks:** Don't tart up your CV to cover barren qualifications. Avoid using exotically original language, such as the "eyelinered genius", a term used by a business graduate applying for an entry-level marketing position in the cosmetics industry. The term may be colourful, but charm communicates better in the interview.

- ✔ **Making employers guess:** Employers hate it when they are asked to decipher your intent. Merely presenting your declared degree is not enough to kick off a gobsmacking job search. Add either an objective to your CV or a skills summary directed at a specific career field. Show potential employers that you've thought about your next move.

- ✔ **Levelling the experience field:** Your CV is no place to give every job equal billing. Many rookie CVs are little more than listings of previous jobs – TV satellite dish sales representative, waiter, gardener, and computer coach, for example. Separate your jobs into an A list and a B list. The A list contains the jobs that relate to what you want to do next, even if you have to stretch them to make a connection. Briefly mention jobs on the B list in a section called "Other Experience or Other Jobs".

- ✔ **Stopping with bare bones:** Some rookies look at a sheet of paper and then at their embarrassing, bedraggled collection of pot-noodle jobs in their work-experience menu. Desperate to get *anything* on paper, they settle for name, rank, and serial number (employer, job title, and dates of employment). The solution is to pull in *all* experience, including volunteer and part-time gigs. Sit, think, think some more, and pull in all relevant skills pointing in the direction in which you hope to get a lift.

✔ **Hiding hot information:** Data entombed is data forgotten. Employers remember best the information you give first in a CV, not the data squished in the middle. Decide what your selling points are and pack that punch up front. Ask three friends to read your CV and tell you what they remember about it right afterwards.

✔ **Highlighting the immaterial:** Featuring the wrong skills and knowledge acquired on each job is an error that many first-time CV writers make. Suppose you want to be a multimedia producer, and one of your work experience citations is your three years of effort for campus student theatrical productions. You painted scenery, sold tickets, and designed sets. It's the experience in designing sets that helps qualify you for multimedia producer, not painting scenery or selling tickets. Costume yourself in the skills that help employers imagine you playing a role in their company.

✔ **Ignoring employers' needs:** Even the smartest new graduates, who may have survived research challenges as rigorous as uncovering the body language of ancient French cave dwellers, make this mistake. They forget to find out what employers want from new employees. In addition to following the standard research techniques mentioned in Chapter 8, if you can find former or present employees willing to share company culture information *from the inside,* go to the head of the StandOut class.

✔ **Writing boastfully:** Appearing too arrogant about your talents can cause employers to question your ability to learn as a junior team member. As one recent graduate says, "It's hard to work in a team structure when you're omniscient". Even when you're just trying to compensate for your inexperience, avoid terminology that comes across as contrived or blatantly self-important. If you're not sure, ask older friends to describe the kind of person they think your CV represents.

Part III
The Making of a StandOut CV

"A very impressive CV, Brother Dominic."

In this part . . .

You find out how to choose the best format for your CV, write the most effective content, choose keywords and action verbs that bring you to the top of an interview scheduler's pile, use worksheet tools, upgrade the appearance of your CV, and deal with job gaps and other dilemmas anyone can face – and some that fewer face.

Chapter 8

Market Yourself with a StandOut CV

. . . .

In This Chapter

▶ Using the StandOut CV to get a better job

▶ Doing your research to create StandOut CVs

▶ Deciding how many CVs you need

. . . .

*Y*ou say you're ready to step out and find a terrific job? You say you're tired of selling off a piece of your life in return for forgettable pay in go-nowhere jobs? Or you're fed up with starving as a student? You say you want a job that speaks fluent money with an interesting accent? Sounds good. But that's not *all* you want, you say? You also want *meaningful* work.

We understand. What you want is a job that you love to get up in the morning to do and that pays major money, has first-class benefits, provides a real sense of self-worth and achievement, doesn't disappear overnight, and maybe sends you off on pleasant travels periodically. Something where the present makes you feel alive, the future makes you feel optimistic, and the whole thing brings a fuzzy warmth to both you and your bank manager.

Those StandOut jobs are going to people who, with StandOut CVs and self-discipline, have found out how to outrun the pack. This chapter tells why you need a StandOut CV to make the new workplace work for you.

 A global knowledge revolution, as far-reaching as the Industrial Revolution, is changing business. And business is changing the job market. No one is immune to being made redundant as the Job For Life goes the way of the dodo. The good news is that more resources to help us find new work connections have appeared during the past decade than in all of previous history.

Really, Must You Have a CV?

Periodically, job guide writers, with bullet-proof self-assurance, assert that CVs are unnecessary baggage. These critics insist that the best way to find a job is to network and talk your way inside. Just ignore them; they're kidding nobody but themselves. The only people for whom the no-CV advice is okay are those who can leave talk-show hosts struggling to get a word in edgewise. Very few people are extroverted and glib enough to carry the entire weight of their employment marketing presentations without supporting materials.

More importantly, you need a CV because most employers say that you need a CV. Employers don't have time to take oral histories when you call to "ask for a few minutes of time to discuss opportunities". Those days are gone. A StandOut CV that's easily read and absorbed saves employers' time and shows that you're aware of this new reality.

Even if – as a corporate executive's child, pal, or hairdresser – you get yourself handed a job on a plate, somewhere along the way you'll need a CV. At some point, people who make hiring decisions insist on seeing a piece of paper or a computer screen that spells out your qualifications. CVs are an important first step on the road to the perfect job.

CVs open doors to job interviews; interviews open doors to jobs.

Your CV as a Sales Tool

A CV used to be a simple, low-key sheet or two of paper outlining your experience and education, with a list of references at the end. That kind of CV is now a museum piece.

By contrast, your StandOut CV is a specially prepared sales presentation. Created as a sales tool to persuade a potential employer that you're the best one to do the job you seek, your CV is a self-advertisement that showcases your skills. With a series of well-written statements that highlight your previous work experience, education, and other background information, your CV helps prove what you say about your achievements, accomplishments, and abilities. It tells an employer you have a positive work attitude and strong interpersonal skills.

As a sales tool, your CV outlines your strengths as a product:

- The skills you bring to the organisation
- The reason you're worth the money you hope to earn

> ✔ Your capacity for doing the work better than other candidates
>
> ✔ Your ability to solve company or industry problems

In every statement, your CV strategically convinces employers that you can do the job, have positive work attitudes, and can get along with others. Your CV – whether stored in the rapidly expanding electronic universe or on paper – helps employers see how they could benefit by interviewing you.

Tailor Your CV to the Company and the Position

When do you need more than one version of your CV? Most of the time. Following the usual approach, you develop a core CV and then amend it to fit specific positions, career fields, or industries. For information on creating a core CV, head to Chapter 10.

Help in discovering what you want to do

Does your career make you feel as if you're treading water just to keep your head above the surface? Then here are a few free Web sites that can help you start moving again. They offer many tips on career decision-making and management:

✔ **The Career Key** (www.careerkey.org) by Dr Lawrence K Jones and other academics specialising in career development. Much of the work is based on legendary John Holland's six basic personality types. You're given a list of jobs that may be appropriate for each of the personality types.

✔ **Online Personality Tests** (www.2h.com) aren't scored but focus on you as a person who works. (When you get to the site, click on *Personality Tests*.)

✔ **Queendom's Best Tests for Career Hunters** (www.queendom.com) doesn't pretend to be scientific, but it does offer a collection of career-focused quizzes, ranging from personality to owning a business. (When you reach the site, click on *Tests & Profiles*.)

✔ **Keirsey.com** (www.keirsey.com) contains links to understanding and taking the Keirsey Character/Temperament Sorter tests, a kissing cousin to the Myers Briggs test.

✔ **Team Technology** (www.teamtechnology.co.uk) – with the slogan "you can't change who you are but you can change the role you play", this site is based around the Myers Briggs test and the role of the individual within teams.

✔ **All the Tests** (www.allthetests.com) – just in case you're getting a taste for this kind of thing, there's no shortage of online test covering personality types and careers and this site presents a sample of what's out there.

Nothing beats a perfect or near-perfect match. Suppose a company sports a job opening requiring A, B, and C experience or education. By designing your CV for the target position, you show that you're well endowed with A, B, and C experience or education – a very close match between the company's requirements and your qualifications.

What should you do when you want to change careers, and you don't know exactly to what? Sorry, but you're not ready to write a StandOut CV. First, you need to clarify your direction through either introspection or professional careers advice. For a jumpstart on mapping out your life's direction, see the sidebar in this chapter: "Help in discovering what you want to do".

The benefits of research

Research is the key to tailoring your CV to the company your want to work for or the job you know you'd excel at.

By researching a company and industry to customise your CV and determine new job prospects, not only do you gain the firepower to create a StandOut CV, but you build an arsenal of data points to use in interviews.

You won't use every scrap of research, of course. Some data will be useful only for impressing your future co-workers at the next office party. The problem is knowing which data is surplus and which is necessary; glean as much information as time and your study habits permit. In general, the higher the level of job you seek, the more research you need to do in order to be seen as the best candidate for the job. Certainly, if you're writing a CV for a dream job, then pull out all the stops.

Finding out about the company

What does your CV reveal about you? Right off the bat, your CV reveals whether you're willing to take the time to discover what a prospective employer wants done that you're well qualified to do. It shows the health of your judgement and the depth of your commitment to work. Your impulse may be to assume that you can write a CV out of your own head and history – that dogged, time-eating research makes a nice add-on but is not essential. Don't kid yourself. At the core of a StandOut CV is research, research, and more research.

For a comprehensive approach, educate yourself about the company's history, growth and acquisition record, products and services, corporate philosophy on outsourcing, sales volume, annual budget, number of employees, division structure and types of people it hires, market share, profitability, location of physical facilities, and how recently and deeply it has downsized personnel.

Research into your prospective company – in this usage, *company* means non-profit organisations and government agencies as well as private companies – lets you glimpse how you may fit into the company and what you can offer it. Research gives you a sound basis for selecting those areas to include in your CV that demonstrate good judgement and commitment to the goals of your prospective company.

When you know what an employer is willing to employ someone to do, you can tell the employer why you should be the one to do it. *In a tight job race, the candidate who knows most about the employer has the edge.*

Resources for company research

Pulling together the information to write StandOut CVs used to be such a chore that CV writers could spend weeks running down all the facts they needed, visiting libraries for books and newspapers, and traipsing down to Companies' House for annual reports. Mercifully, research is far easier today with a multitude of tools at your beck and mouse-call. To be comprehensive, line up the usual suspects in printed form – directories, annual reports, newspapers, magazines, and trade journals. Then scout the Internet. Following are some sites you may find helpful:

- **Prospects** (www.prospects.ac.uk): The official UK graduate careers Web site, Prospects includes advice on what jobs would suit you and a database of UK company profiles.

- **CAROL** (www.carol.co.uk): This site offers company reports online. You name it – balance sheets, profit and loss, financial highlights, and so on – and you can find it here. A valuable source of information that's free to use (registration required though).

- **CEO Express** (ceoexpress.com): This site covers fewer industries than you might expect, but the wealth of research and information about each industry is impressive. The site offers a large number of links to business magazines and business news Web sites.

- **Corporate Information** (corporateinformation.com): Type in the name of a company and get a list of sites that report on that company. Or select an industry and get a list of companies in that industry, plus news, overviews, and a short write-up about the industry.

- ✔ **Herriot-Watt University Careers Service** (`www.hw.ac.uk/careers/empinfo.html`). The information at this site isn't exhaustive, but you can find a useful round up of company sites.

- ✔ **Hoover's Online** (`www.hoovers.com/uk/`): This site offers a business information database with a ton of information about companies, contact information, key officers, competitors, business locations, and industry news.

- ✔ **Europages** (`wwww.europages.com`). A business directory priding itself on 500,000 companies listed from 33 European countries. Just finding out there are 33 European companies can be a bit of a revelation.

- ✔ **Kellysearch** (`www.kellys.reedinfo.co.uk`). Kellysearch is a search engine for UK companies. It breaks the companies down into over 100,000 product headings. Free to use.

- ✔ **Financial Times** (`www.ft.com`). The full glory of the FT online is only available to subscribers, but with the free trial period, you can still make good use of the pink pages without digging deep.

Some companies even have employee message boards – forums where employees swap notes on life in their company. These message boards are usually for employees of large companies and can be a useful way of getting a more human take on what seems like a faceless giant corporation. Be aware of their limitations, though. If *you* know that a company has a dedicated message board, then that company knows as well. If the forum is monitored, either formally or informally by the company, criticism will most likely be muted. By the same token, be careful of the extreme opposite: grievance sites run to criticise large companies. These sites often feature a name that spoofs the company itself, and people post messages to the site anonymously. These sites can also feature a torrent of abuse. Some of the criticism you read at grievance sites may be valid, but anonymity gives some people a feeling of freedom to let rip without reflection, and anyone with a grudge gets to present a one-sided version of events. The proverbial pinch of salt comes in handy.

Finding out about the position

The ultimate StandOut CV, like a custom-made suit, is tailored to the job you want. After researching the target company and position, you can make your CV fit the job description as closely as your work and education history allow.

At minimum, find out the scope of the position and the skills the company is looking for. The next sections give you more information about how to research your next job and what you can do with this information.

Creating a position analysis

Many companies develop what is called a *candidate specification,* which describes the competencies, skills, experience, knowledge, education, and other characteristics believed to be necessary for the job.

Grab this idea and turn it around. Prepare a counterpart – your own *position analysis.*

The content you're looking for to put in your position analysis includes the major responsibilities, technical problems to be solved, and objectives for the position, as well as competencies and skills, education required, and so forth.

Resources for position research

Find the data for your position analysis in a number of places:

- ✔ **Commercial job descriptions:** Buying job descriptions is pricey, so try libraries or friends who work in HR offices. A limited number of free job descriptions are available on the Web; find them with search engines by typing in **job descriptions**.

- ✔ **Recruitment advertising** (print and online): Look online for job ads for the career field and occupation you want. Although some descriptions are notoriously vague, many companies have learnt their lesson and now specify precise requirements for positions to be filled. On the print side, newspaper recruitment ads are happy hunting grounds for the data you need to write your position analysis.

- ✔ **Occupational career guides:** The US Department of Labor's *Occupational Outlook Handbook* (www.bls.gov/oco) contains career briefs that describe the nature of the work for popular occupations. Remember that, while it is still widely referred to over here in the UK, its job descriptions can show its US origins. Double check this information against UK descriptions wherever possible.

After writing your position analysis, you're ready to roll in composing a StandOut CV.

When a friend touts your CV

What should you do when a friend wishes to float your CV among clients and colleagues, and you don't know where it will land? If you value the friendship and can't persuade your friend that you'd appreciate an interview instead, create a general CV reflecting what you most want to do. Complete the worksheets in Part III and then write a CV based on what you'd most like to do, listing the qualifications that support your goal.

When One CV Will Do – or Must Do

The trouble with creating a custom-tailored CV for every job opening is that many busy and beleaguered people feel as though they can barely manage to get to the dentist for a check-up, buy groceries, pick up the dry cleaning, ship the kids off to school on time, run over to sort out Mum's central heating, and generally get through the day – much less write more than one version of an irresistible CV. For these folks, it may come down to this: one great CV or no great CV.

You can generally get by with a single version of your CV if you (A) are a new graduate or (B) have a fairly well-defined career path and intend to work exclusively within the lines of your experience.

Even when you allow yourself the luxury of fielding just one CV, you can't put your feet up, watch the sunset, and sip Chardonnay. With each CV that you distribute, you must attach a personalised cover letter that directly targets the specific job opening. If writing letters isn't your strong suit, *Cover Letters For Dummies,* 2nd Edition, written by Joyce Lain Kennedy and published by Wiley, tells you how.

Chapter 9

Format Means So Much: Choose Wisely

In This Chapter
- ▶ Selecting your best format
- ▶ Using handy templates
- ▶ Comparing format features

*C*V format refers not to the design or look of your CV but to how you organise and emphasise your information. *Different format styles flatter different histories.* This chapter helps you choose a format that highlights your strengths and hides your shortcomings.

An extensive line-up of CV formats follows. A template that you can use for developing your own CV illustrates each of the formats in this chapter. Survey the lot of them before deciding which one best tells your story.

CV Formats

At root, formats come in three family trees:

- ✔ **Reverse chronological:** The reverse chronological lists all employment and education, beginning with the most recent and working backward.
- ✔ **Functional:** The skills-based functional shouts what you can do instead of relaying what you've done and where you did it.
- ✔ **Hybrid:** The hybrid or combination is a marriage of both formats.

These three family types have spawned several other formats:

- **Accomplishment:** highlighting specific achievements rather than general experience
- **Targeted:** point for point directed at a specific job
- **Linear:** relating what you have to offer as a series of short lines
- **Professional:** slightly more long-winded with emphasis on detail of professional qualifications
- **Keyword:** in which words are specially selected to make the CV attractive to keyword-based computer searches
- **Academic curriculum vitae:** very long (up to ten pages) biographical statement usually for academia
- **International curriculum vitae:** a professional format with some modifications to suit target countries with different layout expectations

Table 9-1 gives you a breakdown of which format to use when.

Table 9-1	Your Best CV Formats at a Glance
Your Situation	*Suggested Formats*
Perfect career pattern	Reverse Chronological, Targeted
Rookie or ex-military	Functional, Hybrid, Accomplishment, Targeted, Linear
Seasoned ace	Functional, Hybrid, Accomplishment, Keyword
Tech-savvy	Keyword
Business	Reverse Chronological, Accomplishment, Targeted
Technical	Keyword, Targeted, Accomplishment, Reverse Chronological
Professional	Professional, Academic Curriculum Vitae, Portfolio
Government	Reverse Chronological, Professional
Arts/teaching	Professional, Portfolio, Academic Curriculum Vitae
Job history gaps	Functional, Hybrid, Linear, Targeted
Multitrack job history	Functional, Hybrid, Targeted, Keyword
Career change	Functional, Keyword, Targeted
International job seeker	International Curriculum Vitae
Special issues	Functional, Hybrid, Targeted

The following sections explore each type of CV format so that you can choose the style best for you and your skills.

The narrative format is an outdated chronological format that starts with the oldest facts and works forward to the newest facts. A pretentious variation of the narrative format uses the third person as though you were writing a biography. We don't bother to even discuss them, and we strongly suggest that you don't use either one.

Reverse Chronological Format

The *reverse chronological* (RC) format, shown in Figure 9-1, is straightforward: It cites your employment from the most recent back, showing dates as well as employers and educational institutions (college, vocational-technical schools, and career-oriented programs and courses). You accent a steady work history with a clear pattern of upward or lateral mobility.

Strengths and weaknesses

Check to see whether the RC's strengths are yours:

- ✔ This up-front format is by far the most popular with employers and recruiters because it is so, well, up-front.
- ✔ RC links employment dates, underscoring continuity. The weight of your experience confirms that you're a specialist in a specific career field (social service or technology, for example).
- ✔ RC positions you for the next upward career step.
- ✔ As the most traditional of formats, RC fits traditional industries (such as banking, education, and accounting).

Take the weaknesses of the reverse chronological format into account:

- ✔ When previous job titles are at variance with the target position, this format does not support the objective. Without careful management, it reveals everything, including inconsequential jobs and negative factors.
- ✔ RC can spotlight periods of unemployment or brief job tenure.
- ✔ Without careful management, RC reveals your age.
- ✔ Without careful management, RC may suggest that you were stagnant in a job too long.

REVERSE CHRONOLOGICAL FORMAT

YOUR NAME

Home Address

City, County , Post Code

(###) ###-#### (Phone) (###) ###-#### (Fax) ###@###.# (E-mail)

Objective:

A position that uses your skills.

SUMMARY

- Number of years of work experience, paid and unpaid, relevant to target position
- Achievement that proves you can handle the target
- Another achievement that proves you can handle the target
- Skills, traits, characteristics – facts that further your ability to handle the target
- Education and training relating to the target (if unrelated, bury in resume body)

PROFESSIONAL EXPERIENCE AND ACCOMPLISHMENTS

20## - Present   **Job Title**   Employer, Employer's Location
A brief synopsis of your purpose in the company, detailing essential functions and the
products and customer base you managed.
- An achievement in this position relevant to objective (do not repeat summary)
- A second achievement in this position relevant to current objective
- More accomplishments (awards, recognition, promotion, raise, praise, training)

20## - 20##   **Job Title**   Employer, Employer's Location

Detailed as above.

20## - 20##   **Job Title**   Employer, Employer's Location

Detailed as above but more brief

19## - 20##   **Job Title**   Employer, Employer's Location

Detailed as above but more brief

EDUCATION AND PROFESSIONAL TRAINING

Degree(s), classes, seminars, educational awards and honours.
Credentials, clearances, licenses.

Figure 9-1: The tried-and-true, basic reverse chronological format.

Who should use this format and who should think twice

Use the RC if you fall into any of these categories:

- ✔ You have a steady school and work record reflecting constant growth or lateral movement.

- ✔ Your most recent employer is a respected name in the industry, and the name may ease your entry into a new position.

- ✔ Your most recent job titles are impressive stepping-stones.

- ✔ You're a savvy writer who knows how to manage potential negative factors, such as inconsequential jobs, too few jobs, too many temporary jobs, too many years at the same job, or too many years of age.

Think twice about using the RC under these circumstances:

- ✔ You have a lean employment history. Listing a stray student job or two is not persuasive, even when you open with superb educational credentials enhanced with work experience.

With careful attention, you can do a credible job on an RC by extracting from your extracurricular activities every shred of skills, which you present as abilities to do work with extraordinary commitment and a head for quick learning.

- ✔ You have work-history or employability problems – gaps, demotions, stagnation in a single position, job hopping (four jobs in three years, for example), re-entering the workforce after a break to raise a family.

Exercise very careful management to truthfully modify stark realities. However, you may find that other formats can serve you better.

Instructions

The StandOut way to create an RC is as follows:

- ✔ Focus on areas of specific relevance to your target position or career field.

- ✔ List all pertinent places worked, including for each the name of the employer and the city in which you worked, the years you were there, your title, your responsibilities, and your measurable achievements.

The RC template included in this chapter is generic and doesn't show how to handle problems such as unrelated experience. You can group unrelated jobs in a second work history section under the heading "Other Experience", "Previous Experience", or "Related Experience".

Functional Format

The *functional format,* shown in Figure 9-2, is a CV of ability-focused topics – portable skills or functional areas. It ignores chronological order. In its purest form, the functional style omits dates, employers, and job titles. But employers don't like it when you leave out the particulars, so contemporary functional CVs list employers, job titles, and sometimes even dates – but still downplay this information by briefly listing it at the bottom of the CV. The functional format is oriented toward what the job seeker *can* do for the employer instead of narrating history.

Strengths and weaknesses

The strengths of the functional format are

- A functional CV directs a reader's eyes to what you want him or her to notice. It helps a reader visualise what you can do instead of when and where you learned to do it. Functional CVs salute the future rather than embalm the past.

- The functional format – written after researching the target company – serves up the precise functions or skills that the employer wants. It's like saying, "You want budget control and turnaround skills – I have budget control and turnaround skills". The skills sell is a magnet to reader eyes!

- It uses unpaid and non-work experience to your best advantage.

- It allows you to eliminate or subordinate work history that doesn't support your current objective.

The weaknesses are

- Because recruiters and employers are more accustomed to reverse chronological formats, departing from the norm may raise suspicion that you're not the cream of the crop of applicants. Readers may assume that you're trying to hide inadequate experience, educational deficits, or who knows what.

- Functional styles may leave unclear which skills grew from which jobs or experiences.

- A clear career path isn't obvious.

- This format doesn't maximise recent coups in the job market.

FUNCTIONAL FORMAT

YOUR NAME

Address, City, Postcode (###) ###-#### (Phone), (###) ###-#### (Fax), ###@###.##
(E-mail)

Job Title You Desire

More than (# years paid and unpaid) work experience in target area, contributing to an
(achievement/result/high ranking in industry/top 5% of performance reviews). Add
accomplishments, strengths, proficiencies, characteristics, education, brief testimonial –
anything that supports your target job title.

PROFESSIONAL EXPERIENCE AND ACCOMPLISHMENTS

A Top Skill (pertinent to objective)

- An achievement illustrating this skill and the location/employer where you
  earned it*

- A second achievement illustrating this skill and the location/employer where you
  earned it*

*Omit locations/employers if your work history doesn't present a clear sense of
progression and purpose.

A Second Top Skill (pertinent to objective)

Detailed as above

A Third Top Skill (pertinent to objective)

Detailed as above

A Fourth Skill (optional – must relate to objective)

Detailed as above

A Unique Area of Proficiency (pertinent to objective)

- An achievement testifying to this proficiency, including the location/employer*

- A list of equipment, processes, software, or terms you are familiar with,
  reflecting your familiarity with this area of proficiency*

- A list of training experiences that document your proficiency*

*Omit locations/employers if your work history doesn't present a clear sense of
progression and purpose.

EMPLOYMENT HISTORY

20## – Present	**Job Title**	Employer, Location
20## – 20##	**Job Title**	Employer, Location
19## – 20##	**Job Title**	Employer, Location
19## – 19##	**Job Title**	Employer, Location

PROFESSIONAL TRAINING AND EDUCATION

Degrees, credentials, clearances, licences, seminars, training

Figure 9-2: No experience? Use the functional CV format.

Who should use this format and who should think twice

This CV is heaven-sent for career changers, new graduates, ex-military personnel, seasoned aces, and individuals with multitrack job histories, work-history gaps, or special-issue problems.

Job seekers with blue-chip backgrounds and managers and professionals who are often tapped by executive recruiters should avoid this format.

Instructions

Choose areas of expertise acquired during the course of your career, including education and unpaid activities. These areas become skill and functional headings, which vary by the target position or career field. Note any achievements below each heading. A few examples of headings are: "Management", "Sales", "Budget Control", "Cost Cutting", "Project Implementation", and "Turnaround Successes".

List the headings in the order of importance and follow each heading with a series of short statements of your skills (refer to Figure 9-2). Turn your statements into power hitters with measurable achievements.

Hybrid Format

The hybrid, a combination of reverse chronological and functional formats, satisfies demands for timelines as well as showcases your marketable skills and impressive accomplishments. Many people find the hybrid – or one of its offspring – to be the most attractive of all formats.

Essentially, in a hybrid, a functional summary tops a reverse chronological presentation of dates, employers, and capsules of each position's duties. Figure 9-3 gives you a template for this format.

The hybrid style is similar to the contemporary functional format – so much so that making a case for distinction is sometimes difficult.

HYBRID FORMAT

YOUR NAME

Address, City, Post Code

(###) ###-#### (Phone)

(###) ###-#### (Fax), ###@###.## (E-mail)

Objective: Position as (job title) using (#) years' experience in skills key to target.

SUMMARY OF QUALIFICATIONS

Number of years in area of target position

Related education, training and accreditation

An achievement pertinent to objective

Traits that reinforce your candidacy for this position

Other accomplishments, characteristics, proficiencies

SUMMARY OF SKILLS

Technical skills • Processes • Computer software

ACCOMPLISHMENTS AND EXPERIENCE

Job Title, Top Proficiencies Used   Employer, Location

A Top Skill (pertinent to objective)

- Accomplishments made while in this position
- Several related achievements from position, pertinent to this skill and the objective

Another Skill (pertinent to objective)

- Several achievements pertinent to this skill and the objective

20## - Present

Job Title, Top Proficiencies Used   Employer, Location

Detailed as above

20## - 20##

Job Title, Top Proficiencies Used   Employer, Location

Detailed as above

19## - 20##

PROFESSIONAL TRAINING AND EDUCATION

Degrees, accreditations, licences, clearances, courses

Figure 9-3: The hybrid format – the best of both worlds.

Strengths and weaknesses

A hybrid format combines the strengths of both the reverse chronological and functional formats, so check out those earlier sections. Its weakness is that it contains more "frills" in the form of highlighted accomplishments and achieved goals than a very conservative employer may prefer.

Who should use this format and who should think twice

The hybrid is a wise choice for newcomers, ex-military personnel, seasoned aces, those with job history gaps or a multitrack job history, and individuals with special-issue problems.

Career changers or job seekers needing more appropriate formats, such as functional or portfolio, should skip the hybrid.

Instructions

Build a functional format of ability-focused topics and add employment documentation – employers, locations, dates, and duties.

Accomplishment Format

Definitely not a boring read, an accomplishment format immediately moves your strongest marketing points to centre stage, grabs the reader's interest, and doesn't let go. If you want a rhyme to remember: Use flash and dash to go for cash.

A variation of the hybrid CV, the accomplishment format (shown in Figure 9-4) banners both qualifications *and* accomplishments. This is the format of choice for many executives – particularly in traditionally mobile industries, such as advertising, communications, and publishing.

ACCOMPLISHMENT FORMAT

YOUR NAME

Address   Phone number: (###) ###-####   E-mail: #####@##.##
City, Post Code   Message and/or fax number(s): (###) ###-####

OBJECTIVE: Position as (job title) using skills and experience accumulated over (#) years. (Or use a Summary, as in the hybrid format.)

QUALIFICATIONS:

- Number of years' experience that is pertinent to objective
- Your record of improvement or reputation in the industry
- Specific skills and training related to objective
- Areas of specialised proficiency
- Work ethic traits demonstrating candidacy and a constructive attitude
- Procedural familiarities
- Technological familiarities

ACCOMPLISHMENTS:

In any order, list accomplishments (quantifying with numbers and percentages when appropriate) that elaborate such achievements as

- Competitive skills, technological proficiency, professional aptness
- Improvements, innovations
- Revenue-saving strategies
- Promotions, raises
- Increasing responsibilities, management and troubleshooting functions
- Praise from employers and/or co-workers
- Training rendered, training received

PROFESSIONAL EXPERIENCE:

Job Title	Employer, Location	20## - 20##
Job Title	Employer, Location	20## - 20##
Job Title	Employer, Location	20## - 20##
Job Title	Employer, Location	19## - 19##

EDUCATION:

- Academic and professional accreditation(s), emphasis
- Universities, schools, courses (attended or in progress)

Figure 9-4: The accomplishment format really lets you strut your stuff!

Formats to use when the executive recruiter calls

Executive recruiting is usually a response to an employer's known problem in a given business area. Accomplishment formats, along with reverse chronological and targeted styles, are well equipped to tell employers how you can solve their problems.

When an executive recruiter calls, ask for enough details about the position's problem areas to give you ammunition for whipping out a made-to-order CV. If you're a candidate, the recruiter may be happy to have as many as four readable pages about your background, as long as you grab his or her attention on the first page. Remember that most executive decision makers favour reverse chronological presentations, so use conservative language in drawing attention to your accomplishments on this format. See Chapter 11 for more information about the language of CVs.

Strengths and weaknesses

This format offers benefits similar to those of functional and hybrid styles noted earlier in this chapter. Readers who prefer a reverse chronological style may view the accomplishment format as too jazzed up.

Who should use this format and who should think twice

Use the accomplishment format when

- ✔ You're considering using a functional or hybrid CV style: You're a career changer, new graduate, ex-military personnel, seasoned ace, or have a multitrack job history, work history gaps, or special-issue problems. The accomplishment presentation is especially effective for individuals whose work history may not have been smooth but was, at times, bright with great successes.

- ✔ You're returning to payroll status after a period of self-employment.

If you've climbed career steps without a stumble, use a reverse chronological format instead of the accomplishment format.

Instructions

List accomplishments in order of importance, making chronology a secondary factor. Close with a summarised reverse chronological work history.

Targeted Format

A targeted format, tailored to a given job, is VIP (very important person) treatment. Targeting is persuasive because everyone likes to be given the VIP treatment.

The targeted style is written to match point-for-point a specific job offered by a specific employer.

The template in Figure 9-5 is but one way to build a targeted CV. You can equally benefit with other format options springing from the functional or hybrid branches of the CV family. You choose.

Strengths and weaknesses

The strength of the targeted format is that it shows the employer that you're a good match for the position. Its weakness is that you may not be readily considered for other jobs.

Who should use this format and who should think twice

Pretty much everyone stands out with a targeted CV. Ex-military personnel can translate milspeak to civilianese, newcomers can equate their non-paid experience to employer requirements, and seasoned aces can reach deep into their backgrounds to show, item for item, how they qualify. This format is a good choice for people with strong work histories but a few spots here and there.

The targeted format isn't a great idea for anyone lazy about doing research – the success of the targeted CV depends on lining up data ducks in advance.

TARGETED FORMAT

YOUR NAME

Address, City, Postcode

(###) ###-#### (Phone), (###) ###-#### (Fax), ###@###.### (E-mail)

Objective: Position as (title of job that employer offers) using your (#) of years' experience in skills that are essential and specialised to the position.

SUMMARY OF QUALIFICATIONS

- Number of years in area of target, explaining similarities to objective position/duties

- Related education, training, accreditation – specifically those the employer will appreciate

- An achievement directly related to target

- Traits reinforcing your candidacy for this position, specifically those the employer requires

- Other accomplishments, characteristics, knowledge either rare or prized in the field

SUMMARY OF SKILLS

Technical skills the employer wants • Processes the employer uses • Computer and software skills the employer needs

ACCOMPLISHMENTS AND EXPERIENCE

Job Title   Employer, Location   20## – Present

A Top Skill (pertinent to objective)

- Accomplishments made in this position targeting the employer's priorities or customer base

- Several other related achievements from position, pertinent to skill and objective

Another Top Skill (pertinent to objective)

- Several achievements pertinent to this skill and the objective

Job Title   Employer, Location   20## – 20##

Detailed as above

Job Title   Employer, Location   19## – 20##

Detailed as above

PROFESSIONAL TRAINING AND EDUCATION

Degrees, accreditations, licences, courses

Figure 9-5: Use the targeted format to hit the bull's-eye with a specific employer.

When CVs and research are beyond reach

You say you're not sure you want to do enough research on a position to write a targeted CV? Definitely not a StandOut mind-set, but you're still ahead of an applicant who wrote the following query to the human resources department of a big company (We did not make this up):

Dear Sirs, I would very much like to send a CV to you, but I haven't the slightest idea how to fill out a CV, and I can't remember the dates or addresses for any of it anyway. So if that is going to keep me from being employed by your company, then to hell with it! Otherwise, call me in for an interview and a job.

Instructions

Find out what the position demands and write – fact for fact – how you offer exactly those goods.

If you can meet better than 80 percent of the position's requirements, you've got a shot at an interview; if less than 80 percent, don't hold your breath waiting for your telephone to ring.

Linear Format

A linear format (line by line – hence, *linear*) relates the benefits you offer in short spurts of achievements, winning moves, and the like. An offspring of the reverse chronological format, the linear doesn't get into great detail; it sparks curiosity to meet you and find out more. Check out the template in Figure 9-6.

This spaced-out variation of the reverse chronological format lacks a job objective section and opens with a skills summary instead. Plenty of white space is the hallmark of this achievement-highlighted document.

Career advisers pin a blue ribbon on this format.

LINEAR FORMAT

YOUR NAME

Address, City, Postcode

(###) ###-#### (Phone), (###) ###-#### (Fax), ###@###.### (E-mail)

QUALIFICATIONS SUMMARY

- Number of years' work experience, paid and unpaid, pertinent to objective position

- Accomplishments that prove your unique candidacy for this position

- Skills geared toward the objective position or company

- Other things the employer will like to know – proficiencies, characteristics, achievements, training, credentials, education

PROFESSIONAL EXPERIENCE AND ACCOMPLISHMENTS

20## – Present **Job Title** Employer, Employer's Location

- An achievement made during this position that is pertinent to current objective, detailing job skills and responsibilities

- A second achievement made during this position also pertinent to current objective

- More accomplishments (awards, recognition, promotion, raise, praise, training)

*Divide description according to titles held with employer, listing titles as subheadings.

20## – 20## **Job Title** Employer, Employer's Location

Detailed as above.

EDUCATION AND PROFESSIONAL TRAINING

Degree(s), university, year

Top achievement

Other seminars, awards, honours, credentials, clearances, licences

COMMUNITY LEADERSHIP

Memberships and other offices in community organisations

Figure 9-6: The logical linear format appeals to many employers' eyes.

Strengths and weaknesses

The pluses of linear CVs are

- ✔ Linear CVs are very easy to read quickly, particularly in a stack of CVs a foot high. Instant readability is increasingly important as harried recruiters struggle with the clock, and baby boomers become middle-aged readers whose eyes don't enjoy poring over pages sagging with text.

- ✔ Because the format presents your starring events in a line-by-line visual presentation, your achievements aren't likely to be overlooked as they would be if buried deep in a text paragraph.

The minus is that you can't pack as much information into a linear format (remember the white space), but, with careful planning and good writing, you can pack plenty of sell.

Who should use this format and who should think twice

This format works to showcase career progression – steady as you go. If that's you, use the linear.

Job seekers with gaps in employment, too many jobs, few advancements, or scant experience as well as those who've seen enough sunrises to be on the shady side of 50 should avoid the linear.

Instructions

Write down your achievements and other necessary data, look at the big lumps of text, and then divide and conquer. Think white space.

Professional Format

A professional format, also called a *professional vitae,* is slightly long-winded (say, three to five pages) but factual. It emphasises professional qualifications and activities. This format, shown in Figure 9-7, is essentially a shortened academic curriculum vitae.

PROFESSIONAL FORMAT

YOUR NAME

Address, City, Postcode

(###) ###-#### (Phone), (###) ###-#### (Fax), ###@###.### (E-mail)

EDUCATION AND PROFESSIONAL TRAINING

Degrees, credentials, awards, achievements, honours, seminars, clearances, licences

OBJECTIVE: A position that uses your talents, with an emphasis on your special skills.

SUMMARY

- Number of years' work experience, paid and unpaid, relevant to target

- Accomplishment(s) that prove your unique talents as a candidate for this position

- Strengths geared toward the objective position or company

- Other things the employer will like to know – proficiencies, characteristics, achievements, training, credentials, education

PROFESSIONAL EXPERIENCE AND ACCOMPLISHMENTS

20## – Present   **Job Title**   Employer, Employer's Location

A brief synopsis of your purpose in the company, detailing essential functions and products you managed and your customer base.

- An achievement pertinent to target

- A second achievement also pertinent to target

- More achievements — awards, recognition, promotion, raise, praise, training

19## – 20##   **Job Title**   Employer, Employer's Location

Detailed as above but more brief

*List three previous jobs with the same detail as above; divide jobs according to job title, not employer.

Figure 9-7: The long but effective professional format is perfect for certain careers.

Strengths and weaknesses

The professional CV is mandatory for certain kinds of positions; your choice is whether to send this type or go all the way and send an academic curriculum vitae.

But be aware that professional CVs are reviewed under a microscope; every deficiency stands out. Adding a portfolio that shows your experience-based work skills may compensate for missing chunks of formal requirements. Just make sure that any unsolicited samples you send are high quality and need no explanation.

Who should use this format and who should think twice

Professionals in medicine, science, and law should use this format. Also use it when common sense or convention makes it the logical choice.

For most non-professionals, especially managers, the professional format is tedious.

Instructions

Begin with education, professional training, and an objective. Follow with a summary of the main points you want the reader to absorb. Follow that information with details of your professional experience and accomplishments.

Follow the template in Figure 9-7, paying attention to accomplishments. Just because you present yourself in a low-key, authoritative manner doesn't mean that you can forget to say how good you are.

Keyword Format

Any CV can be a keyword CV. It becomes a keyword CV when you add a profile of *keywords* (nouns identifying your qualifications) anywhere on any type of format. We like front-loading a keyword preface at the top of the CV.

The template shown in Figure 9-8 is a format that works well for computer scanning. Support your keywords with facts but don't repeat the exact phrasing in a keyword profile and in other parts of your CV – vary your language. Repetition must be handled with thought.

Strengths and weaknesses

Virtually everyone benefits from using a keyword profile – it functions like a skills summary. Job seekers sending CVs by e-mail or postings on the Internet should always include keywords.

A minority of recruiters dislike a keyword preface. Their objection: "It appears to be a check-box-oriented approach to doing a CV". This weakness isn't likely to get you rejected out-of-hand, however. If the body of the CV supports your keywords (which it should if it's StandOut quality), and you can do only one CV, it's worth the risk.

Who should use this format and who should think twice

Most job seekers should consider the keyword option. Technical people can't leave home without it.

However, top management executives (the £300,000-a-year-and-up kind) are unlikely to be recruited from CV databases. Executive recruiters do, however, construct their own in-house databases. In building these in-house databases, they may import from public-domain databases that input information from traditional CVs and other sources.

Instructions

As Figure 9-8 shows, you begin with your contact information, followed by a keyword profile, an objective, several strengths, and reverse chronological employment history.

You may choose not to use a front-loaded keyword profile but rather a one-paragraph qualifications summary or a skills section composed of brief (one- or two-line) statements. The more keywords (or skills) in your CV, the better your chances of being summoned for an interview.

KEYWORD FORMAT

YOUR NAME, Address, City, Postcode

(###) ###-#### (Phone), (###) ###-#### (Fax), ###@###.### (E-mail)

Key Words: General nouns, phrases, and terminology known to be valued in the position and industry; specific Key Words descriptive of duties and proficiencies necessary to position; specific terms known to be priority to employer/company applying to, including credentials, years of experience, areas of familiarity, and equipment involved

Objective: Title of opening, using the following highlights of your background:

- Number of years' work experience, paid and unpaid, relevant to target

- Accomplishments that prove your unique suitability for this position

- Strengths geared toward the objective position or company, education, credentials, and training

PROFESSIONAL EXPERIENCE AND ACCOMPLISHMENTS

20## – Present   **Employer, Employer's Location**

Present Job Title

A brief synopsis of your purpose in the company, detailing essential functions and products you rendered and customer base.

- An achievement related to current objective

- A second achievement also related to objective

- More achievements, awards, recognition, promotion, pay rise, bonuses, praise

- Equipment used, processes, procedures (in noun form)

20## – 20##   **Employer, Employer's Location**

Job Title

Detailed as above but more brief

19## – 20##   **Employer, Employer's Location**

Job Title

Detailed as above but more brief

19## – 19##   **Employer, Employer's Location**

Job Title

Detailed as above but more brief

EDUCATION AND PROFESSIONAL TRAINING

Degrees, classes, seminars, awards, achievements, honours, credentials, clearances, licences

Figure 9-8: The keyword CV is a great format to submit to CV databases.

Keep in mind these keyword CV tip-top tips:

✔ Use as many valid keywords as possible in your CV, but if you place a keyword summary at the top of your online CV, 20 to 30 keywords are enough in one dose.

✔ Computers read keywords in any part of your CV, so if you use a summary, avoid redundancy.

If you use an acronym, such as LSE , in your summary or opening profile, spell out London School of Economics later. If you mention that you have "four years of experience with three PC-based software programs", name the programs elsewhere: Excel, RoboHELP, QuickBooks.

Academic Curriculum Vitae

The academic *curriculum vitae* (ACV) is a comprehensive biographical statement, typically three to ten pages, emphasising professional qualifications and activities. A CV of six to eight pages, ten at the most, is recommended for a veteran professional; two to four pages is appropriate for a young professional just starting out (see the "Professional Format" section earlier in this chapter).

If your CV is more than four pages long, show mercy and save eyesight by attaching an *executive summary* page to the top. An executive summary gives a brief overview of your qualifications and experience.

Among various possible organisations, the template in Figure 9-9 (a variation of the hybrid format but with exhaustive coverage) illustrates a line-up of your contact information, objective, qualifications summary, skills summary, and professional background.

Strengths and weaknesses

An ACV presents all the best of you, which is good, but for people with ageing eyes, an ACV is reading-intensive. More important, weaknesses in any area of your professional credentials are relatively easy to spot.

ACADEMIC CURRICULUM VITAE

YOUR NAME

Curriculum Vitae

Address, City, Postcode

(###) ###-#### (Phone), (###) ###-#### (Fax), ###@###.### (E-mail)

Objective (optional): Position as (title of position employer offers) using your (#) of years' experience in (skills essential for and specialised to the position).

SUMMARY OF QUALIFICATIONS

- A summary of your education, proficiencies, and career pertinent to target
- Number of years in objective area, explaining similarities to job and its responsibilities
- Related education, training, and accreditation, reflecting employer's goals/priorities
- An achievement directly related to target
- Traits reinforcing your candidacy for this position, specifically those asked for by the employer and those generally in demand in the field
- Other accomplishments, characteristics, knowledge either rare or prized in the field

SUMMARY OF SKILLS

Topics of speciality or innovation within field • Areas of particular familiarity • Software equipment • Processes • Terminology relevant to target • Languages

PROFESSIONAL BACKGROUND

EDUCATION

Degrees:

> Ph.D., institution, date of degree (or anticipated date), specialisation
>
> M.A./M.Sc., institution, date of degree, emphasis, concentration
>
> B.A./B.Sc., institution, date of degree, class of degree

Courses: Those taken, honours, seminars, number of units, G.P.A. (if a recent graduate)

Other Accreditations: Licences, clearances

Academic Achievements: Appointments, nominations, leaderships, scholarships, grants, awards, praise, recognition, accomplishments

Affiliations: Societies, associations, clubs, leagues, memberships

PH.D. DISSERTATION

> Title, advisor, director
>
> Abstract summary (4-5 sentences) discussing content and methodology

HONOURS, AWARDS, AND ACADEMIC ACHIEVEMENTS

Appointments, nominations, leaderships, awards, praise, scores, recognitions, accomplishments, fellowships, scholarships, grants (including B.A./B.Sc)

Figure 9-9: Brevity definitely isn't a feature of the academic CV.

TEACHING EXPERIENCE

Job Title, Top Proficiencies Used   Employer, Location 20## - Present

  A Top Responsibility (relevant to objective)

- Accomplishments made in this position, targeting the employer's priorities/ mission

- Several other achievements from this position, pertinent to objective

  Another Skill (appropriate to objective)

- Several achievements from this position, pertinent to objective

Repeat pattern for each position.

RESEARCH EXPERIENCE

Positions, locations, dates, descriptions of research pertinent to target position

TEACHING INTERESTS

RESEARCH INTERESTS

PUBLICATIONS

List all those you are willing to show the search committee. Include works in progress or pending. Cite works as follows:

- "Title of work," Name of publication/publisher *(Newsletter*, *Newspaper, Magazine, Journal, Book),* location of publisher , date of publication, volume number (v.##), issue number (#.#), series number (#.#.#), page numbers (# - #).

PRESENTATIONS AND PUBLIC APPEARANCES

Include conference papers and research reports. List as follows:

- "Title of presentation," location of presentation , date (20## - 20##); optional synopsis of content and/or purpose of presentation, audience, results, and so on.

PROFESSIONAL AFFILIATIONS

- A society, association, league, or club with which you associate, position held, 19## - 20##

- And so on.

RECOMMENDATIONS

Names and contact information of three to four references willing to write recommendation letters

CREDENTIALS

Address where the recipient can access your career/placement file

Who should use this format and who should think twice

Anyone working in a PhD-driven environment, such as higher education, think tanks, science, and elite research and development groups, needs to use this format.

Anyone who can avoid using it should do so.

Instructions

Create a comprehensive summary of your professional employment and accomplishments: education, positions, affiliations, honours, memberships, credentials, dissertation title, fields in which comprehensive examinations were passed, full citations of publications and presentations, awards, discoveries, inventions, patents, seminar leadership, foreign languages, courses taught – whatever is valued in your field.

International Curriculum Vitae Format

The international CV is *not* the same document as an academic CV. Think of an international CV as a six-to-eight-page excruciatingly detailed CV (Figure 9-10 gives you a template). Although it solicits private information that's outlawed in the UK, such as your health status, the international CV is favoured in some nations as a kind of global ticket to employment.

The international CV is usually a reverse chronological format that includes your contact information, qualifications summary, professional background, education, and personal information. Some European countries prefer the chronological format, which lists education and work experience from the farthest back to the present.

Strengths and weaknesses

International employment experts say that if you don't use this format, foreign recruiters may think you're hiding something. But keep in mind that the international CV format intrudes into private areas of your life.

INTERNATIONAL CV FORMAT

YOUR NAME

Curriculum Vitae

Home Address, City, State/County, Country, Province, Postcode

Include international codes:

(###) ###-#### (Phone), (###) ###-#### (Fax), ###@###.## (E-mail)

Objective (optional): Position as (title of position employer offers) using your (#) years' experience in (skills essential and specialised to the position).

SUMMARY OF QUALIFICATIONS

- A summary of your education, proficiencies, and career pertinent to target

- Number of years in area of objective, explaining similarities to it/its responsibilities

- Related education, training, and accreditation, reflecting employer's goals/ priorities

- An achievement directly related to target, something that the employer needs

- Traits reinforcing your candidacy for this position, specifically those asked for by the employer and those generally in demand in the field

- Other accomplishments, characteristics, knowledge either rare or prized in the field

- Travelling in field, countries visited, improvements made, distinctions, and so on

SUMMARY OF SKILLS

Topics of speciality or innovation within field • Areas of particular familiarity • Software equipment processes • Terminology relevant to target • Languages

PROFESSIONAL BACKGROUND

EMPLOYMENT

Job Title   Employer, Location   **20## - Present**

A Top Responsibility (relevant to objective)

- Accomplishments made in this position targeting the employer's priorities/mission

- Several other achievements from this position, pertinent to objective

A Skill (appropriate to objective)

- Several achievements from this position, pertinent to objective

Repeat pattern for all jobs.

PROFESSIONAL HONOURS

All honorary positions, awards, recognitions, or titles, with locations, 19## - 20##

Figure 9-10: The international CV is an option when applying for jobs outside your home country.

PUBLICATIONS

- "Title of work," name of publication/publisher *(Newsletter, Newspaper, Magazine, Journal),* location of publisher (country, languages, city and state or major city), date of publication, volume number (v.##), issue number (#.#), series number (#.#.#), page numbers (# - #)

Repeat pattern for all publications.

PRESENTATIONS AND PUBLIC APPEARANCES

- "Title of presentation," location of presentation (country, city, state, province, language), date (20## - 20##); optional synopsis of content and/or purpose of presentation, audience, results, and so on

Repeat pattern for all presentations.

PROFESSIONAL AFFILIATIONS

All societies, associations, leagues, or clubs, positions held, locations, 19## - 20##

EDUCATION

Degrees:

Ph.D., institution, date of degree (or anticipated date), specialisation

M.A./M.Sc., institution, class of degree, date of degree,

B.A./B.Sc., institution, class of degree, date of degree,

Give equivalents of these degrees for other countries

Courses: Those taken, honours, seminars

Other Accreditations: Licences

Academic Achievements: Appointments, nominations, leaderships, scholarships, grants, awards, praise, scores, recognitions, accomplishments

Affiliations: Societies, associations, clubs, leagues, memberships

DOCTORAL DISSERTATION

Title, advisor, director

Abstract summary (four to five sentences) discussing content and methodology

HONOURS, AWARDS, AND ACADEMIC ACHIEVEMENTS

Appointments, nominations, leaderships, awards, praise, scores, recognitions, accomplishments, fellowships, scholarships, grants, (including B.A./B.Sc./equivalents).

PERSONAL INFORMATION

- A sentence or so that describes personal attributes pertinent to employer's interests. Think positively, omit negatives, and highlight goal-oriented, functional characteristics that hold the promise of a good worker-employer relationship and reliably good work product. Present specific work-related examples of these personality highlights and explain how they are significant to the employer. Without exaggerating, accentuate the positive and include all favourable quotes from employers and co-workers, political officials and other public servants, and members of the clergy, volunteer organisations, and non-profit organisations.
- Age, marital status (single, engaged, married)
- Hobbies and leisure activities (travel, clubs, sports, athletics, collections, subscriptions)
- Volunteer service, public service

Who should use this format and who should think twice

Use this format if you're seeking an overseas job and don't object to revealing information that may subject you to discriminatory hiring practices.

Individuals who feel strongly about invasions of privacy or who aren't willing to be rejected out of hand because of gender, religion, race, age, or marital status should avoid this format and negotiate for a bare minimum of personal information.

Instructions

Formality prevails with the international CV. In Japan, for example, job hunters still fill out standard forms, available at Japanese bookshops.

- ✔ If you're applying in a non-English-speaking country, have your CV translated into the appropriate foreign language. Send both the English and the native-language version.

- ✔ Unless it's untrue, mention in the personal section that you have excellent health.

- ✔ Suggest by appropriate hobbies and personal interests that you'll easily adapt to an overseas environment.

- ✔ Hand write the cover letter that goes with your CV – some European countries are keen on handwriting analysis as a screening device. If your handwriting is iffy, enclose a word-processed version as well.

In addition, make sure that your cover letter shows a sincere desire to be in the country of choice.

A Roundup of Other Formats and Styles

A few adventuresome job seekers are experimenting with (or soon will be) newer CV formats, developing distribution technology and imaginative styles of communication. Take a quick look at possibilities that can't be classified as mainstream methods, but may be just the vehicle you need to find the job you want.

Portfolios

Samples of your work, gathered in a portfolio, have long been valuable to fields such as design, graphics, photography, architecture, advertising, public relations, marketing, and education.

Often, you deliver your portfolio as part of the job interview. Some highly motivated job seekers include a brief version of a career portfolio when sending their CVs, although recruiters say that they want less, not more, paper. Still others create online portfolios and try to entice recruiters and employers to review them.

A career portfolio is rarely used today but is a job-searching tool that may rise in future popularity charts as the work force moves more briskly among jobs, often working on short-term projects as contractors. The portfolio is a showcase for documenting a far more complete picture of what you offer employers than is possible with a CV of one or two pages.

Getting recruiters to read it is the problem.

If you believe that a portfolio is your best bet, put it in a three-ring binder with a table of contents and tabs separating its various parts. Mix and match the following categories:

- ✔ **Career goals** (if you're a new graduate or career changer): A brief statement of less than one page is plenty.

- ✔ **Your CV:** Use a fully formatted version in MS Word.

- ✔ **Samples of your work:** Include easily understandable examples of problem solving and competencies.

- ✔ **Proof of performance:** Insert awards, honours, testimonials and letters of commendation, and flattering performance reviews. Don't forget to add praise from employers, people who reported to you, and customers.

- ✔ **Proof of recognition:** Here's where you attach certifications, transcripts, degrees, licenses, and printed material listing you as the leader of seminars and workshops. Omit those that you merely attended unless the attendance proves something.

- ✔ **Military connections:** The military provides exceptionally good training, and many employers know it. List military records, awards, and badges.

Make at least two copies of your portfolio in case potential employers decide to hold on to your samples or fail to return them.

Your portfolio should document only the skills that you want to apply on a job. Begin by identifying those skills; then, determine what materials would prove your claims of competency.

Educator Martin Kimeldorf is responsible for the recent popularisation of career portfolios. Browse a library of Kimeldorf's portfolio samples at `amby.com/kimeldorf/portfolio`.

Direct letters: A CV alternative

The broadcast direct letter – postal mailing or e-mailing to megalists of companies asking for a job – is an old strategy widely panned by career advisors. But in the hands of experts and sent to a targeted list, the strategy can work surprisingly well.

Special reports: A CV supplement

A special report is a white paper of fewer than 10 pages describing your special wisdom to make things run cheaper, faster, better. We cover this highly creative document, which establishes you as an expert in a specific field or niche, in Chapter 4.

E-Mail networking newsletters: A CV supplement

Job seekers, usually over 50, who have special knowledge of a topic (such as classic cars or music) as well as computer savvy, are publishing free newsletters as a vehicle for reminding their network core that they're still between gigs. For more info on the electronic newsletter approach, which is a fairly recent development, take a look at Chapter 16.

Web CVs: HTML

Turn to the chapters in Part IV for discussions of technical savvy CVs and developments related to the Internet.

Choose What Works for You

The big closing question to ask yourself when you've settled on a format is this: Does this format maximise my qualifications for the job I want?

If the format you've chosen doesn't promote your top qualifications, take another look at the choices in this chapter and select a format that helps you shine.

Chapter 10

Contents Make the StandOut Difference

In This Chapter

▶ Understanding the parts of your CV

▶ Making each part impress the reader

*D*eciding what information to put into your CV isn't difficult if you remember the basic purpose of those few sheets of paper – you're showing that you can and will provide benefits to an employer.

Every company wants to be able to read your CV, knowing that you'll be able to "do exactly what it says on the tin". Regardless of how many sophisticated bells and whistles you add, the words of your CV must tell employers just how well you can do the job they want done.

The Parts of Your CV

To make your contents easy to access, organise the facts into various categories. Here are the essential parts that make up a CV:

- ✔ Contact information
- ✔ Objective or summary statement (if appropriate – see below)
- ✔ Education and training
- ✔ Experience
- ✔ Skills
- ✔ Competencies
- ✔ Activities
- ✔ Organisations
- ✔ Honours and awards

You can also include these other sections:

- ✔ Licenses, work samples
- ✔ Testimonials

To increase the likelihood that your CV positions you for an interview, take the time to understand the purpose of the different CV parts, which we explain in the following sections.

Contact Information

No matter which format you choose, place your name first on your CV, followed by contact information:

- ✔ **Name:** If your name isn't first, a computer may mistake Excellent Sales Representative for your name and file you away as "Ms Representative". You may want to display your name in slightly larger type than the rest of the contact information and in boldface, to make it clear who's CV the reader is holding.

- ✔ **Postal address:** Give a street name with the house/flat number, city, county, and post code. If you're a student or member of the armed forces who will be returning home, give both addresses, labelled Current Address and Permanent Address. You can add operational dates for each address. But don't forget to delete a date after it's passed. Otherwise, you will look like a product whose shelf life has expired.

- ✔ **Valid telephone number:** Use a personal number, where you can be reached or where the recruiter can leave a message.

  Don't allow children to answer this line. Don't record a clever message – play it straight, as potential employees might not want to leave a message on an answer phone with an amusing message from Eric Morecambe on it. If you must share a telephone with kids, emphasise the need for them to answer the phone professionally and to keep their calls short. Consider getting a cheap, pay-as-you-go mobile as a unique number/answering machine just for job hunting.

- ✔ **Other contact media:** Use any or all of the following, if available to you: e-mail address, mobile phone number, telephone answering service number, and Web page address.

What about using company resources? Should you ever use your employer's e-mail address or letterhead? Many employers see an employee's use of company resources to find another job as small-time theft. In certain situations, however, you can use your company's help. For example, a company that's downsizing is expected to provide resource support for outplacement. When you're ending a contract project for which you were hired, your employer may allow you to use company resources. Indicate permission to use them in your CV's cover letter: "The project for which I was hired is finishing ahead of schedule; my grateful employer is co-operating in my new search".

 Is it okay to list your work telephone number on your CV? In a decade when employers have been tossing workers out without remorse, it's a tough world, and you need speedy communications. The practical answer is to list your work number – if you have a direct line and voice mail or a mobile phone. To show that you're an ethical person, limit calls to a couple minutes – just long enough to arrange a meeting or an evening call back. Avoid the issue by using your personal mobile phone to call back during your lunch break.

Hooks: Objective or Summary?

Your StandOut CV needs a hook to grab the reader's attention. The hook follows your name and contact information and is expressed as a *job objective* or as an *asset statement* (also called a skills summary, see Chapter 13) – or some combination of the two.

A job objective can look like this:

> *Objective:* Assistant to Executive

A skills summary can look like this:

> *Summary:* Over 14 years of progressively more responsible office support experience, including superior computer skills, with a well-earned reputation for priority-setting and teamwork.

Or a job objective can be linked to a skills summary:

> *Objective:* Assistant to Executive, to keep operations under firmer control, using computer skills, contemporary office procedures, and pleasant manner with people.

However it is fashioned, the hook tells the recruiter what you want to do and/or what you're qualified to do.

 Debate rages among career pros over the topic of objective versus summary.

✔ Objective backers say that readers don't want to slog through a document, trying to guess the type of position you want and how you'd fit into the organisation.

✔ Summary advocates argue that a thumbnail sketch of your skills and other competencies allows you to be evaluated for jobs you haven't identified in your job objective – a serious consideration in this age of CV database searches.

A quick guideline taken from a sampling of six recruiters, as reported in *Job Choices* magazine, is this: "Objective statements are essential for recent graduates, summary statements for seasoned professionals".

On balance, we agree with the recruiters. An objective may be a self-defeating force for seasoned aces with well-established career paths, whose insistence on a particular job objective may be seen as rigid and for those whose CVs will be stored in electronic databases. But an objective is nearly essential for job seekers who are short on experience or don't have a clear idea of what they'd like to do, but know the general direction.

What you really need in your CV is *focus,* whether you style it as a job objective or as a summary.

The job objective statement

Weigh these considerations when deciding how to help readers visualise what you could do in the future for them.

When to use an objective

Use a job objective when:

✔ You're a new graduate or a career changer exiting the military, the clergy, education, or full-time homemaking. A job objective says what you're looking for.

✔ You have a greatly diversified background that may perplex some employers.

✔ You know the job being offered; make that job title your job objective.

Advantages of an objective

Most studies show that employers prefer objectives for quick identification purposes. They like to see the name of their job openings and/or companies at the top of a CV. Because you cite those achievements that support your objective and forget random experiences, the finished product (when done well) shows that you and the desired job are a well-matched pair.

JUDGEMENT CALL

Being objective about objectives

The debate over job objective or a variant of a skills summary continues unabated. These snatches of recruiters' opinions were overheard on a recruiting forum.

✔ "By including their desired job title in the online objective statement, job seekers increase the chances that their CV will match an employer's search string."

✔ "I prefer to see 'Career Summary' in place of 'Objective'. If the objective doesn't match an employer's idea of the job, the CV will probably be discarded. By putting a one-paragraph 'advert' as the very first thing the employer sees, you know that an overview of your qualifications is read."

✔ "As an in-house recruiter, any CV I receive without an objective tells me the applicant is either desperate and will take any job offered, or has not thought about his career enough to know what he wants.

Both are huge red flags. I think an objective is essential."

✔ "We advise candidates to leave off the objective or remove it before sending to a client. Use the objective space to include more information on accomplishments and experience."

✔ "When receiving CVs responding to a specific ad, I really don't have much appreciation for an objective statement. Wanting the job, the candidate will feed back the objective leaving me in the dark about what the candidate is truly looking for. In response to ads, I think a well-prepared cover letter runs circles around an objective statement. But I love objective statements on unsolicited CVs – they're typically more honest. This helps me determine what the job seeker's goals are and if I can even help him or her move to that next level at this time."

Disadvantages of an objective

Do you have the time to write a CV for each position (or career field) to which you apply? A narrow job objective may keep you from being considered by the same employer for other positions. And if the objective is too broadly focused, it becomes a meaningless statement.

The skills summary (asset statements)

A summary statement announces who you are and identifies your strengths and can be stated in paragraph form or in four to six bulleted quick-hits, such as:

✔ Recruited and trained more than 300 people

✔ Installed robotics, standardising product, reducing retraining cost by 16 percent

> ✔ Slashed initial training costs from £800,000 to £650,000 within one year
>
> ✔ Created dynamic training culture to support the introduction of a new product

Take a look at the sections that follow for tips on when a summary statement is best.

When to use a summary

Use a summary statement when:

> ✔ You're a person with widely applicable skills. Recruiters especially like a skills summary atop a reverse chronological CV because it lets them creatively consider you for jobs that you may not know exist.
>
> ✔ You're in a career field with pathways to multiple occupations or industries (an administrative assistant, for example).
>
> ✔ You know that your CV is headed for an electronic database and you want to be considered for multiple jobs.

Advantages of a summary

A summary can be more appropriate to status – senior executives, in particular, can let their records speak for them. Recruiters believe that what you're prepared to do next should be pretty evident from what you've already done. Another argument is premised on psychology: Employers aren't known for being overly concerned with what you want *from* them until they're sure of what you can do *for* them.

Disadvantages of a summary

A summary doesn't explicitly say what you want and why the employer would want you. The technique of specifying a job objective in a cover letter attached to a skills-summary CV is common; the problems arise when the cover letter is inadvertently separated from the CV or the CV is passed out alone, as at a job fair. Furthermore, the fact that a skills summary CV leaves many doors open is a double-edged sword: Your accomplishments don't thrust you toward a specific target, so you may be abandoning a success strategy that's been proven again and again.

Education and Training

While both education and training are all about learning, the first is normally taken to mean more general academic subjects (such as arts or sciences) while the second is seen as vocational or directly job related. In the real world such distinctions are rarely so clear since a literature qualification may be truly job related for a would be publisher, and a certificate in motorbike mechanics may have little bearing on the desired job in stock-broking. Think through all and any of the educational/training qualifications you have to your name and decide which are going to make a potential employer see you as a hot property.

- ✔ List your highest degree first – type of degree, subject you read, college name, and date awarded.

- ✔ New graduates should give far more detail on course work than seasoned aces who've held at least one job for one year or more.

- ✔ Omit secondary school if you have a university degree.

- ✔ If you have a vocational or technical certificate or diploma that required less than a year to obtain, list your secondary school as well.

- ✔ Note continuing education, including seminars related to your work.

- ✔ If you fall short of the mark on the job's educational requirements, try to compensate by expanding the continuing the education section. Give the list a name, such as "Professional Development Highlights", and list every impressive course, seminar, workshop, and conference that you've attended.

Experience

Describe – with quantified achievements – your present and previous positions in reverse chronological order. Include dates of employment, company names and locations, and specific job titles. Show progression and promotions within an organisation, especially if you've been with one employer for aeons.

What's first – education or experience?

The general rule in CV writing is to lead with your most qualifying factor.

With certain exceptions (such as law, where your choice of university may be considered throughout life), lead off with experience when you've been in the workforce for at least three years. When you're loaded with experience but low on credentials, list your school days at the end – and perhaps even omit them entirely if you didn't graduate.

Young people just out of school usually start with education, but if you've worked throughout school or have relevant prior work history, start with experience.

Young readers, if your research shows that a prospective employer wants education and experience, provide a summary linking them together as interdependent. For example, explain how your education was part of your professional experience, or how your experience was an education itself. Following this consolidation, create a heading under which you can merge both sections – such as "Professional Preparation" or "Education, Training, and Employment".

Consider using more than one Experience heading. Try headings, such as "Accounting and Finance-Related Experience", "General Business Experience", and "Healthcare and Administration Experience". This is yet another way of reinforcing your suitability for the job you seek.

Some CV formats use a more rigid approach than others, allowing little leeway as you fill in the blanks. Most formats, however, leave all kinds of room for stacking your blocks in a way that does you the most good.

Skills

Skills are the heart and soul of job finding and, as such, encompass a variety of experiences. These are examples of skills:

> Collaborating, editing, fundraising, interviewing, managing, navigating (Internet), researching, teaching

And here are some more skills:

> Administering social programs, analysing insurance facts, advising homeless people, allocating forestry resources, desktop publishing, co-ordinating association events, designing home furnishing ads, marine expedition problem-solving, writing police reports

And some more:

> Dependable, sense of humour, commitment, leadership, persistence, crisis-resilient, adaptable, quick, results-driven

And these are still more skills:

> Brochures, UNIX, five years, 100 percent quota, telemarketing, senior management, spreadsheet, MBA, major accounting firms

As you can see, a very broad definition encompasses what can constitute a skill, and using skills as a basic element of your CV may surprise you. We include them here because they've taken on new importance, and the concept of "skill" has changed in the past two decades. Skills used to be thought of in the classic meaning of general and industry-specific abilities. Recruiting industry professionals expand the term to include personal characteristics, as well as past employers, special knowledge, achievements, and products.

Because the term is widely used in job searching today, a *skill* is any identifiable ability or fact that employers value and will pay for. That means that "five years" is a skill, just as "word processing" is a skill; employers pay for experience and competence.

Top accomplishments

Top 12 accomplishments that most interest employers:

- ✔ Increased revenues
- ✔ Saved money
- ✔ Increased efficiency
- ✔ Cut overheads
- ✔ Increased sales
- ✔ Improved workplace safety
- ✔ Purchasing accomplishments
- ✔ New products/new lines
- ✔ Improved record-keeping process
- ✔ Increased productivity
- ✔ Successful advertising campaign
- ✔ Effective budgeting

Where do skills belong on your CV? Everywhere. They are the basic ingredients of every CV – so season every statement with skills. Skills are indispensable. Whether you use an e-CV or a traditional paper CV, you must name your skills or be left behind.

Skills are one part of the emerging concept of *competencies,* a discussion of which immediately follows.

Competencies

Competencies is a broader concept than *skills.* Competencies and skills differ in that skills are applications of knowledge to solve a problem or perform an act. The competencies concept includes skills as well as behaviours required in a career field position, such as persuasiveness or persistence in sales and marketing. Richard H Beatty, co-founder and board member of HR Technologies (`www.hrscope.com`), a leading competencies software firm, expands the concept's meaning: "Competencies are the knowledge, skills, characteristics, and behaviours essential to successful performance of a job."

But human resource professionals don't share universal agreement about the precise composition of *competency-based programs.* Some employers establish enterprise-wide *core competencies* that apply to all employees no matter what their position. The employer's signature core competencies (such as teamwork, goal setting, and trustworthiness) are meant to aid in selecting new employees who are aligned with the company's mission and objectives. Essentially, the employer tries to figure out what makes its best performers tick (identify their competencies) and hire more people like them.

Some employers add to core competencies a number of *role competencies* that relate to the position held – an engineer's role competencies differ from an accountant's, for example.

The following overview launches you on the road to understanding the nuts and bolts of the emerging *competency-based recruiting model.*

Competencies in the corporate arena

Most users of competency-based models are large corporations. The idea hasn't yet trickled down to the mass of employers. Each employer chooses the enterprise-wide core and role competencies that it prefers. Some employers articulate only a few enterprise-wide core competencies, and others have a dozen or more. An employer may have hundreds or even thousands of role competencies, assigning 20 or 30 to each position.

The competencies theory is an intellectual child of the 1990s, but its popularity has surged only recently. Although the competencies concept is more commonly used in job interviewing, job seekers are beginning to integrate competencies into their CVs as growing numbers of employers adopt the approach to improving the quality of hiring.

Competencies basically fall into two distinct classifications: *behavioural competencies* and *technical competencies.* Behavioural competencies – where most of the recent employer emphasis has been – are further divided into two distinct types. The two types are behaviours that are *job relevant* (important to job success) and behaviours that are *culture relevant* (important to fitting in well with the organisation's culture of work environment).

Here's an illustration of the differences between the two:

- ✔ **Technical competencies:** These are the specialised knowledge and skills needed to solve the key problems faced in a given position and get the results expected of the job.

  Technical competencies for a sales position include product knowledge, market knowledge, customer knowledge, market trends, pricing, competitor products/ pricing/strategies, closing skills, knowledge of sales tactics, and techniques, for instance.

- ✔ **Behavioural competencies – job relevant:** These are the personal characteristics of excellent performers in the job.

  Descriptions of job-relevant behaviour in a sales position include self-confident, investigative, strategic, open and friendly, relationship builder, networker, good listener, strong communicator, attentive, responsive, and service-oriented.

✔ **Behavioural competencies – culture relevant:** Many of the corporate *core competencies* come into play here. The core competencies reflect the behaviour and attributes that the company's senior management believes are important to the organisation's long-term survival and success.

Descriptions of culture-relevant behaviour in a sales position include team-oriented, client-focused, change agent, strategic visionary, and consistently improvement-oriented.

Competency-based CVs

Most good CVs focus on knowledge, skills, and accomplishments. They only hint at competencies required to do the work. To capture behavioural competencies on a CV, you must show how your accomplishments confirm your competencies. Or to turn it around, you must show how your competencies made it possible for you to hit the back of the net.

Competencies focus on how an employee contributes value (benefits) to the employer and on what's actually accomplished.

As an example, to connect your behaviours with your accomplishments, you can say something like this:

Product development: Created new mid-market segment supporting an annual growth rate of 20 percent in a flat industry, demonstrating high energy and business acumen.

In the above example, the verb "demonstrating" connects the accomplishment (Created new mid-market segment supporting an annual growth rate of 20 percent in a flat industry) with the behaviours, or competencies (high energy and business acumen). Other verbs you can use to bridge the two types of information include the following:

✔ Confirming

✔ Displaying

✔ Exhibiting

✔ Illustrating

✔ Manifesting

✔ Proving

✔ Revealing

Keywords are the magnets that draw non-human eyes to your talents.

Where to Find Keywords

How can you find keywords for your occupation or career field? Use a high-lighter to pluck keywords from these resources.

- **Printed and online help-wanted ads:** Highlight the job skills, competencies, experience, education, and other nouns that employers ask for.

- **Job descriptions:** Ask employers for them, check at libraries for books or software with job descriptions, or search online. To find job descriptions online, just enter the term *job descriptions* on a search engine, such as Google (www.google.co.uk).

- **Your core CV:** Look through to highlight nouns that identify job skills, competencies, experience, and education.

- **Trade magazine news stories:** Text about your career field or occupation should be ripe with keywords. Media that have strictly sober style guides, such as *The Economist* and *The Financial Times* are often good sources of hype-free description.

- **Annual reports of companies in your field:** The company descriptions of key personnel and departmental achievements should offer strong keyword clues.

- **Programs for industry conferences and events:** Speaker topics address current industry issues, a rich source of keywords.

- **Internet search engine:** Plug in a targeted company's name and search the site that comes up. Look closely at the careers portal and read current press releases. You can also use Internet search engines to scout out industry-specific directories, glossaries, and dictionaries.

Just as you should keep your CV up to date, ready to move in a flash if you must, you should also keep a running log of keywords that can help you reconnect to a new job on a moment's notice.

TIP

Mining for keywords in job descriptions

The excerpts below of two job descriptions posted on Business.com (business.com; enter *job descriptions* in the Search box) illustrate how you can find keywords almost everywhere. In these examples, the keywords are underscored.

Vehicle Dismantler:

✔ Knowledge of proper operation of <u>lifts</u>, <u>fork-lifts</u>, <u>torches</u>, <u>power wrenches</u>, etc.

✔ Knowledge of <u>warehouse</u>, <u>core</u>, and <u>stack locations</u>.

✔ Skill to move <u>vehicles</u> without damaging vehicle, other vehicles, or personnel.

✔ Skill to remove <u>body</u> and <u>mechanical parts</u> without damage to part, self, or others.

✔ Ability to read a <u>Dismantler report</u> and assess <u>stock levels</u>.

✔ Ability to accurately assess condition of <u>parts</u> to be inventoried.

Budget Assistant:

✔ Reviews <u>monthly expense statements</u>, monitors <u>monthly expenditures</u>, and gathers supporting <u>documentation</u> for supervisor review and approval.

✔ Performs basic <u>arithmetic operations</u> to calculate and/or verify <u>expense totals</u> and <u>account balances</u>.

✔ Operates <u>computer</u> to enter data into <u>spreadsheet</u> and/or <u>database</u>. Types routine <u>correspondence</u> and <u>reports</u>.

✔ Operates office equipment such as <u>photocopier</u>, <u>fax machine</u>, and <u>calculator</u>.

Get a Grip on Grammar

CV language differs from normal speech in several ways described here. In general, keep the language tight and the tone professional, avoiding the following:

✔ **First-person pronouns (I, we):** Your name is at the top of each CV page, so the recruiter knows it's about *you.* Eliminate first-person pronouns. Also, unless you happen to be royalty, don't use third-person pronouns (he, she, one) when referring to yourself – the narrative technique makes you seem pompous. Simply start with a verb.

✔ **Articles (the, a, an):** Articles crowd sentences and don't clarify meaning. Substitute *retrained staff* for *retrained the staff.*

✔ **Helping verbs (have, had, may, might):** Helping verbs weaken claims and credibility – implying that your time has passed and portraying you as a job-hunting weakling. Say *managed* instead of *have managed.*

✔ **"Being" verbs (am, is, are, was, were):** Being verbs suggest a state of existence rather than a state of motion. Try *monitored requisitions* instead of *requisitions were monitored.* The active voice gives a stronger, more confident delivery. If you activate the grammar checker that accompanies the spell checker in most word processors, it highlights anywhere you have used the passive voice.

✔ **Shifts in tense:** Use the present tense for a job you're still in and the past tense for jobs you've left. But among the jobs you've left, don't switch back and forth between tenses. Another big mistake: Dating a job as though you're still employed (2000–Present) and then describing it in the past tense.

✔ **Complex sentences:** Unless you keep your sentences lean and clean, readers won't take time to decipher them. Try and get your head around this:

> *Reduced hospital costs by 67 percent by creating a patient-independence program, where they make their own beds, and as noted by hospital finance department, costs of nails and wood totalled £300 less per patient than work hours of maintenance staff.*

Eliminate complex sentences by dividing ideas into sentences of their own and getting rid of extraneous details:

> *Reduced hospital costs by 67 percent. Originated patient independence program that decreased per-patient expense by £300 each.*

✔ **Overwriting:** Use your own voice; don't say *expeditious* when you want to say *swift.*

✔ **Abbreviations:** Abbreviations are informal and not universal – even when they're career-specific. Use *Internet,* for example, instead of *Net.*

The exception is industry jargon – use it, especially in digital CVs. Being able to correctly and casually use terms common to the industry in which you're seeking employment adds to your credibility.

Adopt a trick that writers of television commercials use to be sure that they give the most information in the fewest words: Set yourself an arbitrary limit of words to express a unit of information. For example, allow yourself 25 words to explain one of your former jobs. The 25-word limit guarantees that you'll write with robust language.

Remember, when your words speak for you, you need to be sure to use words that everyone can understand and that relate to the job at hand.

Chapter 12

Overcome Deadly Dilemmas

- -

In This Chapter

▶ Squashing the overqualified objections

▶ Standing tall as a woman re-entering the workplace

▶ Dealing with disability issues

▶ Patching over employment gaps and demotions

▶ Adding focus to a busy CV

- -

*I*f you're tempted to skip over this chapter, which deals with reshaping perceptions, go ahead and fly by – just as long as you're no older than 35 and
have five years of experience that precisely matches the requirements for a
job that you want. Otherwise, sit down, read up, and get ready to fight your
corner.

This chapter spotlights major CV components that need spin control to ward
off an early burial for your CV. These components are the quintessential and
potential chance-killing perceptions that stem from your age; the abundance
of your experience; and the experience that seemingly isn't there when you
return to the job market. Other dilemmas include unexplained spaces in your
job history, stumbles in the workplace, or physical characteristics.

All the common rejection issues covered in this chapter call for a spot of CV
spin control, or putting the best face on a perception.

Too Much Experience

Leading off the line-up of CV headaches is the four-letter word that's 10 letters long: *Experience.*

The E word's pejorative status is justified. Not only is inappropriate
experience – too much or too little – often the real reason that you're turned
down, but it's also too frequently a cover story for villainous rejections that
are really based on anything from bias to bad breath.

Too many qualifications or ageism?

A reader who's rounding the 50s curve, writes that his qualifications for a training position are superior but too ample. He explains:

> *Preoccupation with age seems to be the pattern. I'm rarely called for an interview; when I call after sending a CV in response to an ad or a networking contact, I'm told I'm too experienced for the position – "You seem to be overqualified." How can I keep my CV from looking like lavender and old lace?*

Ageism is often the subtext behind the *overqualified* objection. Deal with it by limiting your work history to the most recent positions you've held that target the job opening. To avoid seeming too old or too highly paid, limit your related experience to about 15 years for a managerial job and to about 10 years for a technical job. Concerns about how you moved up so fast will arise if you only go back 10 years for a managerial job, but 10 years is believable for a technical job, many of which won't even have been in existence for that long.

What about all your other experience? Leave it in your memory bank. Or if you believe that the older work history adds to your value as a candidate, you can describe it under a heading of *Other Experience* and briefly present it without dates. Figure 12-1 gives an example of a CV that shows recent experience only.

The recent-experience-only spin doesn't work every time, but give it a try – it shows that you're not stuck in a time warp, and it's a better tactic than advertising your age as one that qualifies you for carbon dating.

If the employer is notorious for hiring only young guns, rethink your direction. Try to submit your CV to employers who can take advantage of your expertise, such as a new or expanding company operating in unfamiliar territory. As things stand, European legislation looks set to make age discrimination illegal by 2006. Not only is that a long time to wait around (and none of us is getting any younger), but past experience suggests that even with legislation on your side, you'll still have to work hard to overcome deeply entrenched prejudice.

Fortunately, a new tool has come along in the past several years admirably suited to this purpose: Savvy job hunters now turn to the Internet's discussion groups to check out job leads, to name names of saint and sinner companies, and to ask about company cultures and anti-discriminatory practices. Based on your occupation, you can choose among the many millions of discussion groups available through forums and newsgroups. You may, for example, want to connect with other architects, financial planners, or technical writers. Use the keywords of your target employment field to find specific discussion forums by searching for **discussion forums** on a UK-focused search engine like www.yahoo.co.uk. Make sure you click on UK Only option unless you want to look at US discussion groups, too. If you are interested in US groups, try taking a peek at forumdirectory.net and forumscentral.com.

RECENT EXPERIENCE ONLY

Work Experience

FEIN AND SONS – Operating from Limehouse, East London.
Sole Proprietor, Broker.

Estate agent, development, asset management, and consulting. Specialising in eight-
and nine-figure acquisitions, shopping centres, and commercial space, obtaining
entitlements and economic analysis. Personal volume: over £ 30 million.

SONNHAARD LTD. – Canary Wharf, London. 2000-20XX.
Marketing Manager.

Real estate development corporation. Primary project: Playa del Sol, a residential
development on Spain's Costa Daurada. Sourced architect, designers, and contractors.
Limited liability company built 60 custom luxury homes by architect Jacques
Donnaeu of Toulouse. Supervised 10 sales representatives. Sales gross exceeded £10
million, selling 58 homes ahead of project schedule by six months.

EUROPEAN CONFEDERATION OF ESTATE AGENTS – London. 1992-
2000. **Executive Vice President.**

International trade association with 190 member companies, 15 affiliated
organisations, and 300 service members who provide goods and services to members.
Annual convention attended by over 2,000 executives. Responsible for creating
formal information-sharing programme and database on local and pan-European real
estate legislation. Increased membership by 200%, administering seven-figure budget,
with staff of five professionals.

Other Experience

• BBH & Co., **Executive Vice President.** Administered six-figure budget and
supervised 27 managers. Directed recruitment and marketing activities.

• CSU Manchester, **Development Director.** Managed £10 million project to expand
university campus grounds by 30%. Maintained campus construction budget within
promised budgetary and time constraints, including contracting and materials.

• TRADE ALTERNATIVE, **Commercial Properties Manager.** Marketed, leased,
and acquired £300,000 in commercial property. Catered to such upmarket clientele
as high-end law firms.

Figure 12-1: Focusing on recent experiences is an effort to avoid the problem of being seen as too old.

A bit harder to navigate, but with a complete 20-year archive, Google Groups (`http://groups.google.co.uk`) allows you to wade through most newsgroups.

What if the overqualified objection is just that and not a veil for age discrimination? The employer legitimately may be concerned that when something better comes along, you'll be out the door like greased lightning.

If you really prefer to take life easier or to have more time to yourself, you can be forthcoming with that fact in your CV's objective. Writing this kind of statement is tricky. You risk coming across as worn-out goods, ready to kick back and listen to babbling brooks while you bank the salary. When you explain your desire to back off an overly stressful workload, balance your words with a counter statement reflecting your energy and commitment, as in the example in Figure 12-2.

Figure 12-2:
This positive statement shows that, although you no longer want a leadership role, you still want to be a productive employee.

Energetic and work-focused, but no longer enjoy frenzied managerial responsibility; seek a challenging non-managerial position.

Too much experience in one job

A reader writes:

I've stayed in my current and only job too long. When my company cut thousands of workers, we received outplacement classes. I was told that job overstayers are perceived as lacking ambition, uninterested in learning new things, and too narrowly focused. What can I do about this?

Spin strategy A: Divide your job into modules

Show that you successfully moved up and up, meeting new challenges and accepting ever more responsibility. Divide your job into realistic segments, which you label as Level 1, Level 2, Level 3, and so on. Describe each level as a separate position, just as you would if the levels had been different positions within the same company or with different employers. If your job titles changed as you moved up, your writing task is a lot easier.

Spin strategy B: Deal honestly with job titles

If your job title never changed, should you just make up job titles? *No.* The only truthful way to inaugurate fictional job titles is to parenthetically introduce them as "equivalent to . . ." Suppose that you're an accountant and have been in the same job for 25 years. Your segments might be titled like this:

- ✔ Level 3 (equivalent to supervising accountant)
- ✔ Level 2 (equivalent to senior accountant)
- ✔ Level 1 (equivalent to accountant)

To mitigate the lack of being knighted with increasingly senior job titles, fill your CV with references to your continuous salary increases and bonuses and the range of job skills you mastered. In a world in which people are often rewarded with grandiose titles instead of pay rises or responsibility, the fact that you have been rewarded with more solid benefits may speak well of you.

Spin strategy C: Tackle deadly perceptions head-on

Diminish any perception that you became fat and lazy while staying in the same job too long by specifically describing open-ended workdays: "Worked past 8 pm at least once a week throughout employment."

Derail the perception you don't want to learn new things by being specific in describing learning adventures: "Attended six terms of word-processing technologies; currently enrolled in adult education program to master latest software."

Discount the perception that you're narrowly focused by explaining that, although your employment address didn't change, professionally speaking, you're widely travelled in terms of outside seminars, professional associations, and reading.

Spin strategy D: When nothing works, try something new

When you have followed these recommendations note for note but are still sitting out the dance, take a chance on something new.

Highlight the issue

In a departure from the normal practice of omitting from your CVs reasons for leaving a job, consider indicating why you're making a change after all this time.

Neutralise the issue burning in every employer's mind: "Why now? Why after all these years are you on the market? Excessed out? Burned out?" If the question isn't asked, that doesn't mean it isn't hanging out in the recruiter's mind. Even though you may be seen as a mouldering antique, reveal yourself as interested in current developments by adding this kind of phrase in your objective:

Focusing on companies and organisations with contemporary viewpoints

In an even more pioneering move to solve the same problem, create a whole new section at the tail of your CV, headed *Bright Future,* with a statement such as the one in Figure 12-3.

Figure 12-3:
This add-on may make the difference between being seen as stodgy and unambitious and being seen as dynamic and experienced.

BRIGHT FUTURE
Layoffs springing from a new management structure give me the welcomed opportunity to accept new responsibilities and bring a fresh challenge to my work life.

Consider contract work

An employer's perception of highly experienced people may be that they're too rigid and hold expectations that the new environment will replicate the old – a perception that assassinates their job prospects.

Sometimes, going the extra mile to prove you're dynamic and experienced, as well as generous and forward-looking, still doesn't generate job offers. This is particularly true for professionals over 40 in technical fields.

An example from a reader:

"I have a PhD in physics and more than 20 years of computer programming experience, including Fortran, C/C++, ADA, HTML, and Java. At my own substantial expense, I'm currently completing a year's course work in Cobol, Visual Basic, Web-page administration, and advanced LAN theory."

The reader laments that he hasn't had a nibble on a job interview. Yes, he's tried the work experience remedy.

I enrolled for work experience, but after I donated 40 hours to the company, building five computers for free for them, the company pulled out of the programme, negating a verbal agreement to give me hands-on experience. Because I have a doctorate, almost routinely I'm asked, "Why would you want to be a programmer?" The implication is that I'm overqualified. The reality is that ageism is alive and well, and employers are unwilling to pay for senior talent.

In such cases, we advise seasoned personnel to consider contract work. For contract work, start your CV with a keyword profile and include as many skills as you legitimately can.

In addition to following the CV tips for seasoned aces offered in Chapter 4, get other ideas of how technical personnel can surmount "overqualified" objections and age discrimination from Web sites such as Math and Engineering Links (www.phds.org). More UK specific sources of help, include the Campaign Against Age Discrimination in Employment (CAADE) which you can contact at www.caade.net. There's also a guide to the relevant legislation at The Employers Forum on Age – a body campaigning for "an age diverse workforce" in the UK (www.efa.org.uk). For the government line on encouraging age diversity, there's also Age Positive, which has advice on job seeking as well as useful links (www.agepositive.gov.uk).

Too Long Gone: For Women Only

A woman re-entering the world of work still has it tough. Usually, Mum's the one who puts her career on hold to meet family responsibilities. When she tries to re-enter the job market, by choice or economic necessity, she feels as though she's been living on another planet, as this letter shows:

Employers don't want to hire women if they've been mothers and out of the market for more than a year or two. You know what, for the last 10 years, I've worked my rear-end off! Don't they understand that? Doesn't intelligence, willingness to work hard, creativity, attention to detail, drive, efficiency, grace under pressure, initiative, leadership, persistence, resourcefulness, responsibility, teamwork, and a sense of humour mean anything these days?

Every characteristic that this reader mentions is still a hot ticket in the job market, but the burden is on mothers to interpret these virtues as marketable skills.

✔ Grace under pressure, for example, translates to *crisis manager,* a valuable person when the electricity fails in a computer-driven office.

✔ Resourcefulness translates to *office manager,* who is able to ward off threatening calls from credit collection agencies.

✔ A sense of humour translates to *data communications manager,* who can cajole a sleepy technical whiz into reporting for work at two in the morning for emergency repair of a satellite hovering over Europe.

You can't, of course, claim those job titles on your CV, but you can make equivalency statements: "Like a crisis manager, I've had front-line experience handling such problems as electrical failures, including computer crashes."

If you're a returning woman, develop a StandOut CV, like the one shown in Figure 12-4, that connects what you can do with what an employer wants done using the tips in the following sections.

Look back in discovery

Review your worksheets (see Chapter 13) to spot transferable skills that you gained in volunteer, civic, hobby, and domestic work. Scout for adult and continuing education, both on campus and in non-traditional settings.

Re-examine the informative television programs that you've watched, the news magazines that you've monitored. Go to the library and read business magazines and trade journals to make a lexicon of up-to-date words, such as "Please compare my skills" and not "I'm sure you will agree".

Avoid tired words like *go-getter* and *upwardly mobile.* Yesteryear's buzzwords, such as *management by objective* and *girl Friday* won't do a thing to perk up your image, and will, in fact, make you look as old as Rosalind Russell – the original girl Friday.

In recounting civic and volunteer work, avoid the weak verbs: *worked with* or *did this or that.* Instead say, *collaborated with.* What other strong verbs can you think of to sound more businesslike? Try taking a look at Chapter 11; Win with Words for Inspiration.

Incorporate professional terms

The use of professional words can help de-emphasise informal training or work experience. But you must be careful when doing this to show good judgement about the work world.

REENTRY

JOY R. NGUYEN

12 Watt Road, Northampton, Northants, NN40TJ   01933 456 123

SUMMARY OF EXPERIENCE

More than five years' experience in event-planning, fundraising, administration, and publicity. More than nine years' experience in administration for retail and manufacturing firms. B.A. in Business IT with Human Resource Management.

NONPROFIT/VOLUNTEER SERVICE

2002-Present   **Wellingborough Women's Association, Wellingborough**
                          Membership Committee Chair

Planning, organising programs, exhibits and events to recruit association members. Coordinated annual new member events.

1994-2002   **Northants Telephone Samaritans**
                       Member, Board of Directors and Executive Committee

Spearheaded expansion of Telephone Samaritans organsiation. Designed programs, procedures, and policies, monitoring trustees in the conversion of a £1 million switchboard and greeting rooms facility. Led £75 million fundraising campaign.

- **Fundraising Chair**, 1994-1996, Raised funds for entire construction project, establishing hundreds of donors and supervising project. Sourced contractors and directed fundraising activities, using strong interpersonal and networking skills.

HOME MANAGEMENT EXPERIENCE

- **Scheduling**: Assisted business executive and two children in the scheduling of travel and 16,000 miles of transportation. Arranged ticketing, negotiated finances of £5,000 in travel expenses.
- **Conflict Resolution**: Arbitrated personal, business issues. Effective interpersonal skills.
- **Relocation**: Took care of the relocation of entire family, coordinating moving services, trucks, and packing schedules.
- **Budget & Purchasing**: Managed family finances, including budgeting, medical, dental insurance packages, two home purchases, three car purchases, expenses and taxes. Developed financial skills.

ADDITIONAL PROFESSIONAL EXPERIENCE

1994-1996   **Sunrise Books, Northampton**
                       Assistant Manager, Sales Representative

Managed daily operations of coffee house and bookshop, managing a staff of 11. Supervised entire floor of merchandise and stock. Purchased all support goods.

- Spearheaded store's first sales campaign, resulting in tripled sales.
- Designed system for inventory analysis, streamlining purchasing and display control.
- Redirected staff duties for more effective work hours.
- Promoted from sales to supervisor in 38 days; three months later to asst. mgr.

EDUCATION

Bachelor of Arts (Hons), Business Information Technology with Human Resource Management, 1994, Coventry University

Figure 12-4: A sample CV showcasing the skills of a domestic specialist re-entering the work world.

Professionalising your domestic experience is a tightrope walk: Ignoring it leaves you looking like a missing person, yet you can't be pretentious or naive. Don't say *housewife;* say *family manager.* Be very wary of using the word *domestic* when describing what you do because the term has been pretty much hijacked and tends to conjure up images of Nigella Lawson. Refer to *home management* to minimise gaps in time spent as a homemaker, and be sure to fill the home management period with transferable skills relevant to the targeted position.

Delve into what you did during your home management period. You did not hold a paid job, but you did do important unpaid work. Dissect your achievements to find your deeds – they can be impressive. Examples range from time management (developing the ability to do more with less time) to budgeting experience (developing a sophisticated understanding of priority allocation of financial resources). Other examples include using the telephone in drumming up support for a favourite charity (developing confidence and a businesslike telephone technique) and leadership positions in school committees (developing a sense of authority and the ability to guide others).

Selected home-based skills

Don't overlook these skills that you may have acquired inside the home. We've included a few examples of occupations in which they can be used. This illustration assumes that you lack formal credentials for professional-level work. If you do have the credentials, upgrade the examples to the appropriate job level.

✔ **Juggling schedules:** Paraprofessional assistant to business executives, physicians. Small service business operator, dispatching staff of technicians.

✔ **Peer counselling:** Human resources department employee benefits assistant. Substance abuse programme manager.

✔ **Arranging social events:** Party shop manager. Non-profit organisation fund-raiser. Art gallery employee.

✔ **Conflict resolution:** Administrative assistant. Customer service representative. School secretary.

✔ **Problem-solving:** Any job.

✔ **Decorating:** Interior decorator. Interior fabric shop salesperson.

✔ **Nursing:** Medical or dental office assistant.

✔ **Solid purchasing judgement:** Purchasing agent. Materials buyer.

✔ **Planning trips, relocations:** Travel agent. Corporate employee relocation co-ordinator.

✔ **Communicating:** Any job.

✔ **Shaping budgets:** Office manager. Department head. Accounting clerk.

✔ **Maximising interior spaces:** Commercial-office real estate agent. Business furniture store operator.

Despite more than three decades of media attention to skills developed by homemakers, employers continue to be dismissive of parenting and other abilities acquired inside the home. Many employers believe that identifying yourself as a domestic specialist is no more workplace-useful than claiming to be a "seasoned husband" or "experienced friend".

Make your homemaker skills difficult to disrespect by showing their relevance to a given career field. Be careful to avoid sounding as though you attended a workshop where you memorised big words, however.

Whatever you do, you can't ignore the issue – like where have you been for the past few years? When you lack skills developed outside the home in community work, you have to do the best you can to pull out home-based skills.

Use years or use dates – not both

Some advisers suggest that, in referring to your home management years, you use a *years-only approach* and list years, not dates, as in Figure 12-5, to avoid the gap in paid work experience.

Figure 12-5:
Examples of the years-only approach to list household management skills.

• *Family Care 10 years*
Child care, home operations, budgeting, and support for a family of four. Participation in parent/school relations, human services, and religious organisation

• *Leadership Positions*
Vice President, St. Aidan's County High School PTA; Chair, Fund-Raising, Carlisle Oxfam shops; Subcommittee Chair, Budget Committee, First Baptist Church

This approach is unlikely to make a favourable impression on a person who hires often. Employment professionals prefer concrete facts and dates. But the years-only CV can work at small businesses where the hiring manager also wears several other hats and doesn't pay much attention to hiring guidelines.

Don't make the mistake of using both forms on the same CV, assigning dates to your paid jobs but only years to your homemaker work.

Know the score

Gender bias lives, and, of course, you should omit all information that the employer isn't entitled to, including your age, marital status, physical condition, number and ages of children, and husband's name. Even though the law is on your side, in today's interview-rationed job market, your CV must qualify you more than the next applicant. If you've been out of the job market for some years, you have to work harder and smarter to show that you're a hot hire. To help in your quest, seek out seminars and services offered to women re-entering the job market.

Job Seekers with Disabilities

2003 was the European Year of Disabled People, and to usher it in, the UK government promptly announced a disability bill aiming to update the Disability Discrimination Act of 1995. Much of the bill is concerned with access to public transport and services, but when it became law, it also affected the workplace by widening the definition of disabled to include those diagnosed with HIV or cancer.

As it stands, British law states that any employer with over 15 employees is legally bound to give disabled workers the same rights as their able-bodied colleagues. That covers any part of the employment process, including job interviews, career development, and promotion. As part of this, the employer must try to accommodate the disabled by changing work hours where necessary, arranging relevant training, and physically changing the workspace for accessibility where required. Of course every case is different, and some disabilities will rule out suitability for certain types of jobs, but grey areas like these can be tackled case by case with a bit of help. The Disability Rights Commission (DRC) is there to help you, and your local job centre should have a Disability Employment Adviser (DEA) to talk to about potential problems. You can also find a helpful overview of the Disability Discrimination Act at www.disability.gov.uk and further help from the Advisory, Conciliation, and Arbitration Service (ACAS) at www.acas.org.uk.

To find out whether you're covered by existing disability discrimination legislation, take a look at the definition of disabled at the Disability Rights Commission (DRC) Web site (www.drc-gb.org) or phone them. A confidential advice service, the Benefit Enquiry Line for People with Disabilities, is also available on 0800 882200.

Deciding when and whether to disclose a disability

The DRC watches your back to prevent discrimination based on your disability, but recruiters may still weasel around the law to avoid what they perceive as a liability. Use street smarts: When you can't win and you can't break even, change the game. In your game, spin control begins with choosing whether to disclose your disability on your CV. Use these tips:

- ✓ **If your disability is visible, the best time to disclose it is after the interview has been set and you telephone to confirm the arrangements.** Pass the message in an offhanded manner: "Because I use a wheelchair for mobility, I was wondering if you can suggest which entrance to your building would be the most convenient?"

- ✓ **Alternatively, you may want to reserve disclosure for the interview –** it's a personal judgement call and while it is illegal for a potential employer to discriminate against you on the basis of a disability this is a less than perfect world. Some people prefer not to give employers any extra time in which to dwell on the disability before having the chance to meet the abled part of the package.

- ✓ **If your disability is not visible, such as mental illness or epilepsy, you need not disclose it unless you'll need special accommodations.** Even then, you can hold the disclosure until the negotiating stage once you've received a potential job offer.

No matter what you decide to do, be confident, unapologetic, unimpaired, and attitude-positive.

Explaining gaps in work history

Disclosure in the job-search process is a complex quandary. What can you do about gaps in your work history caused by disability? Data protection laws mean that an employer isn't likely to be able to get hold of your medical records, so you may be tempted to bury, or at least camouflage, gaps in your work history. Think twice about this. Honesty may well be the best policy, not least because without the correct information an employer may jump to worse conclusions about your absence from the work scene.

If your illness-related job history has so many gaps that it looks like a rugby player's teeth, we've never heard a better suggestion than writing "Illness and Recovery" next to the dates. It's honest, and the "recovery" part says, "I'm back and ready to work!"

If you have too many episodes of "missing teeth," your work history will look less shaky in a functional format, discussed in Chapter 9. Online CV discussion groups can serve as further sources of guidance on this difficult issue.

Asking for special equipment

If you need adaptive equipment, such as a special kind of telephone, we wouldn't mention it – even if the equipment is inexpensive or you're willing to buy it yourself. Instead, stick with the "time-release capsule" method of sharing information: Dribble out those revelations that may stifle interest in hiring you only when necessary. Never lose sight of your objective: to get an interview.

When Demotion Strikes

Kevin Allen (real person, fake name) was the district manager of five retailers in a chain when he was demoted to manager of a single shop. The higher-ups were sending him a message – they hoped he'd quit so that they could avoid awarding a severance package of benefits. Kevin ignored the message, retained a lawyer, kept his job, and started a job hunt after hours.

He finessed his CV by listing all the positions he had held in the chain, leaving out dates of when each started and stopped.

>
> **Demoting Chain, Big City**
>
> District Manager, 5 shops
>
> Store Manager, Windy City
>
> Store Assistant Manager, Sunny City
>
> Store Clerk, Sunny City

Throwing all of Kevin's titles into one big pot seemed a clever idea, but it didn't work for him. After a year of searching, Kevin got interviews, yes; but at every single face-to-face meeting, he was nailed with the same question: "Why were you demoted?" The interviewers' attitudes seemed accusatory, as if they'd been misled. Kevin failed to answer the question satisfactorily – he did not receive a single offer during a year's search. How did all the potential employers find out the truth?

Among obvious explanations: (A) Kevin worked in a "village" industry where people know each other and gossip. (B) Employers ordered checks on his employment details.

No one knows what really happened, but in hindsight, Kevin may have done better had he accepted the message that the chain wanted him out, negotiated a favourable severance package that included good references, and quit immediately while his true title was that of district manager.

After two humiliating years of demotion status, Kevin took action by "crossing the River Jordan," a Biblical phrase that universities have adapted. It refers to those who seek a new beginning by returning to college for a law or business degree. Kevin enrolled in law school. (A happy ending: Six years later, Kevin is a happily employed lawyer.)

In cases like Kevin's, a strategy that's forthright but doesn't flash your demotion in neon lights may work better than trying to cover up the demotion. Combine only two titles together, followed quickly by your accomplishments and strengths, as shown in Figure 12-6.

Figure 12-6:
Sample of combining a demotion with a higher position.

1999–2002 Demoting Company Name
Assistant Manager, Manager
As assistant manager, supported the manager and carefully monitored detailed transactions with vendors, insuring maintenance of products and inventory; used skills in invoicing, billing, ordering, and purchasing. As manager, supervised all aspects of purchasing, display, and merchandise sales. Trained team of more than 30 employees in two-week period. Trained three assistant managers in essential functions of customers, employees, and finance. Increased sales revenues 25 percent in first six months.

No matter how well you handle your CV entry, the reference of the demoting employer may ultimately damage your chances of landing a new job that you want. In trying to mend fences, you may appeal to the demoting employer's fairness or go for guilt. Point out how hard you worked and how loyal you've been. Find reasons why your performance record was flawed. Ask for the commitment of a favourable reference and a downplaying of the demotion. In practice, most companies are very twitchy about putting anything negative into a reference. Even if they choose to avoid giving you a reference altogether (the most likely result of a bad employer relationship), that isn't necessarily a problem since so many companies now avoid giving anything but employment dates as a reference. In the nightmare scenario of getting a real stinker of a reference, you may want to see a lawyer and see whether that changes your former employer's mind.

The basic way to handle demotions throughout the job-hunting process is akin to how you handle being fired: by accentuating the positive contributions and results for which you are responsible. *But being demoted is trickier to handle than being fired.* Surprisingly, being fired no longer suggests personal failure – being demoted does.

Gaps in Your Record

Periods of unemployment leave black holes in your work history. Should you (A) fill them with positive expressions such as *family obligations,* (B) fill them with less positive but true words such as *unemployed,* or (C) show the gap without comment?

Choosing B, *unemployed,* is dreary. Forget that! Choosing C, *leave-it-blank-and-say-nothing,* often works – you just hope that it isn't noticed. My choice, however, is A: Tell the truth about what you were doing but spin it in a dignified, positive way. A few examples: "independent study", "foreign travel", and "career renewal through study and assessment".

An infoblizzard of tips has been published on how to repair CV holes. Unless you were building an underground tunnel to smuggle drugs, the principles are simple:

- ✔ Present the time gap as a positive event.

- ✔ Detail why it made you a better worker – not a better *person,* but a better worker with more favourable characteristics, polished skills, and mature understanding, all of which you're dying to contribute to your new employer.

How can these principles be applied? Take the case of a student who dropped out of college to play in a band and do odd jobs for four years before coming back to finish his biology degree and look for a job. The student knows that employers may perceive him as uncommitted. In the CV, he should treat the band years like any other job: Describe the skills that were polished as a band leader. Identify instances of problem solving, teamwork, leadership, and budgeting.

You do the real problem solving in the cover letter that accompanies such a CV, as for example in Figure 12-7.

Figure 12-7: Excerpt explaining a job gap in a cover letter. After completing two years of undergraduate study, it was necessary for me to work to continue my education. Using my talents as a musician, I organised a band and after four years was able to continue my education. I matured and learned much about the real world and confirmed that an education is extremely important in fulfilling my career goals.

The chief mistake people make is assuming that a positive explanation won't sell. Instead, they fudge dates from legitimate jobs to cover the black holes. You may get away with it in the beginning. But ultimately, you'll be asked to sign a formal application, a legal document. If you haven't been entirely frank or up front, then those fudges may come back to haunt you. In the event of a company wanting to dump staff without paying severance benefits, the first thing they'll do is check for those they can claim got their positions under false pretences. Lies on applications, even if they surface years into a subsequent career, can be used by a cynical company to save money on severance. Lying isn't worth the risk – it's a mistake.

Another method of papering-over glaring gaps is to include all your work under "Work History" and cite unpaid and volunteer work as well as paid jobs.

Suppose that you've been unemployed for the past year. That's a new black hole. Some advisers suggest the old dodge of allowing the recruiter to misperceive the open-ended date of employment for your last job: "2000–" as though you meant "2000–Present." The open-ender solution often works – until you run into a reader who thinks that it's way too calculating.

Black holes are less obvious in a functional format, as discussed in Chapter 9. *If you can't find a positive explanation for a black hole, say nothing.*

If you possess a not-so-pristine past, stick with small employers who probably won't check every date on your CV.

The consultant/entrepreneur gap

Professional and managerial job seekers are routinely advised to explain black holes by saying that they were consultants or that they owned small businesses. Not everyone can be a consultant, and there's substantial risk in the small-business explanation.

If it should happen to be true that you were a consultant, name your clients and give a glimmer of the contributions you made to each. If you really had a small business, remember: Employers worry that you'll be too independent to do things their way or that you'll stay just long enough to learn their business and go into competition against them. Strategic antidotes: Search for a business owner who is within eyeshot of retirement and wouldn't mind your continuing the business and paying him or her a monthly pension. CV antidotes: Describe yourself as "manager," not "CEO" or "president," and if you have time, rename your business something other than your own name: "River's End Associates" not "Theresa Bronz, Ltd"

Here a Job, There a Job, Everywhere a Job, Job

We once interviewed a man who had held 185 jobs over the course of his 20-year career, encompassing everything from dishwasher to circus clown and from truck driver to nursing aide. He wrote to us, not requesting CV advice, but to complain that a potential employer had the nerve to call him a *job hopper!*

Talk about an antiquated term – in the 21st century, the notion of job hopping is as far out of a reality circle as the concepts of job security, company loyalty, and a guaranteed company pension. The Great Corporate Dumping Machine will continue to chew up and spit out people who then may have to take virtually any job they can to survive.

Omit inappropriate data

The best way to handle some land mines on your CV is to ignore them. Generally, revealing negative information on a CV is a mistake. Save troublemaking information for the all-important job interview, where you have a fighting chance to explain your side of things.

Stay away from these topics when constructing a CV:

- Firings, demotions, forced resignations, and early termination of contracts

- Personal differences with co-workers or supervisors

- Bankruptcy, tax evasion, or credit problems

- Criminal convictions or lawsuits

- Homelessness

- Illnesses from which you have now recovered

- Disabilities that don't prevent you from performing the essential functions of the job, with or without some form of accommodation

Should you ever give reasons for leaving a job? In most instances, CV silence in the face of interview-killing facts is still the strategy of choice. But the time has come to rethink at least one special issue: losing a job.

Now that jobs are shed like so many autumn leaves, losing a job is no longer viewed as a case of personal failure. It may be to your advantage to state on your CV why you left your last position, assuming that it was not due to poor work performance on your part. If you were downsized out, the recruiter may appreciate your straightforward statement, "Job eliminated in downsizing."

But remember, if you elect to say why you lost one job, for consistency, you have to say why you left all your jobs – such as for greater opportunity, advancement, and the like.

Adding insult to injury, some employers cling to a double standard – hiring and firing employees like commodities, then looking with disfavour on applicants who have had a glut of jobs by circumstance, not by choice.

You're not alone

Large numbers of people have to write CVs that explain holding too many jobs in too short a time. The harsh realities of business may force you to detour from a single career path to alternative tracks where you can acquire new skills and experiences, even if they're not skills and experiences of choice. If so, you need serious creative writing to keep your CV focused on the work history that is relevant for the next job sought.

Use these tips when you find that you have too many jobs in your history:

- ✔ Start by referring to your *diversified* or *skills-building* background.
- ✔ Use a functional or hybrid CV format (see Chapter 9) and present *only your experience relevant to the job you seek.*
- ✔ Express your work history in years, not months and years.

Focus your CV

Too many jobs in your background threaten your focus. *Unfocused* is an ugly word in job-search circles. Being judged as "unfocused" is saying that you lack commitment, that you're perpetually at a fork in the road. It's a reason not to hire you.

When your CV looks as though it will collapse under the weight of a hotchpotch of jobs unconnected to your present target, eliminate your previous trivial pursuits. Group the consequential jobs under the heading "Relevant Work Experience Summary".

What if this approach solves one problem – the busy CV – but creates another, such as a huge, gaping black hole where you removed inconsequential jobs? Create a second work history section that covers those holes, labelling it "Other Experience". Figure 12-8 shows an example.

Dealing with an unfocused career pattern on paper is easier when it's done under the banner of a temp agency. The spin in this case lists the temp agency as the employer. You choose one job title that covers most of your assignments. Under that umbrella title, identify specific assignments. Give the dates in years next to the temp agency, skipping dates for each assignment. Figure 12-9 shows an example.

IMPACTED CV WITH FOCUS

Professional Experience

UNITECH, Hamburg, Germany
Computer Laboratory Assistant, 2002-Present
> Manager and chief trouble-shooter for all hardware and software systems.
> Tasks include data recover, programming architecture, and hardware/software installation.
> Assist a team of 18 engineers.

TECHNIK TECH, Hamburg, Germany
Assistant to System Analysts, 1998-2001
> Participated in construction, repair, and installation of systems at local businesses.
> Diagnosed faulty systems and reported to senior analysts, decreasing their workload by 25%.

TRADE NET, Berlin, Germany
Applications and Network Specialist, 1996-1998
> Set up and monitored a Windows based BBS, including installation, structure, security, and graphics.
> Authored installation scripts for Trade Net, licensing U.S. software use in Europe.

Other Experience

AMERICAN BOOK STORE, Berlin, Germany, Sales Representative, 2001-2002
> Arranged and inventoried merchandise, directed sales and customer relations.
> Developed strong interpersonal skills and gained knowledge of retail industry.

CAMP INTERNATIONAL, Frankfurt, Germany, Activities Director, 1996-1998
> Organised daily activities, including sports, recreation, and day classes, for over 300 children from English-speaking countries.
> Supervised 10 counsellors and kitchen staff of five, developing responsible and effective management skills.

Figure 12-8: Solving the black-hole problem in a jobs-impacted CV by creating a focus plus a second work history section.

FOCUSSING WITH TEMP JOBS

Professional Experience

Relia-Temps, Birmingham   **2002-present**

Executive Secretary

- West Midlands Banking Group
  Performing all clerical and administrative responsibilities for 10-partner investment and loan firm, assisting each partner in drafting contracts, reviewing proposals, and designing various financial programs. Supervision of 7 staff members. Introduced 50% more efficient filing system, reducing client reviews from 4 to 3 hours.

Administrative Assistant

- Mosaic Advertising
  Supervised 3 receptionists and 4 clerical specialists, reporting directly to MD. Administered daily operations of all accounting and communication transactions. Using extensive computer knowledge, upgraded company computer networks with Windows 2000.

- Blakeslee Environmental, Inc.
  Assisted 8 lawyers at environmental "Due Diligence" agency, scheduling meetings and conferences, maintaining files, and updating database records. Redesigned office procedures and methods of communication, employing superior organisational skills.

Figure 12-9: Listing your temporary job assignments without looking unfocused.

What if you work for several temping agencies at the same time? The simple answer is that you use the same technique of dating your work history for the temp agencies, not for the individual assignments. This dating technique is a statement of fact; you legally are an employee of the temp agency, not of the company that pays for your temporary services.

When excess jobs or focus isn't a problem, you may choose an alternative presentation for a series of short-term jobs, as illustrated in Chapter 4. The alternative doesn't mention the staffing firm(s) but only the names of the companies where you worked.

When Substance Abuse Is the Problem

In the US substance abuse, including alcoholism, is a disability under the Americans with Disabilities Act. Here in the UK, it isn't – so don't feel tempted to disclose previous substance abuse on your CV.

Cover gaps in your work history with the "Illness and Recovery" statement (see the "Job Seekers with Disabilities" section earlier in this chapter) or simply don't address the issue at all. Be careful what information you put on a job application – remember that it's a legal form and that lies can come back to haunt you (see the "Gaps in Your Record" section earlier in this chapter).

Unless you're applying for a particularly sensitive job (for example as a carer or in a legal profession), being cautioned (or even arrested) for smoking pot or being intoxicated is a fact that's unlikely to come back and haunt you. For a start, the normal rules of disclosure are not as stringent as those for sensitive careers, and unless the offence entailed a month or more jail sentence, then it will eventually expire from your record like points on a driving license.

The upshot: Avoid mentioning booze or drugs, be careful about application forms, and be honest at interviews – *if* you have recovered or *if* the experience was a brief fling or two.

If you're still held prisoner by a chronic, destructive, or debilitating overuse of a chemical substance that interferes with your life or employment, no CV tweaks will benefit you. Get help for your addiction.

A Bad Credit Rap

Job seekers who won't be handling money are surprised that employers may routinely check credit records. Don't necessarily expect them to tell you that's what they're doing either; they can use the services of credit information brokers who run the basic check without telling the person concerned. If anyone does run a check, by the way, a record of that is made as well.

Credit histories from credit information companies can cost as little as £12 and be offered as a same day service making it easy for an employer to check the electoral roll, your addresses to date, County Court Judgements (CCJs), information about any insolvency or bankruptcy, and a list of who else has run a credit check on you.

Employers are wary of hiring people awash in debt because they fear that stress will impact job performance, that you have inadequate management skills, or even that you may have sticky fingers with the company's funds.

Credit assessments are an imprecise art, and there are many stories of people being refused credit because of the record of a previous tenant at the same address. If you think that credit checking may pose a problem for you, then forewarned is forearmed: Make sure you get hold of your own record first. If it's inaccurate, you have the right to demand that it be amended. It the report is accurate, you have the chance to prepare your explanations first. In an era of student loans and credit card folly, debt is not as shameful as it may have been to our great grandparents. Bankruptcy can even be spin doctored as part of a go-getter prepared to risk all for the business. CCJs expire from the record after six years, so don't be haunted by memories of that unpaid electricity bill five years ago when you were a student.

For details of your credit history, go to Equifax or Experian; the two Credit Reference Agencies in the UK, either of which will supply you with your own record for the cost of a couple of quid. To contact Experian, go to its Web site (www.experian.co.uk) or telephone (0115 941 0888). Equifax's Web address is www.equifax.co.uk and its telephone number is 0845 600 1772. To find out more about what information can and can't be held on you, take a look at the Information Commissioner's page at www.dataprotection.gov.uk

Credit checking isn't a CV concern as such, but after you understand how a negative report – true or erroneous – can torpedo your employment chances, you'll want to take it into account if applying for any credit-sensitive work. (We discuss background-check concerns in Chapter 1.)

Resources to Solve Many Dilemmas

The array of CV dilemmas known to humankind is too long, too challenging, and too complex to comprehensively chronicle in this dollop of space.

The topic of strategies for ex-offenders, for instance, needs its own book to adequately address this issue. Fortunately, there are a few people out there to help. For advice on job hunting with a less than desirable record, try getting in touch with the Apex Trust, which aims to promote employment opportunities for ex-offenders. You can find the Apex Trust at www.apextrust.com or call on 0870 608 4567.

Spin Control Is in the Details

A white ruffled blouse stained only slightly with one dab of spaghetti sauce is 99 percent clean. But every person who sees you wearing it at a public event remembers the red spot, not the white part of the blouse. Similarly, you can have a 99 percent StandOut CV, but any one of the deadly perceptions identified in this chapter can ice it without your knowing why. Practice spin control – present possible negative perceptions in a flattering light.

A positive explanation goes a long way in overcoming a CV land mine. It doesn't work all the time, but it works some of the time, and all you need – for now – is one good offer to hit the job jackpot.

Chapter 13

Move from Worksheets to Finished CV

. . . .

In This Chapter

▶ Focusing on what you want and do not want

▶ Sizing up your education and training

▶ Examining your skills and competencies

▶ Writing worksheets, summaries, and asset statements

▶ Producing great-looking CVs

. . . .

*I*f there were a Grand Prix pit crew to fine-tune your CV in this modern age, it would consist of you, you, and you.

That is, everything in your StandOut CV starts with what you want and can do, and how effectively you write it down. This chapter helps you do exactly that by guiding you through the compilation of three self-discovery documents. You work through this task in the following three steps:

1. **Detailed worksheets** on which you write all employment-related aspects of your life to date.

2. **Summary worksheets** on which you write key information drawn from your detailed worksheets.

3. **Asset statements** (power-packed self-marketing statements drawn from your summary worksheets), which you can use to open your CV or cover letter with a flourish.

Step 1: The Detailed Worksheets

The worksheets in this chapter are your first line of defence against repeating sour experiences in your previous jobs, and they also help you to reincarnate cherished experiences in your future jobs. If you haven't held a job before, this chapter can help guide you to the kind of position that you'll most appreciate.

Think of the worksheets in this chapter as a kind of Swiss Army Knife, giving you the tools to get in touch with your innermost thoughts and desires about the following:

✔ The real reasons you left previous jobs

✔ Beneficial transferable lessons you learned in previous jobs

✔ The components that you really must have in a job to be happy

✔ The skills and responsibilities that you most enjoy using

✔ The skills and responsibilities that you never want to use again

Knowing what you have to offer

You can't present the best of yourself until you have a handle on the goods and that means a lot more than simply listing your better points and looking for inspiration in your successes.

William Bolitho, a writer and journalist for what was then *The Manchester Guardian,* pretty much summed it up when he exclaimed: "The most important thing in life is not to capitalise on your gains. Any fool can do that. The really important thing is to profit from your losses."

On these pages you get a chance not only to capitalise on your gains but also to profit from your losses in your chosen career. Make copies of the New Job Worksheet, which begins on the next page, for each job you want to review.

If, at the end, you think that maybe your chosen career was the problem then back up and pursue the issue of career choice in *Changing Careers For Dummies,* by Carol L McClelland, PhD (Wiley).

New Job Worksheet

(Photocopy and complete one worksheet for each relevant job.)

Reasons for Leaving Job

Employer: _____ From:_____(Year) To:_____(Year)

What did you most like about your job here, and why did you apply for it in

the first place? _____

_____

_____

_____

_____

_____

_____

What did you most dislike about your job here? _____

_____

_____

_____

_____

_____

Why did you choose to leave (pay, title, no promotion, unfulfilling)? _____

_____

_____

_____

_____

Areas of Highest Performance

Of the skills you used here, which gave you the most satisfaction
(give example)? Why? _____

_____

_____

_____

_____

_____

Of the duties, which made you feel your best? Why? _____

_____

_____

_____

_____

_____

Which skills and responsibilities would you like to use in your next job? __

_____

_____

_____

_____

_____

What You Never Want to Do Again

Of the skills you used here, which were the least fulfilling? _____

_____

_____

_____

_____

Which tasks did you dread most? Why? _____

_____

_____

_____

_____

_____

Your Most Attractive Attributes

In your leisure activities, which competencies and skills have you used that

can transfer to your next job? _____

_____

_____

_____

_____

Note: Don't bother writing a summary of this exercise; its message will be indelible in your mind.

Working the worksheets

Each worksheet that follows looks at your life in a wide-angle, rear-view mirror and then narrows the focus by suggesting that you target the most useful and vital accomplishments and competencies.

Many people lose the CV derby because they merely report where they have worked and enumerate the duties they were assigned. That information alone won't roll over the competition. You need to provide effective answers to the following questions:

- ✔ What did you accomplish?
- ✔ What value and competencies did you bring to a specific position?
- ✔ What did it matter that you showed up at the office most days?
- ✔ How have you put your education to work?
- ✔ What good has your education done anyone?

Harried career? Use worksheets to rethink your direction

Do you find yourself working too many hours a week and neglecting other parts of your life – friends, family, hobbies, community, and spiritual activities?

Women are especially prone to burnout from the work-go-round grind of rising early, struggling through the day, falling asleep wondering how they'll get it all done, and then getting up again the next morning and starting all over.

Do you really want a career change?

If you're overwhelmed and overworked, the worksheets in this chapter can help you with more than CV preparation. You may be ripe for a career change – or a flexible work schedule, telecommuting, or starting your own business.

Use the worksheets as a diary for discovery.

Use these worksheets to fuel an introspective look at who you are and where you've been. Think of them as a kind of work/life diary to identify the experiences you most enjoyed and did well at, as well as those you never want to repeat.

The personal inventory you create in these worksheets can take you a long way toward identifying solutions to a work/life dilemma that's eating away at your happiness. You may realise that you really don't want a career that's all-consuming – you want one with more balance. The personal inventory you create for CVs also serves as a straightforward tool to guide you toward a more fulfilling future.

The *identification* and *measurement* of *results, outcomes,* and *achievements* are what make recruiters book you for interviews.

Begin your personal inventory now. Fill out these worksheets, which appear on the following pages:

- ✔ **Education and Training Worksheet:** This worksheet outlines your education and training experiences.

- ✔ **Paid Work Worksheet** and **Unpaid Work Worksheet:** These worksheets help you identify your competencies, knowledge, and abilities.

- ✔ **Hobbies/Activities-to-Skills Worksheet:** This worksheet helps you translate your hobbies and activities to skills that employers look for.

- ✔ **Employability Skills Worksheet:** This worksheet helps you identify your personal characteristics.

Education and Training Worksheet

Name of institution/program _____

Address/Telephone _____

Year(s) attended or graduated _____

Degree/diploma/certificate_____

Class rank (if known) _____

Work-relevant study

(Photocopy and complete one worksheet for each relevant course.)

Course_____

Knowledge acquired_____

_____

_____

Skills acquired _____

_____

Accomplishments (with concrete examples) _____

_____

Relevant projects/papers; honours _____

_____

Keywords/StandOut words_____

Quotable remarks by others (names, contact data) _____

_____

_____

Paid Work Worksheet

(Photocopy and complete one worksheet for each job.)

Name of employer _____

Postal address, e-mail address, telephone _____

_____

_____

_____

Type of business/career field _____

Job title_____ Dates _____

Direct supervisor's name, contact information (if good reference; otherwise, note co-workers or sources of good references) _____

_____

_____

_____

Major accomplishments (Promotion? Awards? Business achievements – "increased sales by 30 percent" or "saved company 12 percent on office purchases"? What credit can you claim for creating, implementing, revamping, designing, saving? Jog your memory by recalling problems faced and action taken.) _____

_____

_____

_____

Problems faced _____

_____

_____

Action taken _____

_____

_____

_____

Skills acquired _____

_____

_____

_____

Knowledge/abilities acquired _____

_____

_____

_____

Job responsibilities _____

_____

_____

_____

Keywords/StandOut words _____

_____

_____

_____

_____

Quotable remarks by others (names, contact data) _____

_____

_____

_____

_____

Unpaid Work Worksheet

(Photocopy and complete one worksheet for each relevant unpaid job.)

Name of employer _____

Type of organisation _____

Volunteer job title _____Dates _____

Direct supervisor's name, contact information _____
_____

Major accomplishments (What credit can you claim for creating, implementing, revamping, designing, saving? Jog your memory by recalling problems
faced and action taken.) _____
_____
_____
_____

Problems faced _____

Action taken _____

Skills acquired _____

Knowledge/abilities acquired_____

Keywords/StandOut words_____

Quotable remarks by others (names, contact data) _____
_____
_____
_____

Hobbies/Activities-to-Skills Worksheet

(Photocopy and complete one worksheet for each relevant work-related activity.)

Name of hobby, organisation, club (location)_____

Dates _____

Title/position (officer/member) _____

Elected (yes/no) _____

Accomplishments_____

_____

_____

_____

Work-related skills acquired _____

_____

_____

Knowledge/abilities acquired_____

_____

_____

Keywords/StandOut words_____

_____

_____

Quotable remarks by others (names, contact data) _____

_____

_____

_____

Employability Skills Worksheet

(Photocopy and complete one worksheet for each relevant position.)

Name of company/supervisor _____

Aspects of your work ethic that the employer appreciated _____

_____

_____

Example _____

Facets of your personality that the employer valued _____

_____

_____

Example _____

Name of co-worker/client/industry contact _____

Aspects of your work ethic that the person appreciated_____

_____

_____

Example _____

Facets of your personality that the person valued _____

_____

_____

Example _____

Keywords/StandOut words_____

_____

_____

Step 2: The Summary Worksheets

The worksheets you filled out in the preceding section are rich in raw material for the worksheet summaries in your next step toward a glorious StandOut CV. On your worksheet summaries, highlight the data that most clearly show how well you qualify for the job (or jobs) you desire.

Photocopy the blank Summary Worksheet and fill out one copy for each job that catches your eye. In the left column, jot down what the employer wants. You obtain this information from job ads, job descriptions, and occupational literature. If you're working with a recruiter, the data should be easy to get.

In the right column, drawing from your worksheets, make note of how well you fill the bill. How good is the fit between each requirement and your qualification?

When the job calls for specific skills, an employer doesn't necessarily care how or where you obtained the requisite skills in the summary worksheet, so the headings in the left column merely say Skills Required.

By contrast, the headings in the right column of the summary worksheet correspond to other worksheets in this chapter. They are noted specifically as yet another reminder to include your skills obtained from any source, paid or unpaid.

The more successful you are at tailoring your CV to fit a specific job, the more likely you are to be in the final running.

Summary Worksheet

The Employer Wants ➡ You Have

Education and Training Required	Education and Training Skills Including Achievements
1)	
2)	
3)	
4)	
5)	
6)	
7)	
8)	
9)	
10)	
Skills/Knowledge/Abilities Required (Competencies)	**Paid** Skills/Knowledge/Abilities
1)	
2)	
3)	
4)	
5)	
6)	
7)	
8)	
9)	
10)	

(1 of 2)

Summary Worksheet

The Employer Wants ➡ You Have

Skills/Knowledge/Abilities Required (Competencies)	**Unpaid** Skills/Knowledge/Abilities
1)	
2)	
3)	
4)	
5)	
Skills/Knowledge/Abilities Required (Competencies)	Hobby/Activity Skills Including Achievements
1)	
2)	
3)	
4)	
5)	
Employability Skills Required (Personal Characteristics)	Employability Skills Including Achievements
1)	
2)	
3)	
4)	
5)	

(2 of 2)

Step 3: Drafting Asset Statements

To open a CV or cover letter, you may want to use an *asset statement.* An asset statement is essentially a skills summary – although other ingredients of competencies can be inserted, specifically your knowledge, abilities, and personal characteristics. An asset statement is known by many names in the recruiting industry. Some of these other names are:

- ✔ Highlights statement
- ✔ Keyword summary (or profile)
- ✔ Marketing summary
- ✔ Objective summary
- ✔ Power summary
- ✔ Professional history capsule
- ✔ Profile section
- ✔ Qualifications summary
- ✔ Synopsis

The asset statement typically contains the three to five best skills (sales points) that support your job aspiration. The exception to this definition is the keyword profile, which uses a listing (rather than sentences) of virtually all the relevant skills you possess.

The data in your asset statement need not be proven with examples in this brief section – for now, it stands alone as assertions. In effect, you are saying, "Here's who I am. Here's what I can do for you." This is a tease, encouraging the reader to hang in there for proof of what the opening claims.

The information you've written in the previous worksheets paves the way for your powerful asset statements. Figure 13-1 gives you examples of power-packed asset statements.

Human Resources manager

Well-rounded experience in all human resource functions. Focus: Benefits and Staff Relations. Managed an HR staff of 200,000-population city. Reputation for progressive programmes attractive to both city and employees.

Marketing account executive

Award-winning marketer with impressive performance record in Internet merchandising. Proficient in international conventions and customs. Attentive to details while focusing on the big picture. Excellent at organising, tracking, and managing projects. Relate well to both customers and co-workers.

Construction manager

General construction-manager experience covers all areas: start-up and financing, site selection, building design, and construction. Hire and train. Work ahead of schedules. Rehired several times by same developers.

Communications graduate

Entry opportunity in print or broadcast news. Completing rigorous communications degree. Work experience as editorial associate in newspaper columnist's office, achieved top performance review; editor of college newspaper; instructor of adult students at writing lab.

Figure 13-1: Asset statements that turbo-charge a CV.

Why you need asset statements

An asset statement opens your CV with a bang but provides several other benefits as well:

- ✔ **Summary page:** Asset statements can be expanded to an entire summary page, which you place atop a reverse chronological CV (in effect turning your reverse chronological CV into a hybrid CV format, as discussed in Chapter 9).

- ✔ **Old successes:** An asset statement can revive a fading job achievement. Suppose you have an achievement that took place four or five years ago and is now needed to qualify you for a job. By amplifying the old achievement in a summary statement (and perhaps choosing a functional format for your CV), you don't bury it in a bazaar of your past jobs. When crystallised in a focused power summary, the golden oldie achievement still works for you.

- ✔ **Basis for achievement statements:** Asset statements provide the raw material for achievement sections (paragraphs) and brief (one- or two-line) high-voltage statements that you use later in your CV.

Data in achievement statements must be proven by *examples,* the best of which are *quantified.* Measure, measure, measure!

What's the difference between an asset statement and the achievement statements that are used later in your CV? The difference is that in an *achievement statement*, you should incorporate documentation, or "storytelling," to authenticate what you're saying. By contrast, *asset statements* are credible without examples or results.

E-Z asset statements

Remember, you don't have to prove what you say right there in the opening statement or summary – but you do have to prove it later in your CV in achievement statements. Here's a collection of fill-in forms to start you off. Just fill in the blanks.

- ✔ After __ (number of years, provided the number is not too high) years in _____ (your occupation), seek opportunity to use extensive experience and _____ (your favourite skills) as a (your target position).

- ✔ Knowledge of (your expertise) and familiarity with _____ (type of product, industry, or clientele). Seek position as _____ (job title) using intensive experience as a _____ (occupation).

✔ Developed new _____ which resulted in increased _____; maintained an aggressive _____ program that increased employer's revenues by __%. Seeking a position as a _____ (your objective) in an organisation needing expertise in _____ (your top skills).

✔ A position as a _____ (a job slightly higher in rank than your top employment), specialising in _____ (a skill unique to you).

✔ A _____ (type of) position that needs _____ (list skills and accomplishments). Demonstrated by _____ (list of paid and volunteer responsibilities and successes). Will _____ (an improvement that your prospective employer appreciates).

✔ Offering _____ (your field) skills in _____ (related industry), with ability to solve _____ (one or more problems common in the field), including _____ (your top skills).

✔ Encyclopaedic knowledge of _____ (your top skills in technical aspects of position), familiarity with _____ (qualifying duties of position), and effective management of _____ (your lesser job-related skills).

Aim for powerful but true statements

Wait until the next day to review your finished asset statement. Did you get carried away with fantasy writing? Ask yourself, "Can I live up to this advance billing?" If not, tone it down to reality – that is, your *best reality*. Unfortunately – you smooth writer, you – when you land a job based on hype that you can't back up, you'll be renewing your job search.

After working your way through Step 1 (worksheets), Step 2 (summary worksheets), and Step 3 (asset statements), you're ready to put your keyboard in action, either electronically or on paper. The following tips apply chiefly to paper, but some suggestions apply to formatted online CVs as well.

Write Until It's Right

Can you write a decent CV in nanoseconds? Several CV books on the market sport titles insisting that you can do just about that. Don't be taken in. A well-developed CV requires adequate ripening time to form, mellow, and develop – you must think, write, think some more, rewrite, proof-read, get feedback, and rewrite.

All too many job hunters scatter hundreds of thrown-together CVs. Then they wait. Nothing happens. Why do you think nobody bothers to call with an interview offer? Perhaps thrown-together too often gets thrown out?

If you don't want to be left behind because of a thrown-together CV, write a StandOut CV. It works.

After tailoring your StandOut CV, must you also customise a cover letter? Here's the *wrong answer:* No, just roll out the old I-saw-your-ad-and-I-am-enclosing-my-CV cliché. Here's the *right answer:* Yes, a tailored cover letter is the perfect sales tool for a tailored CV. But that's a topic for another book. Check out *Cover Letters For Dummies,* 2nd Edition (Wiley), for everything you need to know about cover letters and more.

Paper CVs That Resonate

Although the market is moving away from paper CVs toward digital CVs, tree-and-ink products are here for the foreseeable future. Here's how to look out-standing on paper and make the first cut in the employment screening process.

Take the time to make sure your CV is as strong as it can be to attract the employer who has the right job for you. The CV samples in Chapter 17 can give you a good idea of the variety of clean-cut, appealing CV designs you can adopt.

Word processing

You need a computer equipped with word-processing software to produce your CV. Typewritten copies are still acceptable, but most people don't type well enough to produce crisp, clean, sparkling copies. If word processing is not yet one of your skills, scout out a word-processing class – you'll need this ability in nearly any job you take. In the meantime, find a friend who can key in your CV. If you have the skill but not the tools, can you use a friend's computer? How about a computer at a school's computer lab or career centre, or a Web café, or your local public library? If none of these is possible, take your hand-written CV to a professional office support firm and hire someone to do the production work.

Unemployed people can use computers for free at job centres and libraries across the country.

Printing

Producing your CV on a laser or inkjet printer is today's standard. The old-fashioned dot matrix printers lack the firepower to print CVs that compete in today's job market. If you photocopy a core CV – rather than custom-tailor each CV to the job at hand – make sure that the copies look first-rate. No blurring, stray marks, streaks, or faint letters.

Paper

How good must your paper be? For professional, technical, managerial, and executive jobs, the stock for a paper CV should be quality paper with rag content, perhaps 25 percent, and a watermark (a faint image ingrained in the paper). Office supply stores, small printing firms, and speciality-paper mail-order catalogues offer a wide range of choices. Restrict the colour of your paper to white or off-white, eggshell, or the palest of grey. Print on one side of the sheet only.

The ink on a StandOut CV is evenly distributed across each page, which is best achieved with a smooth paper stock. The image evoked by a high-quality paper is diminished when it looks as though the ink just didn't flow consistently – the print looks alternately dark or faded, may be streaky or smeared. Linen (_textured_) paper is impressive, but the ink from a laser printer or photocopier may not move smoothly across a sheet, making your CV hard to read. Try before you buy. If there's the slightest doubt about readability, switch to laid (_smooth_) paper.

The quality of paper is immaterial when your CV is to be scanned into job computers or spun across the Internet. Hiring managers never see the quality of paper or printing you have selected.

Open spaces

Which style of reading do you prefer: A paper so packed with text that your eyes need a spa treatment before tackling it or a paper so generous with white space that you _want_ to read it? Too many people, hearing that they must not exceed one page, try to cram too much information in too little space.

A ratio of about one-quarter white space to text is about right. Line spacing between items is vital. Do not justify the right side of the page – that is, do not try to have the type align down the right side of the page – leave it ragged. Right justification creates awkward white spaces. An overcrowded page almost guarantees that it will not be read by younger recruiters and hiring managers who grew up in an age of television and web pages. And older readers? Their eyes won't take the wear and tear of too many words crashing in too small a space. White space is the master graphic attention-getter.

Typefaces and fonts

A *typeface* is a family of characters – letters, numbers, and symbols. A *font* is a specific size of typeface. Helvetica is a typeface; Helvetica 10-point bold, Helvetica 12-point bold, and Helvetica 14-point bold are three different fonts.

No more than two typefaces should appear on one CV; if you don't have an eye for what looks good, stick to one typeface. Either Times Roman or Helvetica used alone is a fine choice for your CV. But if you want to mix the two typefaces, We recommend that you choose Helvetica for the headings and Times Roman for the text and lesser headings.

Paying attention to the spacing of your CV contributes much to its readability. Printing your name in small capital letters can be pleasing. Using larger type for headings (12 or 14 pt.) or boldface can give necessary prominence. Use italics sparingly – you don't want to overdo emphasis, and italicised words lose readability in blocks of text.

Design structure

Your name and contact information can be left aligned, centred, or right aligned. Look at examples in Chapter 17. Here are some other tips:

Some recruiters suggest that you type your name right aligned because they thumb through the right-hand corner of CV stacks.

Aim for a tasteful amount of capitalisation and bold lettering for emphasis.

Important information jumps in the recruiter's face when set off by bullets, asterisks, and dashes.

Typos and spelling errors are unacceptable. They are seen as carelessness or a lack of professionalism. It is far better that we have spelling mistakes in this book than you have one in your CV. In the tens of thousands of CVs mistakenly sent to us for review, spelling has, at times, been creative. One man claimed to be *precedent* of his company. Do you think he was a good one? Use your computer's spell-check feature, read your finished CV carefully, and ask a friend to read it also.

The CV design: Does it make a difference?

Recruiters essentially agree that CV design counts, as these excerpts from an online recruiting forum reveal:

Recruiter #1: "Is there a 'best' CV design? I'm told by a self-proclaimed expert that a format with about one third of the page left blank on the left-hand side (for example, a heading of 'Education' all the way to the left margin, then information is indented about one third of the way into the page) is best. This space allows recruiter/interviewers to have a place to make notes".

Recruiter #2: "Recruiters and interviewers should not be writing on anyone's CV".

Recruiter #3: "Attention to detail should not be overlooked. But to say that there should be a margin here or there, or everything should be on one page, is an outdated point of view. CV design can be indicative of someone's personality, telling much more from the beginning".

Recruiter #4: "The CV design makes a great deal of difference. Most managers don't have time to search through a CV looking for information. If it's not easy to spot, the CV will go into the 'do not call' pile. The better the design of the CV, the more likely we are to interview".

Do not staple together a two- or three-page CV or put it in a folder or plastic insert. The CV may be photocopied and distributed, or it may be scanned into a database. To minimise the risk of a page becoming an orphan, put a simple header atop each page after the first: your name and page number. In a multiple-page CV, you may want to indicate how many pages there are ("page 1 of 2", for example) in case the pages get separated. You can also put the page number at the bottom.

Part IV
StandOut CVs Online

"It says here, you are artistic and a
good knowledge of typefaces —
Do you have any samples handy?"

In this part . . .

You find the latest news about e-CVs: what's in, what's out. You get insider tips on how to decide which technology to entrust with your StandOut CV, including the exact words to use.

Chapter 14

The Changing E-CV:
Technology in Transition

. . . .

In This Chapter

▶ Defining e-CVs

▶ Gaining e-CV benefits

▶ Understanding keyword scams

▶ Asking how to submit e-CVs

▶ Using an easy work-flow model

. . . .

*T*he e-CV has gained ground during the last few years in the transition from paper to electronic self-marketing. Although paper won't go away in our lifetime, it's now on the downward slope of the popularity curve.

Paper will always be valued with some traditional employers and at job interviews when cranking up a computer is distracting. For most job seekers, a dual-CV track – with a heavy dose of e-CVs – is the one to follow in the opening years of the twenty-first century. Whether you're a digital debutante or a confirmed cyber-CV creator this chapter takes you through the tips and tricks of this most crucial CV development.

Defining the E-CV

If you're new to the mysterious world of the e-CV, a quick scoot by a few terms gets you clicking on the right keys. (If you're an old e-CV hand, go straight to "The Invisible Keyword Scam" section later in this chapter.)

An e-CV may be called a *digital* or *online* CV because it appears in digital format (meaning that it's electronic, not printed on paper) and is sent through a computer connected to a computer network. The term *e-CV* can mean any of the following:

- ✔ A file sent as an e-mail attachment; usually, the distribution format is MS Word or WordPerfect. Less frequently, it's Adobe Acrobat's PDF (portable document format).
- ✔ A CV that is incorporated into the body of an e-mail message.
- ✔ A CV posted on a commercial Web job site, such as Monster.
- ✔ A CV submitted to a company Web site's career portal.
- ✔ A CV/portfolio on a Web page created by a job seeker.
- ✔ A CV/portfolio on a CD-ROM.

If you're wondering why the word "scannable" didn't make the cut, it's because a scannable CV starts out as a paper (printed) document and becomes an e-CV only after it is scanned into an electronic database.

The Rise of the E-CV

The Net (Internet) is the world's biggest computer network. The Web (World Wide Web) is a graphical overlay on the Internet that makes possible sound, film, video, and various special effects, as well as text.

With the Net and the Web as background, boundless change is inevitable in the way we do business, and the CV industry is no exception. The transformation within the CV industry is irreversible. The newest trends are described in Chapter 1, but these two developments underpin all CV change:

- ✔ An amazing acceleration of computer software over the past 15 years drives the reinvention of the way you *prepare and submit CVs* and in the way others *read and manage them.*
- ✔ The Internet, in connecting the globe's computers, continues to restructure forever the way CVs are sent from one place to another.

These two developments sparked the explosion of the e-CV. Millions and millions of e-CVs float like inexhaustible soap bubbles throughout cyberspace each day. Their collective volume threatens to overwhelm the recruiting industry.

The Invisible Keyword Scam

Feeling as if they're stuck in a rerun of the movie _Groundhog Day,_ recruiters searching CVs online are seeing the same dozen people perched atop search results again and again.

Suppose an applicant named Charlie Brown turns up high on search results for an HR representative and high again on search results for a sales representative. Applicant Gina Graham is a top-rated contender for medical assistant and top-rated for respiratory therapist as well. How can this be? Do superworkers walk among us?

Not exactly. The reason the same people keep turning up at the top of search results for many job openings is not that they're supremely talented in multiple directions. The reason is online shenanigans.

Some technically sophisticated job seekers have discovered the "Invisible Keyword Scam". These crafty individuals are packing e-CVs with every keyword they can find, whether or not the words actually describe their qualifications. They highlight keywords they don't want to show up, then change the font colour from black to white to match the background colour. In a normal onscreen review, the eye doesn't see the misleading keywords.

Why go to all this trouble? They hope to improve their employment chances by scoring a high ranking in search results when search engines, sifting through a database of qualified applicants, find those keywords and raise them to the top of the electronic heap.

Unravelling the ruse is simple but time consuming, irking the recruiter who's doing the digging. To discover hidden keywords, the recruiter highlights the applicant's entire CV, then pastes it into an MS Word document. Next, the recruiter highlights the text and changes the font colour to black. That's when the recruiter sees the deceit: Standing between the paragraphs are all the keywords that were not visible or printable until they were highlighted and the font colour changed from white to black.

How do the understandably irritated recruiters respond when they come across the hidden keyword gambit? Just what you think: They bin it. The offending applicants who truly may be desperate are perceived as such – and desperate doesn't sell. Moreover, all versions of CVs from applicants who pepper their documents with inappropriate keywords are kicked out of that company's database. The company-wide wipe-out means the offending applicant not only loses one particular job, but all jobs there.

If use of the invisible word trick grows, clogging e-recruiting systems that rely on keyword searches and turning their databases into swamps of unqualified job seekers, the systems will be severely damaged, perhaps even disabled.

Employers' countermeasures to combat hidden keywords and other less dramatic causes of database overload are being debated as you read these words.

But the e-CV, in all its variations, is effectively the Elvis of the recruiting industry – the king who will live forever. Recruiters say they're underwater, soaked with maddening swells of e-CVs and gasping for air. The overload has created problems that could well affect your job search.

Get the Loot, Not the Boot

To avoid the cyberwall-to-cyberwall competition in e-CVs described in the previous section, do you automatically throw up your hands, forget about e-CVs, and claim you'd rather dig ditches for a living? No, because if you do decide to "just forget about doing an e-CV", a shovel may well become your only work tool.

Except for small businesses that don't use computers and companies that prefer you come into the employment office and fill out an application for hourly work, e-CVs have become essential.

Instead of swearing off e-CVs, review the aspects and advantages of an e-CV, especially if you are on the world's "A list" of job seekers – a younger person with a bit of experience and hot skills in demand:

- **Career management tool:** Using a variety of privacy-protecting methods, a number of employed people position themselves to trade up jobs by parking their CVs on carefully chosen job sites that use (computer) personal job agents. (See Chapter 2.) When a better job turns up that matches their requirements, they're notified by e-mail. This category of employed person is termed *passive job seeker* and is the most prized of recruits; a widely held theory says that the person who has been hired by someone must be a desirable candidate.

- **CV of choice:** Recruiters and hiring managers increasingly prefer to receive e-CVs because they are easier to deal with than stacks of paper.

- **Fewer CV readers:** The downsizing of a vengeful employment god over the past 25 years has taken its toll on human resource departments like everywhere else. The old conventional dilemma: The leaner staffs are drowning in paper CVs. The new conventional dilemma: The leaner staffs are submerged in e-CVs. Even so, browsing e-CVs is easier than scaling paper-CV mountains.

✔ **Ever-changing workforce:** Flexible employees – temporary, part-time, contract, and self-employed – need efficient connections for quick job changes. E-CVs may shorten search and response time.

✔ **Information technology workforce:** Anyone in IT fields must use an e-CV or else be considered IT's Biggest Plonker.

✔ **Tightening recruitment budgets:** Employers say that online recruiting costs less than most other kinds of recruiting and that's why they're using more of it. Newspapers aren't standing still for job site competition for advertising: Newspapers are combining online with print ads for a slight additional cost or even for free. Online recruiting typically calls for e-CVs.

✔ **Requests for online response:** Job ads increasingly instruct applicants to send e-CVs. Some advertisers refuse to reveal postal mail addresses.

✔ **Modernisation of recruitment agencies:** Virtually all third-party recruiting agencies (read *headhunters*) use digital databases to manage their CV volume.

Stop and Ask Directions

When you're not sure what technology is being used where you send your CV (which, today, is most of the time), telephone or e-mail the employer's human resource department or company receptionist and ask the following question:

In submitting my CV, I want to be sure I'm using the correct technology at your organisation. Can I submit my CV to your company electronically?

If the answer is yes, then ask:

Can I send my CV as an attachment?

If the answer is yes, then ask:

If I send my CV as an attachment (MS Word, WordPerfect), will managers see my CV in the original format, or do you convert the attachment to text?

If the company converts the original CV to a pure text CV, avoid a bad wrap. Send your CV as a plain text (ASCII) file (Chapter 15 has info on ASCII CVs). Why? Some systems that convert an attachment to text do so at the expense of readability. They mess up the line-wrapping formatting so badly that the result looks as though your typing is tacky. Figure 14-1 shows an example of a plain text CV that began life as an attachment.

```
TARGET COMPANY
Category:  Consulting Services
Description of my ideal company:
To obtain a position in the Information Technology field which
provides a challenging atmosphere conducive to professional
achievement and the ability to advance while contributing to
organisational goals. To work for a company that lives a credo
and holds commitment to personal integrity and pursuit of
excellence as core values.
TARGET LOCATIONS
Relocate:  Yes
UK South West/East      France        Germany
Spain
WORK STATUS
I am an EU resident authorised to work in the UK or any other
EU member state.
EXPERIENCE
7/2000 - Present         Broadbase Software, Inc.
Thames Valley Business Park,
Reading Application Consultant
?     Install and configure Broadbase Foundation and Brio
Enterprise Server to create a decision support environment.
?     Customise out-of-the-box Broadbase Applications and Brio
Reports to customers decision support needs.
?     Reverse engineer transactional databases with Erwin to
build a logical dimensional model for physical deployment onto
Broadbase db.
?     Create custom applications in Broadbase Foundation
Application Workbench to perform ETL into physical dimensional
model within Broadbase db.
?     Administer Broadbase db.
?     Provide support after engagement is over for problems
that may arise.
?     Work mainly on transactional systems in SQL Server,
Sybase, and Oracle. To develop dimensional models for
analytical reporting from Brio or MS OLAP server.
9/1999 - 7/2000  Genesis ElderCare       Kensington, London
Senior Application Analyst (Applications DBA)
Designed an assessment database to track patient medical
outcomes and company defined scoring system
```

Figure 14-1: What can happen when you don't use ASCII.

CV Production, 1-2-3!

Are you puzzled about where to begin, what to write first, and what to do next? Follow these steps that we recommend to fire up your CVs after you've created the core document, from which all targeted CVs flow.

1. **Create your CV in a word-processing program, such as MS Word or WordPerfect.**

   Stylise the CV to reflect your persona by choosing a typeface you like. Visually emphasise focal points with boldface, bullets, and underlined characters, as well as words. Save as "yourname.doc" (like "SteveShipside.doc"). This document is your fully formatted CV for general usage. Print paper copies as needed.

   Limit yourself to using characters found on a standard keyboard so that they translate correctly. For example, use asterisks to mark bulleted items, and forget about using the fancy arrows you can choose in the MS Word program.

2. **Convert your formatted CV (MS Word or WordPerfect) into plain text by following these steps:**

   1. Choose Edit⇨Select all.

   2. Click the Start button; then click Programs⇨Accessories⇨Notepad. When a Notepad window opens, and paste your CV from the fully formatted original in Step 1.

   3. Still in Notepad, choose Format⇨Word Wrap.

      Some minor tweaking may be necessary to line up dates and job titles if they were indented or you used bullets in your formatted CV.

   4. Save the resulting document in Notepad (by choosing File⇨Save) as **yourname.txt** (for example, SteveShipside.txt).

   This is your plain text (ASCII) e-CV, which is compatible with all systems for use in e-mailing and posting to job sites.

3. **Use either your .doc file (created in Step 1) or .txt file (created in Step 2) to import your e-CV to other applications, such as an Adobe Acrobat PDF file.**

   You also can save your MS Word document as HTML from MS Word's Save As dialog box.

That's it. You're ready to roll.

Chapter 15

Fading Technology: Scannable and Plain Text CVs

Scannable CVs were all the rage in the 1990s. These days, scannable CVs are on their way out. Plain text CVs (also called ASCII CVs) are sauntering toward history, too – just more slowly.

New technology is the reason scannable and plain text CVs are joining DOS operating software in computer museums. Recruiters now prefer slick intake systems that allow CVs to travel smoothly online and move straight into an electronic CV management database with no muss, no fuss.

Older systems that pass CVs through scanners often require manual doctoring to correct goofy readings. As for plain text CVs, well, recruiters and line managers say they're ugly and hard to read.

Even so, don't bin the scannable and plain text versions of your CV just yet. If an employer or job site directs you to send a CV that can be scanned or to send an online plain text CV, do it. This chapter gives you what you need to know.

Help Computers Find Your Scannable CVs

A *scannable CV* is a paper CV scanned into a computer as an image. It can be mailed by post, hand delivered, faxed on a fax machine, or faxed from your computer to the employer, printed on paper, and then scanned into a computer.

Scanning of CVs into electronic databases is done by human resource departments (which often outsource the task to service-bureau-like firms) and also by third-party recruiters.

A computer's scanning technology is programmed to extract (pull out) a summary of basic information from each CV image. This info includes name, address, telephone number, skills, work history, years of experience, and education.

The extracted information summary is stored in the electronic database along with the CV image. The summary is categorised by qualifications or kept as a searchable *plain text document* (described later in this chapter in the section called Fast Key to ASCII).

CVs and their extracted summaries sleep peacefully until an HR specialist or recruiter searches (usually by keywords) the summaries to retrieve applicants who match the requirements of the job opening. The technology ranks the applicants from the most qualified to the least qualified. The relevant CVs get a wake-up call and pop to the recruiting screen.

Your mission: Take the correct steps to make your scannable CV *searchable* and *retrievable*. Make sure that scanning technologies can distinguish the letters and that your keywords (see Chapter 11) are spelled correctly so computers can find them.

When your CV goes AWOL in a database, your name just never comes up for the right jobs, or maybe any jobs. Fortunately, you can take steps to prevent scanning errors from putting you on the sidelines. By following the technical tips in Table 15-1, you can ensure that your CV survives 99.9 percent of all types of scanning software in CV databases. Figure 15-1 shows a CV prime for scanning, and Figure 15-2 demonstrates many of the items from the "No, Don't Do This" columns of Tables 15-1 and 15-2.

Table 15-1	Tips to Charm Computer Eyes
Yes, Do This	*No, Don't Do This*
Do use white A4 paper.	Don't use coloured paper. Paper that's too dark (or type that's too light) is a risky read for computers. Don't use paper that has a background pattern of any type: marble, speckles, lacy, or abstract designs. The software tries to read the designs and gets very mixed up. Avoid odd-sized paper. Especially don't use A3 paper and fold it over like a presentation folder (the fold-over has to be cut apart and painstakingly fed through the scanner's automatic document feeder on the front side and then again on the back side). A corollary is don't use coloured typeface.
Do print on one side of the paper.	Don't print on two sides of the paper.
Do provide a laser-printed original that has good definition between the type and the paper. Your CV needs all the help it can get if it's faxed from one location to another: Each successive generation of copying degrades the quality of the reproduction.	Don't send a typewritten original (it makes you look like an old fuddy duddy), a photocopy (unless you're certain that its reproduction quality is tops), or dot matrix printouts. Inkjet printers can be okay, but with the wrong paper, slightly smeared ink can cause the letters to bump into each other.
Do use standard typefaces, such as Helvetica, Futura, Optima, Univers, Times, Courier, New Century Schoolbook, and Palatino.	Don't use a condensed typeface. White space separates letters; no space squishes them together. Letters must be distinctively clear with crisp, unbroken edges. Avoid arty, decorative typefaces.
Do make sure that none of the letters touch together; in some typefaces, for example, the letter *r* touches the following letter and looks like an *n*. Computers relate to correctly spelled words, and so a "misspelled" word won't be read.	Don't try to crowd too much on one page by using 8-point or 9-point fonts. (Technically, some 9-point fonts are computer readable, but older human eyes may hate squinting to read your prose packed tightly with petite type.)

(continued)

Table 15-1 *(continued)*

Yes, Do This	*No, Don't Do This*
Do feel free to use larger fonts for section headings and your name: 14 to 16 points are good. Larger headings look better on the electronic image of your CV when humans read it (which they don't always do). Personally, we like the body of CVs in a 12-point font size, the section headings in 14-point, and the name in 16-point.	Don't worry about using 12-point fonts for your section headings and name if that's what you prefer. Scanning software convert everything into the same size font no matter what's on the image, and you may need the space taken up by larger fonts to add a skill point.
Do use boldface and/or all capital letters for section headings.	Don't use any of these bad-scan elements: • Italics or script • Underlining • Reverse printing (white letters on a black field) • Shadows or shading • Hollow bullets (they read like the letter *o*) • Number (#) signs for bullets (the computer may try to read the line as a phone number) • Boxes (computer try to read them like letters) • Two-column formats or designs that look like newspapers • Symbols (such as a logo) • Vertical lines (computers read them like the letter *l*) • Vertical dates (use horizontal dates: 2002–2007)
Do keep your scannable CV simple in design and straightforward – what recruiters call "plain vanilla."	Don't overdo the use of special characters when alternatives are available. Rather than write "telephone/fax number", write "telephone-fax number".

Yes, Do This	No, Don't Do This
Do use white space to define sections.	Don't overdo the use of horizontal lines, and leave plenty of white space (about ¼ inch) around each section.
Do follow these formatting guidelines: • Place your name on the top line. If your CV runs more than one page, put your name as the first text on the other pages. • Use a standard address layout below your name. List each telephone number on its own line; list your e-mail address on its own line; list your Web site on its own line. If you combine contact information, such as your telephone and e-mail address on the same line, put six spaces of white space between them.	Don't use unusual placements of your name and contact information.
Do send your CV without staples. Paper clips are okay.	Don't use staples (can cause processing of two pages as one).
Do send your CV flat in a A4 envelope; remember to add extra postage.	Don't fold or crease your CV. Laser print and copier toner may flake off when your CV is folded, or the software may just look at the fold and shrug in defeat.

After you examine the mechanics of scanner-savvy CVs, consider the content. Table 15-2 contains tips and tricks for human scanners.

Table 15-2	Tips to Charm Human Eyes
Yes, Do This	No, Don't Do This
Do include a one-page cover letter to all employers and recruiters, or when special instructions are needed. Be sure to use keywords (see Chapter 11) in your cover letter.	Don't bother to send a cover letter if you're sending your CV to a CV database where its insertion into the database is understood. An exception: When you're posting in a company database where the match between your CV and the job may not be obvious — an engineer applying for a sales engineering position, for instance.

(continued)

Table 15-2 *(continued)*

Yes, Do This	*No, Don't Do This*
Do realise that multiple-page CVs are not discouraged. Computers can easily handle multiple-page CVs, allowing you to give more information than you might for a formatted (paper) CV. As soon as the computer begins to search and retrieve for skills and other points of background, it laps up information to determine whether your qualifications match available positions. Generalised guidelines: • New graduates, one page (two with heavy facts) • Most job seekers, one to two pages • Senior executives, two to three pages • Academic CV users, three to six pages	Don't cram-jam so much data onto a single page that it looks like the fine print on an insurance policy. Be concise, but use the pages you need to effectively sell your abilities.
Do consider putting a keyword profile of approximately 20 to 30 words at the beginning of your CV. It's an attention grabber and a thumbnail portrait of the essence of your qualifications and experience. Although a keyword profile isn't technically necessary – computers can extract your skills anywhere on your CV – leading off with a keyword preface assures that human eyes see your strengths on the first screen, enticing them to scroll down and see in what context your skills are offered. If you fail to grab readers' interest on the first screen, they find it too easy to click to the next CV. And creating a keyword profile forces you to specifically think of the keywords you need to use.	Don't be redundant by layering summary upon summary. If you use a keyword summary, don't follow up immediately with a qualifications summary.
Do be generous with your keywords to define your skills, experience, education, professional affiliations, and other marketable points of background. Generally, keywords are such nouns as *writer, Excel,* and *Spanish.* Refer to Chapter 11 for info on keywords	Don't assume that your action verbs will place you among the candidates chosen for an interview.

Yes, Do This	No, Don't Do This
Do incorporate the CV-writing guidance given in other chapters of this book (with the exception of heavy reliance on action verbs). For example, focus your CV. If you use a job objective with a keyword profile, remember to make sure that the profile supports your objective.	Don't throw out all you've ever learned about writing formatted paper CVs; the problem-solving concepts also apply to scannable CVs.
Do handle with care shortfalls in experience. Suppose that the job ad calls for five years' experience in manufacturing technology, and you have only three years, but you have an engineering degree. Computers don't handle the counting of years of experience very well. If you've had two jobs in manufacturing technology but one lasted two years and the other three years, the computer won't add it up. So just say it: "Have five years' experience equivalent: three years' direct experience plus two years' college training in subject". In this technique, use "years' experience in" (apostrophe replaces the preposition "of") instead of "years of experience." *Remember:* The five years' experience requirement may be somewhat arbitrary. What employers want are skills; if you can come close to the requirement and you've got the skills, you've got an excellent chance of being chosen.	Don't (in an educational shortcoming) put down two dates (the date you started and the date you left college) beside the name of your college. Double dates flag your disqualification as a college graduate. If you're a graduate, the graduation year is enough. Don't write more years than a job ad asks for. If the job requires five years and you write that you have eight years, some software programs will whiz right by your CV. So write "more than five years' experience." By mimicking the job's requirements, older applicants also get a fair chance to be seen. Suppose you've got 30 years' experience. You still write "more than five years' experience."
Do keep your CV updated with new keyworded skills and achievements; computers automatically date and call up the last CV received with your name and telephone number.	Don't send multiple CVs with differing objectives to the same database, using the same name and telephone number – you'll look unfocused.
Do call to follow up and be assured that your CV was received, is in the database, and has been routed to the appropriate line managers. If you can determine which line managers received your CV, try calling them during normal business hours.	Don't end your follow-up with a call to a specified number for an employer's automated applicant tracking system. An impersonal inquiry to an automated response system android won't do much to advance your cause.

(continued)

Table 15-2 *(continued)*

Yes, Do This	*No, Don't Do This*
Do use industry jargon and familiar, standard words that computers are likely to search for. Say "candidate sourcing", not "candidate locating", for example. Some scanning software can come up with synonyms, but other software can't. If you use initials (LSE) in a keyword preface, spell it out later in the text (London School of Economics).	Don't use unfamiliar words that computers may not be programmed to search for. Industry jargon is an exception to this caution – employers almost always use jargon in searching for the best candidates. They expect you to understand the lingo if you're in the industry.

Fast Key to ASCII: The Plain Text Option

ASCII is pronounced "AS-kee." It's an acronym that stands for *American Standard Code for Information Interchange* and is used to describe *plain text* files that have no graphics, no rule lines, no bullets, no italics, and so on.

No-frills files may be referred to simply as ASCII, or plain text, or ASCII plain text; all three terms mean the same thing – files that can be universally understood by computers everywhere in the world. An ASCII message is straight text and allows for almost no formatting.

ASCII is so dreary in design that even its mother (if it had one) couldn't love it. Even so, almost everyone has been using this one-size-fits-all file to avoid communications miscues between such popular word-processing programs as MS Word and WordPerfect, which run on various computer platforms, such as PCs, Macintosh, UNIX workstation, or mainframe terminals.

Although ASCII CVs are heading into the sunset, until the recruiting world is totally living large with handsomely formatted e-CVs, you may be stuck with the plain-Jane look. So here's the drill.

To create a plain text CV, start with your formatted, printable CV. Open your formatted CV, make a copy of the computer file, name it *yourname*.txt (or anything else with the .txt extension) and tell the computer to save it as a *text-only* document.

Alternatively, type your electronic version from scratch in your favourite word-processing program, saving it as a *text-only* document and naming it *yourname*.txt.

BAD SCANNABLE CV

PETER IMPERFECT

44 Dryden Lane
Little Trenthide, Dorset, DT6 ZVY

Messages: 0796 332-2999
Home: 01297 332-8765

EXECUTIVE MANAGEMENT ... BUSINESS DEVELOPMENT
MBA

PROFESSIONAL EXPERTISE

Product Marketing

Sales Management

Business Development

Customer Service

Operations Management

Manufacturing Processes

Material Flow

Inventory Management

Accounting & Finance

Financial Justification

Risk Management

Human Resources

Public Relations

EDUCATION:

M.B.A. Degree
University of Manchester

B.A. Business Economics
University of Nottingham

PROFILE

A professional manager with many years of successful business experience gained in private industry, non-profit and government sectors. Accustomed to profit and loss responsibilities. Effective leader with imagination and vision. Marketer of industrial equipment in multi-level channels. Former President/CEO and Regional Sales Manager.

FUNCTIONAL SUMMARY OF EXPERIENCE
General Administration
Thoroughly experienced in managing the efforts of others. Direct leadership involvement in accounting, banking, credit, insurance, and risk management. Experience with hiring, training, redirection, and safety programs. Examples of general administration accomplishments:

- As President/CEO of a start-up material handling equipment company, exercised full profit and loss responsibility for all operations.
- Planned and implemented company strategy, including selection of product lines, fabrication to accommodate special applications, outsourcing manufacture of component parts.

Marketing & Sales Management
Diversified experience marketing industrial equipment products through established and new independent distributors.
Experienced in all types of product marketing, including co-operative advertising programs, selecting and training new distributors, encouraging and replacing established distributors, interacting with customers; assisting in the bidding process; preparing sales reports and forecasts. Examples of marketing accomplishments:

- As Regional Sales Manager with a major industrial hardware manufacturer, managed annual sales of £1.5 million across the southwest while faced with shrinking product offering, many production problems, sales office reallocations and major personnel changes.
- Developed and implemented marketing strategies to maintain profitability as many competitors were failing.

Figure 15-1: Hold on, there! This CV's not ready yet!

GOOD SCANNABLE CV

Mitesh Patel
27 Twickenham Road
Canton Cardiff
CF00 1ZA
(029) 456-7890
e-mail: mpatel@nosuch.co.uk

Note Linear Treatment
with Ample Keywords

OBJECTIVE

Microcomputer network administration/analysis/training

PROFILE

10 years' A+ Certified Computer Service Technician/ Includes laser printer maintenance and repair, network administration, PC hardware and software configuration

Professional societies are keywords that employers often search for.

- Software: MS DOS, All Windows inc. Windows 2000/XE HTML
- "Excellence in Customer Service" award
- Member and past officer, Welsh Computer Tech's Association
- Systems integration, analysis and trouble shooting experience
- PC, Macintosh, and multi-user system experience

EXPERIENCE

Electrismart Inc.   Cardiff   2002 to Present
Consultant/Webmaster

Consultant for local Internet Service Provider (ISP).

Turn solid bullets into asterisks, make type all one size and substitute uppercase for boldface to make e-mail friendly

- Assist with e-mail setup and configuration.
- Provide instruction for use with Macintosh and IBM/Compatible computers.
- Help new clients with web page design.

FreshImports Inc.   Cardiff   1998-2001
Marketing and Sales Representative

- Marketing and product management of electronic microcomputer components for electronic manufacturing company.
- Managed all help-desk technical support, troubleshooting (hardware/software), integration and interface to PC compatibles (desktop and notebook), Macintosh, and server environments.
- Created support manuals and user guides for proprietary and distributed products. "Improved overall customer service and technical support by 65% "(Employer's quote).

EDUCATION

MPhil – University of Wales, Swansea
- Pursuing, expect to complete in 2008.

Figure 15-2: This baby's ready to roll!

Because your CV now has ASCII for brains, it won't recognise the formatting commands that your word-processing program uses. So be on guard against the common errors in the following sections.

Typeface/fonts

Don't expect a particular typeface or size in your ASCII CV. The typeface and fonts appear in the typeface and size that the recipient's computer is set for. This means that boldface, italics, or different font sizes won't appear in the online plain text version.

Word wrap

Don't use the word wrap feature when writing your CV because it either won't work or will look as weird as a serial letter *E* running vertically down a page. Odd-looking word wrapping is one of the cardinal sins of online CVs. Use hard carriage returns (just press the Enter key) to insert line breaks.

You can see what your ASCII document looks like by opening it in a simple text editor (like Notepad on Windows). If you want to be really sure to avoid features that won't translate to ASCII, try writing your CV in Notepad instead of Word (remembering those hard carriage returns).

Proportional typefaces

Don't use proportional typefaces that have different widths for different characters (such as Times Roman). Instead, use a fixed-width typeface (such as Courier). When you avoid proportional fonts, you know that, if you compose and send your CV in Courier 12 and it's received in the Arial typeface, it should still work well with most e-mail programs, surviving transport with a close resemblance to the original line length.

Special characters

Don't use any characters that aren't on your keyboard, such as "smart quotes" or mathematical symbols. Special characters don't convert correctly, and your CV will need fumigating to rid itself of squiggles and capital U's.

You know that you're off in the wrong direction if you have to change the preferences setting in your word processor or otherwise go to a lot of trouble to get a certain character to print. Remember that you can use dashes and asterisks (they're on the keyboard), but you can't use bullets (they're *not* on the keyboard).

Although you can't use bullets, bold, or underlined text in a plain text document, you can use plus signs (+) at the beginning of lines to draw attention to part of your document. You can also use a series of dashes to separate sections and capital letters to substitute for boldface. When you don't know what else to use to sharpen your ASCII effort, you can always turn to Old Reliable – white space.

Tabs

Don't use tabs because they get wiped out in the conversion to ASCII. Use your spacebar instead.

Alignment

Don't expect your CV to be full-justified. Your ASCII CV is automatically left-justified. If you need to indent a line or centre a heading, use the spacebar.

Attachments

Paste your CV with a cover note (a very brief cover letter) into the body of your e-mail. You can, if you want, also attach a nicely formatted CV.

Page numbers

Don't use page numbers. You can't be certain where the page breaks will fall, and your name and page number could end up halfway south on a page.

Spell check

Don't forget to spell check *before* you save your CV as an ASCII file.

The subject line

The subject line of an e-mail can bring you front and centre to a recruiter's attention.

- ✔ When responding to an advertised job, use the job title. If none is listed, use the reference number.

- ✔ When you send an unsolicited CV, write a short "sales" headline. Consider these examples:

    Bilingual teacher, soc studies/6 yrs' exp.

    Programmer, experienced, top skills: Java, C++.

Never just say Bilingual teacher or Programmer. Sell yourself! Keep rewriting until you've crammed as many sales points as possible into your "marquee".

Should you show a "cc" for "copy sent" on your CV? If you're e-mailing a hiring manager (such as the accounting manager), copy the human resources department manager; that saves the hiring manager from having to forward your CV to human resources and is more likely to result in your landing in the company's CV database to be considered for any number of jobs.

Do a Final Check

After you think that your CV is ready to roll, write a short cover note (using the same technical guidelines as for your CV). Leading off with the cover note, cut and paste the text of both your note and CV into the body of an e-mail message. Send the message to yourself and to a friend, and then compare responses. This last check should reveal flaws in your technique, giving you a chance to mend before you send.

Look over the following plain text CV for Della Hutchings (Figure 15-3), and you can see why it should never leave home without a bag over its face.

An example of how so called "plain text" can actually be hard to read since there is little to lead the eye to the key information.

```
PLAINTEXT CV

Della Hutchings
183 Clarence Parade
Southsea
Portsmouth
PO1 H09
E-mail: dellah@aol.com
   Admin Assist, 4 yrs exp, 6 software pgms, time mgt skills

   SUMMARY
   ============================================================
   Word. WordPerfect. Lotus. Excel. PageMaker. QuickBooks.
   Bilingual: Spanish. Time management. Budgeting.
   Organisational skills.

   EMPLOYMENT
   ============================================================
   University of Portsmouth, 2003-Present



   ASSISTANT TO DIRECTOR OF ACADEMIC TECHNOLOGY
   Use and support a wide variety of computer applications
   Work with both Macintosh and IBM computers
   Communicate with clients in Europe
   Apply troubleshooting and problem solving skills
   Maintain complex scheduling for employer, staff, self
   Responsible for dept. budget administration; 100% balanced

   Mothers for Wildlife, 2002-2003
   ADMINISTRATIVE ASSISTANT

   Edited/wrote newsletter
   Organised rallies and letter-writing campaigns
   Maintained mailing lists
   Saved organisation £1,200 changing equipment

   EDUCATION
   ============================================================
   University of Portsmouth
   BA with honours in International Studies, May 2000

   Won Gilsmith award for best honours thesis on European
   Integration
```

Figure 15-3: Blimey! What a mess! It continues on the next page.

```
AFFILIATIONS
================================================================
Portsmouth Hispanic Students Association
Amnesty International
Concept of Colours (Multi-cultural modelling group)

HOBBIES
================================================================
Like details: Writing and Web design

AWARDS
================================================================
On present job: Administrative Assistant of the Month four
times
Recognised for productivity, organisation, attention to
detail, and interpersonal skills.
```

E-Forms: Fill in the Blankety-Blanks

The e-form is just a shorter version of the plain text CV, usually found on company Web sites. The company encourages you to apply by setting your plain text into designated fields of the forms on the site.

The e-form is almost like an application form, except that it lacks the legal document status an application form acquires when you sign it, certifying that all facts are true.

Follow the on-screen instructions given by each employer to cut and paste the requested information into the site's template. You're basically just filling in the blanks with your contact information that's supplemented by data lifted from your plain text CV.

E-forms can't spell check, so cutting and pasting your CV into the e-form body, instead of typing it in manually is your best bet. Because you spell checked your CV before converting it to ASCII (of course, you did!), at least you know that everything is likely to be spelled correctly.

Virtually all company Web sites now encourage you to apply online through their applicant portals. You're asked either to cut and paste your CV or to fill out an online form. Some companies ask you to answer demographic questions about race, gender, and so forth as a way of collecting data for the *Equal Opportunities Commission* (EOC). You aren't required to include this information to be considered for employment and remember that an employer is not legally allowed to discriminate on the basis of it. Nevertheless, women and minorities are well advised to oblige the demographics request. What if you're a white male? Your call.

When you're finished, send your e-form. That's all there is to it. No big deal.

E-forms work well for job seekers in high-demand occupations, such as nursing, but they don't work so well for job seekers who need to document motivation, good attitude, and other personal characteristics and achievements that computers don't search for. When you rely on an e-form to get an employer's attention, you're playing 100 percent on the employer's turf.

A Game Plan for Scannable and Plain Text CVs

To cover all bases, create multiple versions of your CV. You may never need to provide a scannable or plain text CV, but then again, you might. Plan ahead. Follow this straightforward process:

1. **Write a core CV formatted to flatter your background and styled in an eye-appealing manner with boldface, indentation, underlining, italics, and any graphic features that look good. Use all the action verbs you want.**

   Hold on to this good-looking, formatted CV and take copies with you to job interviews.

   Advantage: SUPER PRESENTABLE.

2. **Working from your formatted CV, strip away the graphic baggage of underlines, italics, designs, and so forth.**

   Advantage: SCANNABLE.

3. **Add muscle to your scannable CV with keywords even if you have to delete some action verbs (check out Chapter 11 for keywords).**

   Advantage: SEARCHABLE.

4. **Working from your scannable CV, convert your CV to plain text (ASCII).**

   Advantage: SENDABLE.

5. **Add a Keyword Summary at the top of your plain text CV if it doesn't already have one.**

   Advantage: SALEABLE.

6. **Working from your plain text CV, copy and paste requested data into employers' e-forms posted on their Web sites.**

   Advantage: SPELLCHECKABLE.

Save all versions of your CV on your hard drive, ready to print, revise, update, or e-mail in an instant.

Chapter 16

In Search of an Uncommon E-CV

"*L*et me try something new!" your inner creative person screams. "I'm comfortable in my skin, and I want to be comfortable in my CV. The colourless, button-down, one-dimensional CV isn't me."

Well, if that's the tune running through your head, you don't want to miss this chapter, which explains the variety of high-tech CV options available.

Before the tour begins, you should know that recruiting professionals discourage atypical CVs, adamantly arguing that they don't work. Recruiting professionals tell me that a mere *5 percent* (or fewer) of e-CVs venture out of the mainstream, and those that do are often ignored.

By *mainstream,* we mean straightforward documents that are fully formatted and technologically born again to ride the online rails as attachments to e-mail (see Chapter 1), usually MS Word attachments. Those, of course, are in addition to mainstream CVs that journey across the Internet as ASCII plain text documents (see Chapter 15).

But despite the overwhelming body of employment industry insiders – like 95 percent – who advise against being *too* different, you may find just the right uncommon e-CV to entice a recruiter or employer who is in the market for an independent thinker.

Having explained the odds, let the tour begin.

Seven CVs You Don't See Every Day

Although recruiting professionals generally dismiss offbeat CVs, you may think one of the following seven creations could carry your message with style.

- ✔ PDF file
- ✔ Web and e-portfolio
- ✔ E-newsletter
- ✔ Beamer
- ✔ Smart card
- ✔ Talker
- ✔ Flash

These slightly off-kilter but potential star CV presentations, described in the following sections, prove once again that everything under the sun has not yet been invented.

PDF CV

"PDF" really stands for *portable document format,* but a document using this format comes to readers looking *pretty darned fine* – exactly the way you sent it. PDF CVs have experienced a recent surge in popularity. They are particularly attractive to recruiting professionals who spend hours and hours in front of a computer reading coma-inducing ASCII text CVs.

A PDF CV is a *read only* document. That is, it can't get bent out of shape when a reader, say an in-house corporate recruiter, is looking at a CV on a computer monitor, then somehow manages to graffiti it up by dropping a book on the keyboard or inadvertently tapping a key or two and changing the content. A non-PDF CV (a Word attachment, for example) could be altered to a wacky, tacky version and sent downstream to hiring managers who would wonder, "Why am I getting this messy CV?" But a PDF CV won't change – it has the equivalent of a protective coating around it.

PDFs are an invention and trademark of Adobe. You've probably seen online catalogues with all the lines, text, and pictures in the right places and no bulging in the middle – the catalogues were created as PDFs. Now, the technology is increasingly turning up in online CVs.

PDFs can be viewed by any computer platform – Windows, Macintosh, even Linux. You can download the latest version of the Adobe Acrobat Reader software for free at adobe.com. However, to create your own PDF files (for a CV), you need to have the Adobe Acrobat program (which unlike the Adobe Acrobat Reader is not free) installed on your computer. You can purchase the latest version from Adobe (adobe.com) for less than £250. Or you can look at online competitive shopping sites such as Cnet.com (cnet.com) for cheaper prices. Better yet, see if you can "rent" a copy in a Web café or print shop.

To convert your CV into a PDF, you first review it to be certain it's precisely the way you want it – very little editing can be done after your CV is effectively set in PDF stone. Then you open MS Word (or the word processor you used to create your CV), open your CV document, and select Print. In the Print dialog box, select the PDF print driver as your "printer". This process converts your CV into PDF format viewable by Acrobat Reader.

Readers viewing your attached PDF CV also need the free Adobe Acrobat Reader. You should include a hyperlink in your CV that allows a quick download of the Reader in case the employer or recruiter doesn't already have it.

Web CV and e-portfolio

Web CVs and e-portfolios have not caught on broadly across the employment spectrum because they're generally viewed as too time-intensive for recruiters. Even tech-savvy job seekers are advised to use Web CVs as a supplement to one-dimensional versions.

Web CVs

Web CVs – also called HTML CVs – are electronic documents posted on a personal Web site, permitting easy transmission to links of information that flesh out your basic CV facts – samples of your work, for instance. With the right "tags", your CV will appear on numerous search engines and be easily accessible to recruiters and employers. Companies that pride themselves on being cutting edge or that do a lot of e-commerce business are prime prospects for Web CV job seekers.

Web CVs, with their links to sound and graphics, are a glamorous alternative to the one-dimensional CV. Although a Web CV can't pop to life in the pages of a book, I have included a heavily-linked version in Figure 16-1 created by Glenn Gutmacher, who teaches advanced online recruiting techniques to companies and staffing agencies. (The CV is real but the dates are fictional.) Gutmacher's CV is lined with links. This version is cut to two pages, and the links are represented by underlined text. You can see the entire CV and click through the links on Gutmacher's Web site, recruiting-online.com.

Web CVs are very useful for people who need to show their work, such as individuals in engineering, architecture, art, or modelling, and when you're working as a free agent marketing your workplace wares on various job sites that cater to contract gigs.

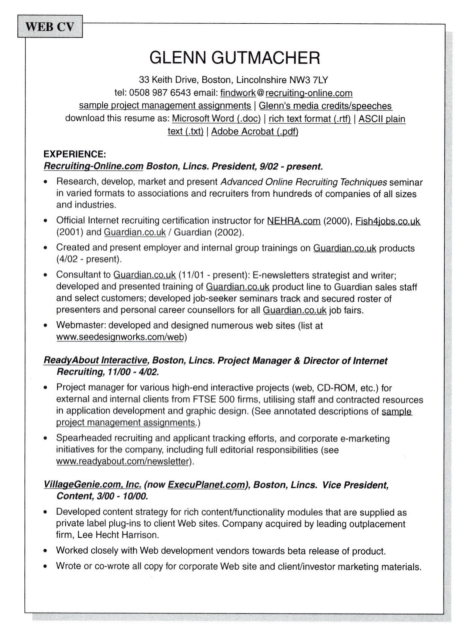

WEB CV

GLENN GUTMACHER

33 Keith Drive, Boston, Lincolnshire NW3 7LY
tel: 0508 987 6543 email: findwork@recruiting-online.com
sample project management assignments | Glenn's media credits/speeches
download this resume as: Microsoft Word (.doc) | rich text format (.rtf) | ASCII plain
text (.txt) | Adobe Acrobat (.pdf)

EXPERIENCE:
Recruiting-Online.com Boston, Lincs. President, 9/02 - present.

- Research, develop, market and present *Advanced Online Recruiting Techniques* seminar in varied formats to associations and recruiters from hundreds of companies of all sizes and industries.
- Official Internet recruiting certification instructor for NEHRA.com (2000), Fish4jobs.co.uk (2001) and Guardian.co.uk / Guardian (2002).
- Created and present employer and internal group trainings on Guardian.co.uk products (4/02 - present).
- Consultant to Guardian.co.uk (11/01 - present): E-newsletters strategist and writer; developed and presented training of Guardian.co.uk product line to Guardian sales staff and select customers; developed job-seeker seminars track and secured roster of presenters and personal career counsellors for all Guardian.co.uk job fairs.
- Webmaster: developed and designed numerous web sites (list at www.seedesignworks.com/web)

ReadyAbout Interactive, Boston, Lincs. Project Manager & Director of Internet Recruiting, 11/00 - 4/02.

- Project manager for various high-end interactive projects (web, CD-ROM, etc.) for external and internal clients from FTSE 500 firms, utilising staff and contracted resources in application development and graphic design. (See annotated descriptions of sample project management assignments.)
- Spearheaded recruiting and applicant tracking efforts, and corporate e-marketing initiatives for the company, including full editorial responsibilities (see www.readyabout.com/newsletter).

VillageGenie.com, Inc. (now ExecuPlanet.com), Boston, Lincs. Vice President, Content, 3/00 - 10/00.

- Developed content strategy for rich content/functionality modules that are supplied as private label plug-ins to client Web sites. Company acquired by leading outplacement firm, Lee Hecht Harrison.
- Worked closely with Web development vendors towards beta release of product.
- Wrote or co-wrote all copy for corporate Web site and client/investor marketing materials.

Figure 16-1: Sometimes, employment comes through a well-linked CV. This example continues on the next page.

Community Newspaper Co., Boston, Lincs. Interactive Product Manager and Commercial Content Editor, 10/98 - 3/00.

- Oversaw launch of and maintained CommunityClassifieds.com and its component sites: Town Online *Working* (CNC's career resources Web site for Lincolnshire); ParentandBaby.com (parenting resources); Town Online *Real Estate* (for *Lincolnshire Homes*, etc.); Town Online *Newcomers* (Newcomers Guide); and Town Online *Introductions* (online personals).
- Developed and systematised new sources of online content to complement what comes from print publication weekly (e.g., career experts for live chats, special columnists, etc.).
- Wrote and supervised compilation of content from various departments for corporate intranet.

Home Box Office, Lincolnshire. Secretary, Area Marketing, 8/96 - 4/98.

- Researched and maintained periodic marketing campaign reports.
- Liaison between corporate departments and regional sales staffs to help handle field issues.

EDUCATION, DISTINCTIONS AND SKILLS:

- Cambridge University (St John's college), B.A. Hons, Cantab, Psychology/Organisational Behaviour, 5/96.
- Archibald MacLeish Prize, Cambridge University. For graphic and literary style in a college
newsletter, 5/96.
- MS Office; graphics and publishing software; web site development tools; medium Spanish fluency.

BOARDS AND MEMBERSHIPS:

- Northeast Human Resource Association (NEHRA), Member, 2000 - present and Internet recruiting certification instructor, 2002 - present.
- Maple Common Neighbourhood Association, Trustee/Officer, 4/02 - present.
- National Association of College Broadcasters, Cambridge. Chairman of the Board, 1/95 - 1/96.

OTHER KEYWORDS:

seminar developer, seminar courseware writer, user documentation writer, training course documentation writer, seminar instructor, course instructor, training instructor, seminar trainer, online content editor, online content manager, online content writer, internet content editor, internet content manager, internet content writer, internet recruiting trainer, internet recruiting consultant, marketing collateral writer, print collateral writer, javascript, html, Microsoft Office 2000: word, excel, powerpoint, outlook, project, access; visio, sourcesafe; photoshop, pagemaker, quarkxpress, filemaker pro, infogist, copernic, adobe acrobat, eudora, ulead, quickbooks pro

E-Portfolios

What is the difference between Web HTML CVs and e-portfolios? E-portfolios are so similar to link-loaded Web CVs that many people say there's little difference. Kimeldorf, a noted champion of the CV portfolio, separates the two by describing the Web CV as a work of words and the e-portfolio as a work of pictures.

In times gone by, only artists and other creative professionals who needed to show their work carried big leather cases filled with work samples to job interviews. Now the leather-bound portfolio has been reincarnated as a CV portfolio that goes to interviews and employee evaluation meetings. Professionals share their portfolios online. Institutions of higher education everywhere have grown enthusiastic about the portfolio concept as a job-hunting tool to give employers a big picture of who their students are.

Your e-portfolio should include, at minimum, a copy of your CV; your skills and abilities; samples of your own work; testimonials and letters of recommendations; awards and honours; conferences and workshops; transcripts, degrees, licences, and certifications; military records, awards, and badges; and three to five references.

You may want to check out some Web sites that feature portfolio information. Once classic example is the Kimeldorf Portfolio Library (`amby.com/kimeldorf/portfolio`).

Beamers

Dateline: CV of the Future Department . . . A *beamer* – or beamable CV – is a quick version of your CV read on a *personal digital assistant* (PDA) or wireless handheld device or digital phone. Your handheld electronic device broadcasts your contact information, qualifications, and experience in a format suitable for a small screen.

Cutting-edge recruiting professionals say that millions of these CVs will silently travel through the airwaves of future conferences, business meetings, and power lunches. Most of the technology already exists, but some standardisation issues are yet to be resolved. The potential for the design and delivery of the beamer CV may be enormous. "Beam me up" takes on whole new shades of meaning.

E-newsletters

In Chapter 4 we saw how Jack Chapman uses Special Reports to attract attention to knowledge or skills in an appealing way. E-newsletters are simply the same approach using the Web as a (virtually free) publishing medium for networking. The appeal for others is that you are sharing your expertise, the attraction for you is that this establishes just how good you are.

Knowledge of all things intergalactic isn't a prerequisite to qualify you to send out an e-newsletter as a networking tool for job leads, but knowing what you're talking about is essential.

Fred Pike and Tom Tucker have experimented with e-newsletters (e-mailed to recipients) with encouraging results. Their discovery: The trick is to give something in return for the assistance you hope to get. That something is *information.*

Fred Pike's online newsletter

Pike's four-page communication – *Fred Pike's News from the Job Search Front –* is presented in a layout swimming in white space for easy reading. Small graphics brighten the newsletter throughout, complimenting the editorial content, which offers original philosophical and business-oriented essays.

In an early issue, Pike discussed the topic of "Differentiation" as a marketing tool, explaining how it could help your business succeed. Following the essay, Pike concludes with a brief job pitch, which he light-heartedly calls "My Shameless Plug," and the graphic is, yes, an electric plug.

After selling a successful business several years ago, Pike now wants back in the game. He explains in "My Shameless Plug" the type of managerial position he's looking for, and he then closes with a polite and warm request for job leads: "If you know any companies where I could be a good fit, or any people I should contact as part of my ongoing networking, please let me know!"

A reader's overall impression is not one of being pressured, but of an opportunity to lend a networking hand to a charming and very knowledgeable job searcher. At press time, Pike was considering two offers.

Tom Tucker's online newsletter

Tips from Tom Tucker opens with a crowd pleaser – a photo of Tucker's classic 1967 Corvette. Tucker's gift to the reader is a collection of important tips for maintaining old cars and aeroplanes, Tucker's hobby for 25 years.

Sample tip: "Change the engine oil if the car has been in storage for any length of time. Why? (a) Allowing the bearings to set in dirty oil will cause problems later and (b) To insure there is no moisture in the oil so that your engine won't rust internally."

Tucker's newsletter has an engaging feel to it, and quickly after launching, an old school pal who runs a trucking company saw the newsletter and asked Tucker to take a contract stint as his trucking company's safety director until Tucker lands a permanent executive position.

Smart card

A *smart card* is a piece of plastic embracing a microchip capable of storing data, as well as a microprocessor to pass it on to a computer network. The essential smart card is a thirtysomething in the world of technology. Since the 1970s, the smart card been used for a multitude of purposes – from campus meal plans to security key systems to banking debit cards.

Technically, CVs can be adapted to smart cards and swiped through smart card readers to be downloaded into a system. The hitch is that smart card readers are relatively scarce and standardisation issues stand in the way. Another concern: Losing your smart card CV is a privacy loss as great as losing your wallet. The smart card as a CV platform is definitely a wait-and-see.

Talkers

Surprisingly it was we Brits, rather than our more talkative Trans-Atlantic cousins, who started the talking streak to transform the CV into a multimedia version with voice and video. Known more formally as the talking CV, there isn't much difference between the talking CV software model and the video online job interview that I describe in *Job Interviews For Dummies* (Wiley).

After the talking CV (or interview) is completed, you, the owner of the chatty document, give out a private ID and password to recruiters whom you want to view and listen. You can see illustrations of talking CVs at `www.talkingcv.com`.

This format could take off as broadband online service (high-speed Internet) becomes more widely available.

Flash

Reflecting the ultimate in animated movement and rock-concert audio, this CV product is made possible by Flash software. You never know what theme you'll find on a Flash CV, from space-age motifs to Spiderman to video games.

The Flash CV package may include additional elements, such as a photo (a big no-no in the recruitment world because of possible discrimination) and cover letter. The Flash model isn't for bankers or accountants, but it could net you a job as a Web or club designer.

Creative specialists at video game companies, theme park workplaces, advertising agencies, graphics studios, or virtually any enterprise requiring inventive thinking could find a flash of excitement to be just what the bored recruiter ordered.

Type **Flash CVs** into your favourite search engine for examples and companies that provide the service.

Part V
Samples of StandOut CVs

"A pop-up C.V. — how very original."

In this part . . .

You find CV examples that have been carefully crafted so you can be inspired by different ways to handle your own StandOut effort. Your CV is your marketing spokesperson. So give it your best.

Chapter 17

A Sampling of StandOut CVs

*P*repare to meet the graduates of StandOut boot camp, from entry- to management-level job seekers. Real people wrote the originals of these CVs, but we tore them up and rewrote them to meet StandOut standards. All names and contact information are fictional, but the raw selling power behind every one is real.

Although StandOut formats (illustrated by the templates in Chapter 9) are loaded with selling-power, they're by no means rigid – not every section heading works for every CV. Choose your section headings carefully to flaunt your strengths.

In the interest of not chopping trees, we chopped material – that is, some CVs in this chapter would have been two pages had we not eliminated text. Occasionally, as another conservation measure, we used ampersands (&) to replace the word *and*. Should you use ampersands on your own CV? Yes, but very gingerly. Ampersands are okay for

✔ Company names

✔ Copyrights

✔ Logos

✔ Phrases common in the targeted industry, such as "P & L Statements" (Profit & Loss)

Otherwise, spell out the word *and*.

This chapter gives you a selection of StandOut model CVs.

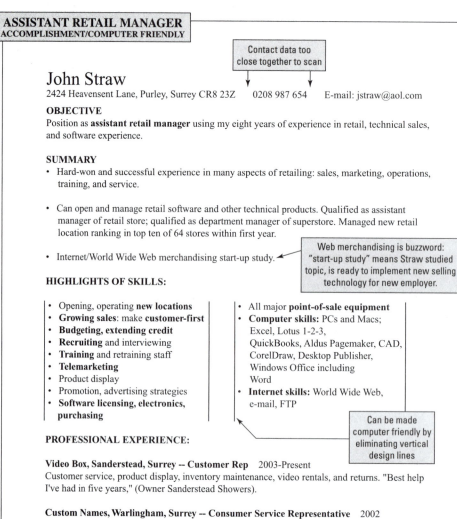

ASSISTANT RETAIL MANAGER
ACCOMPLISHMENT/COMPUTER FRIENDLY

> Contact data too
> close together to scan

John Straw

2424 Heavensent Lane, Purley, Surrey CR8 23Z   0208 987 654   E-mail: jstraw@aol.com

OBJECTIVE

Position as **assistant retail manager** using my eight years of experience in retail, technical sales, and software experience.

SUMMARY

• Hard-won and successful experience in many aspects of retailing: sales, marketing, operations, training, and service.

• Can open and manage retail software and other technical products. Qualified as assistant manager of retail store; qualified as department manager of superstore. Managed new retail location ranking in top ten of 64 stores within first year.

• Internet/World Wide Web merchandising start-up study.

> Web merchandising is buzzword:
> "start-up study" means Straw studied
> topic, is ready to implement new selling
> technology for new employer.

HIGHLIGHTS OF SKILLS:

• Opening, operating **new locations**
• **Growing sales**: make **customer-first**
• **Budgeting, extending credit**
• **Recruiting** and interviewing
• **Training** and retraining staff
• **Telemarketing**
• Product display
• Promotion, advertising strategies
• **Software licensing, electronics, purchasing**

• All major **point-of-sale equipment**
• **Computer skills:** PCs and Macs; Excel, Lotus 1-2-3, QuickBooks, Aldus Pagemaker, CAD, CorelDraw, Desktop Publisher, Windows Office including Word
• **Internet skills:** World Wide Web, e-mail, FTP

> Can be made
> computer friendly by
> eliminating vertical
> design lines

PROFESSIONAL EXPERIENCE:

Video Box, Sanderstead, Surrey -- Customer Rep   2003-Present
Customer service, product display, inventory maintenance, video rentals, and returns. "Best help I've had in five years," (Owner Sanderstead Showers).

Custom Names, Warlingham, Surrey -- Consumer Service Representative   2002
Extensive retail sales and technical support for software, computer equipment, satellite TV, electronics, and home theatre equipment. Maintained average monthly sales of £20,000, ranking fourth in sales. Heavy telemarketing component.

The Cutting Edge, Whyteleafe, Surrey -- Assistant Manager   2000-2002
Serviced upscale clientele in high-end software, electronics, and video game shop. Handled sales, purchasing, staff training, work schedules, product inventory and display, technical support for electronics and software, bank deposits, and staff management.

(1 of 2)

John Straw

Software Bug, South Croydon -- Night Manager   1997-2000
Evening management of software retailer. Innovative sales strategies brought shop from 47th in sales ranking to 8th in a 64-store chain. Other work: employee recruiting and dismissal, training, retraining, scheduling, staff management, technical support. Awarded Employee of Month four separate months.

Temp-a-Medic, West Croydon -- Healthcare Staffer   1996-1997
Matched healthcare temps with hospitals in Croydon and surrounding areas. Developed organisational skills, calm resilience when chaos threatened, and acceptance of high-pressure, detail-reliant environment. Sold new accounts at seven hospitals.

EDUCATION
Two-thirds of the way through an Open University Bachelor of Arts degree; expect degree ◄
June 2004.

VOLUNTEER AND PERSONAL EXPERIENCE

– Coach, Warlingham Warlocks Water Polo team. Team drawn from across Surrey of more than 30 youths, ages 7-12. Grateful for opportunity to develop strong interpersonal, cross-generational, cross-cultural, and community networks. Proven talent with teamwork, organisation, people of various economic classes.

– Interests include computers, electronics, water polo, swimming, computer drafting, and freehand illustration.

> Straw's goal is completion of college degree. To indicate intent to enroll for more than 3-6 hours per semester while working in retail, noted for long hours, would be risky.

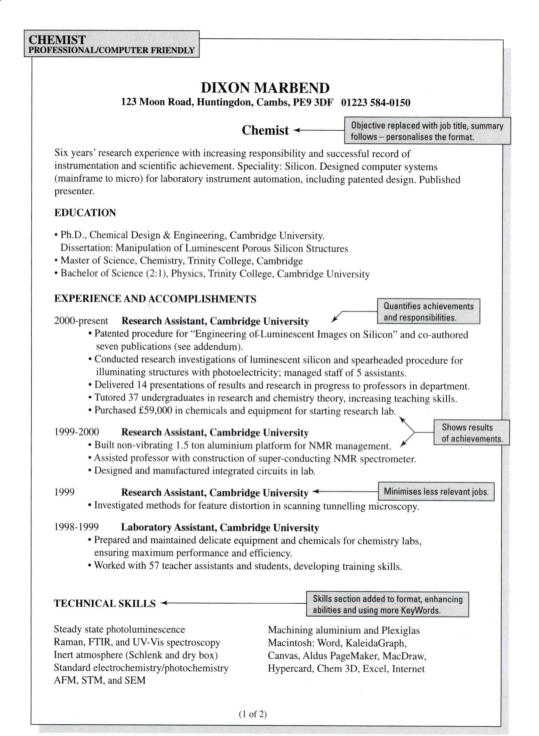

CHEMIST
PROFESSIONAL/COMPUTER FRIENDLY

DIXON MARBEND
123 Moon Road, Huntingdon, Cambs, PE9 3DF   01223 584-0150

Chemist ◄

> Objective replaced with job title, summary follows – personalises the format.

Six years' research experience with increasing responsibility and successful record of instrumentation and scientific achievement. Speciality: Silicon. Designed computer systems (mainframe to micro) for laboratory instrument automation, including patented design. Published presenter.

EDUCATION

- Ph.D., Chemical Design & Engineering, Cambridge University.
  Dissertation: Manipulation of Luminescent Porous Silicon Structures
- Master of Science, Chemistry, Trinity College, Cambridge
- Bachelor of Science (2:1), Physics, Trinity College, Cambridge University

EXPERIENCE AND ACCOMPLISHMENTS

> Quantifies achievements and responsibilities.

2000-present   **Research Assistant, Cambridge University**
- Patented procedure for "Engineering of Luminescent Images on Silicon" and co-authored seven publications (see addendum).
- Conducted research investigations of luminescent silicon and spearheaded procedure for illuminating structures with photoelectricity; managed staff of 5 assistants.
- Delivered 14 presentations of results and research in progress to professors in department.
- Tutored 37 undergraduates in research and chemistry theory, increasing teaching skills.
- Purchased £59,000 in chemicals and equipment for starting research lab.

1999-2000   **Research Assistant, Cambridge University**
- Built non-vibrating 1.5 ton aluminium platform for NMR management.
- Assisted professor with construction of super-conducting NMR spectrometer.
- Designed and manufactured integrated circuits in lab.

> Shows results of achievements.

1999   **Research Assistant, Cambridge University** ◄
- Investigated methods for feature distortion in scanning tunnelling microscopy.

> Minimises less relevant jobs.

1998-1999   **Laboratory Assistant, Cambridge University**
- Prepared and maintained delicate equipment and chemicals for chemistry labs, ensuring maximum performance and efficiency.
- Worked with 57 teacher assistants and students, developing training skills.

TECHNICAL SKILLS ◄

> Skills section added to format, enhancing abilities and using more KeyWords.

Steady state photoluminescence
Raman, FTIR, and UV-Vis spectroscopy
Inert atmosphere (Schlenk and dry box)
Standard electrochemistry/photochemistry
AFM, STM, and SEM

Machining aluminium and Plexiglas
Macintosh: Word, KaleidaGraph,
Canvas, Aldus PageMaker, MacDraw,
Hypercard, Chem 3D, Excel, Internet

(1 of 2)

DIXON MARBEND
01223 584-0150

PUBLICATIONS

"Engineering of Luminescent Images on Silicon." Marbend, Patent No. 1,234,567; Jan 1, 2003

"Silicon Technology." Saynor and Marbend in *2003 Cambridge University Press Yearbook of Science Technology*; C.U.P. 2003, 123-4

"Optical Cavities in Silicon Film." Saynor, Curbin, and Marbend in *Electrochemic Journal*, 2003, 21

"Emission from Etched Silicon." Marbend and Piner in *Material Research Symposium,* 2002, 12, 3456-7

"Colour Image Generation on Silicon." Marbend and Saynor in *Chemical Science*, 2002, 123, 4567-8

"Porous Silicon Micro-Dension." Marbend and Saynor in *Physics Applied*, 2002, 45, 678-9

"Stoichiometric Cadmium Electrodeposition." Krass and Marbend, *MaterialChem*, 2001, 1, 23

HONOURS, MEMBERSHIPS & PRESENTATIONS

Chemical Symposium Research Fellow, Undergraduate Honours Fellows, Winter Research Fellow

Chemical Symposium, Chemical Alliance, Electrochemistry Association

Marbend, Saynor and Curbin. *Emission from Etched Silicon.* Presented at 123rd Chemical Symposium, Oxford, January 2003

Marbend. *Porous Silicon Micro-Dension.* Presented at 234th Chemical Alliance, London, January 2003

New scanning software reads italics; old ones do not. Marbend telephones RezReader to determine scanning software. When old programs are used, Marbend substitutes a second version of his CV, replacing italics with quotes around same typeface used in rest of CV.

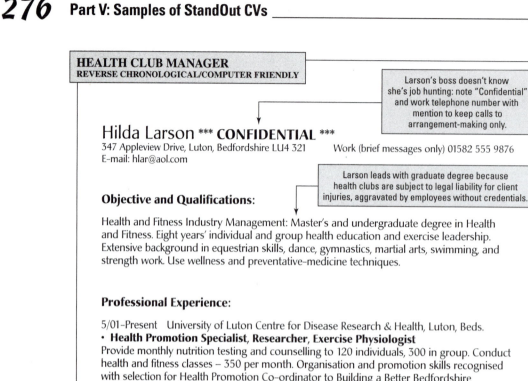

HEALTH CLUB MANAGER
REVERSE CHRONOLOGICAL/COMPUTER FRIENDLY

> Larson's boss doesn't know she's job hunting: note "Confidential" and work telephone number with mention to keep calls to arrangement-making only.

Hilda Larson *** CONFIDENTIAL ***

347 Appleview Drive, Luton, Bedfordshire LU4 321   Work (brief messages only) 01582 555 9876
E-mail: hlar@aol.com

> Larson leads with graduate degree because health clubs are subject to legal liability for client injuries, aggravated by employees without credentials.

Objective and Qualifications:

Health and Fitness Industry Management: Master's and undergraduate degree in Health and Fitness. Eight years' individual and group health education and exercise leadership. Extensive background in equestrian skills, dance, gymnastics, martial arts, swimming, and strength work. Use wellness and preventative-medicine techniques.

Professional Experience:

5/01–Present   University of Luton Centre for Disease Research & Health, Luton, Beds.
• **Health Promotion Specialist, Researcher, Exercise Physiologist**
Provide monthly nutrition testing and counselling to 120 individuals, 300 in group. Conduct health and fitness classes – 350 per month. Organisation and promotion skills recognised with selection for Health Promotion Co-ordinator to Building a Better Bedfordshire Programme.

10/99–5/01   Wheaton College Health and Fitness, Wheaton, Beds
• **Instructor and Program Consultant**
Produced bimonthly newsletter, wellness counselling, and campus-wide publicity, leading to 25% membership increase in health and fitness club in 3 months.

11/99–5/01   Fitness Plus Enterprises, Luton, Beds
• **Personal Fitness Trainer, Group Exercise Instructor**
Taught group exercise classes and designed personal fitness programs for 550 individual clients. Popular trainer among special groups (disabled and elderly).

5/99–7/99   Aerobics Activity Centre, Luton, Beds
• **Assistant to the Associate Director**
Designed activity program, teaching, lecturing, and performing market research.

9/98–5/99   University of Luton, Beds
• **Graduate Teaching Fellow**
Designed and taught. Advised 24 independent study projects for undergraduate students. Wrote two proposals to Health/Fitness Department Chair, initiating development of new graduate instruction program, resulting in a £3,000 grant.

(1 of 2)

Hilda Larson   01582 555 9876

Education:

It's okay to list the education section on the 2nd page because Larson refers to it in the Qualifications section.

Master of Health Science, University of Luton, 2000
Bachelor of Science, **Honours**, Kinesiology, University of Luton, 1996
Guest Scholar, Physical Education Professional Division, University of Luton, Winter and Spring 1999

Certifications:

2003   RSA Exercise to Music Certification
2001   British Amateur Body Building Association certificate
2000   Central YMCA Personal Trainer qualification

Presentations:

- Building a Better Bedfordshire Programme, Summer 2003
- Sport Cardiologists and Nutritionist National Conference, Spring 2000
- Buen Salud Annual Gathering, Madrid, Spain, Spring 2000
- University of Luton Individual Fitness Design, Autumn 1999

Conferences:

- World Fitness IDEA International Conference, Olympia, London, 2003
- IDEA Personal Trainer's Conference, Luton, Beds, 2003
- Better Bedford Wellness Conference, Bedford, Beds, 1999

Awards and Honours:

- Academic Honours, University of Luton, 1993 and 1994
- Cross Cultural Awareness Award – CRE/Better Bedford, 1984
- Prize for Dance and Gymnastics, University of Luton, 1984

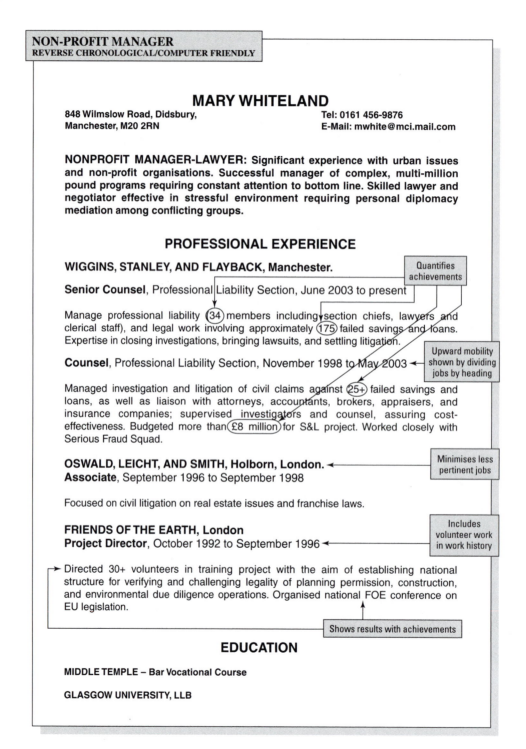

NON-PROFIT MANAGER
REVERSE CHRONOLOGICAL/COMPUTER FRIENDLY

MARY WHITELAND

848 Wilmslow Road, Didsbury,
Manchester, M20 2RN

Tel: 0161 456-9876
E-Mail: mwhite@mci.mail.com

NONPROFIT MANAGER-LAWYER: Significant experience with urban issues and non-profit organisations. Successful manager of complex, multi-million pound programs requiring constant attention to bottom line. Skilled lawyer and negotiator effective in stressful environment requiring personal diplomacy mediation among conflicting groups.

PROFESSIONAL EXPERIENCE

WIGGINS, STANLEY, AND FLAYBACK, Manchester.

Quantifies achievements

Senior Counsel, Professional Liability Section, June 2003 to present

Manage professional liability (34 members including section chiefs, lawyers and clerical staff), and legal work involving approximately (175) failed savings and loans. Expertise in closing investigations, bringing lawsuits, and settling litigation.

Upward mobility shown by dividing jobs by heading

Counsel, Professional Liability Section, November 1998 to May 2003

Managed investigation and litigation of civil claims against (25+) failed savings and loans, as well as liaison with attorneys, accountants, brokers, appraisers, and insurance companies; supervised investigators and counsel, assuring cost-effectiveness. Budgeted more than (£8 million) for S&L project. Worked closely with Serious Fraud Squad.

OSWALD, LEICHT, AND SMITH, Holborn, London.
Associate, September 1996 to September 1998

Minimises less pertinent jobs

Focused on civil litigation on real estate issues and franchise laws.

FRIENDS OF THE EARTH, London
Project Director, October 1992 to September 1996

Includes volunteer work in work history

Directed 30+ volunteers in training project with the aim of establishing national structure for verifying and challenging legality of planning permission, construction, and environmental due diligence operations. Organised national FOE conference on EU legislation.

Shows results with achievements

EDUCATION

MIDDLE TEMPLE – Bar Vocational Course

GLASGOW UNIVERSITY, LLB

SPEECH-LANGUAGE PATHOLOGIST
PROFESSIONAL & TARGETED/COMPUTER FRIENDLY

Brian N. Hawes

123 Northumbridge Avenue, Newcastle-upon-Tyne NE1 7RU
Tel: (0191) 456-7891 • Email bhaw@aol.com

Speech-Language Pathologist

> Replaces objective with job title

EDUCATION

1996 to 1998, and 2000   **Durham University**
   Ph.D., 1993; dissertation pending
   Minor: Audio/Visual Media

1994 to 1995   **Durham University**
   Master of Science in Speech-Language Pathology
   Wrote and produced radio and television commercials and promotional videos

1985 to 1989, and 1995   **Sunderland University**
   Upper Second (2:1) Bachelor of Arts in Language
   Out-placement work experience serving as multimedia laboratory
   Assistant, student government representative, and club president

> Shows extracurricular achievements

> Skips summary – saved for cover letter

PROFESSIONAL EXPERIENCE AND ACCOMPLISHMENTS

1997 to Present   **Radius Vox Laboratories, Newcastle**   **Director**

Firm delivers computer and video imaging and audio signal analysis (voice spectrography). Marketing targets hundreds of physicians and healthcare providers treating laryngeal, craniofacial, dental, and neurologic disorders.

> Describes prestigious employer

1996 to 1997   **Durham University**   **Lecturer, Researcher**

Restructured research laboratory, adding new facilities for voice analysis, videoendoscopy, and biofeedback. Employed sound spectrography, stroboscopy, photography, and electrophysiologic measurement techniques. Lectured to 233 linguists on articulation and voice disorders analysis. Supervised Orofacial Clinic (staff of 37), developed familiarity with fiberoptic endoscopy, videofluoroscopy, and nasometry.

> Quantifies advancements

1995 to 1997   **The Sound & Sight Centre, South Shields**   **Speech-Language Pathologist**

Provided assessment and therapy to over 3,000 patients (neurologic, orofacial, vocal, and pediatric). Designed medical forms and computer-based therapy, decreasing procedure time by 30%. Co-ordinated patient referral plans with local medical centres.

> Shows industry knowledge

OTHER SKILLS AND CERTIFICATIONS

Computer: Windows (latest version), numerous applications, Microsoft certified, AI (Prolog), SAS, and SPSS.
Specialised Certifications: American Speech Association, International Association of Forensic Phonetics, Association of Phonetic Sciences, Zertifikat Deutsch, Goethe Institute Summer Abroad Fellowship, and Lake Search and Rescue Team. Licensed Tennessee Speech-Language Pathologist, FCC Radiotelephone Operator's Permit.

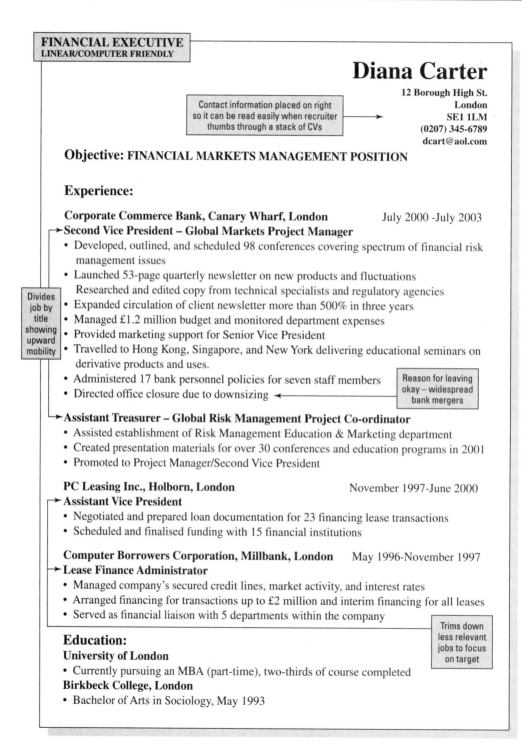

FINANCIAL EXECUTIVE
LINEAR/COMPUTER FRIENDLY

Diana Carter

12 Borough High St.
London
SE1 1LM
(0207) 345-6789
dcart@aol.com

Contact information placed on right
so it can be read easily when recruiter
thumbs through a stack of CVs

Objective: FINANCIAL MARKETS MANAGEMENT POSITION

Experience:

Corporate Commerce Bank, Canary Wharf, London   July 2000 -July 2003
Second Vice President – Global Markets Project Manager
- Developed, outlined, and scheduled 98 conferences covering spectrum of financial risk management issues
- Launched 53-page quarterly newsletter on new products and fluctuations Researched and edited copy from technical specialists and regulatory agencies
- Expanded circulation of client newsletter more than 500% in three years
- Managed £1.2 million budget and monitored department expenses
- Provided marketing support for Senior Vice President
- Travelled to Hong Kong, Singapore, and New York delivering educational seminars on derivative products and uses.
- Administered 17 bank personnel policies for seven staff members
- Directed office closure due to downsizing

Divides job by title showing upward mobility

Reason for leaving okay – widespread bank mergers

Assistant Treasurer – Global Risk Management Project Co-ordinator
- Assisted establishment of Risk Management Education & Marketing department
- Created presentation materials for over 30 conferences and education programs in 2001
- Promoted to Project Manager/Second Vice President

PC Leasing Inc., Holborn, London   November 1997-June 2000
Assistant Vice President
- Negotiated and prepared loan documentation for 23 financing lease transactions
- Scheduled and finalised funding with 15 financial institutions

Computer Borrowers Corporation, Millbank, London   May 1996-November 1997
Lease Finance Administrator
- Managed company's secured credit lines, market activity, and interest rates
- Arranged financing for transactions up to £2 million and interim financing for all leases
- Served as financial liaison with 5 departments within the company

Trims down less relevant jobs to focus on target

Education:
University of London
- Currently pursuing an MBA (part-time), two-thirds of course completed
Birkbeck College, London
- Bachelor of Arts in Sociology, May 1993

NUCLEAR ENGINEER
REVERSE CHRONOLOGICAL

Technical jargon – or keywords – used
throughout so this is also a keyword CV.

Anthony Barbosa

Graceland Avenue
Leiston, Suffolk
01728 456 7890 Home
0777 321 4567 Mobile
atbarbosa@earthlink.net

CONFIDENTIAL CV

Entire CV stresses accomplishment,
impressive striving to demonstrate skill

EXPERIENCE

2003-Present   Giant Power & Light Co.
Reactor Operator, Sizewell C

- Chosen by management to attend Reactor Operator Qualification course

- Passed the National NVQ Exam with a score of 93%

2001-2003 Giant Power & Light Co.
Auxiliary Operator Nuclear, Sizewell C

- Member of operations unit which upgraded the Sizewell C Reactor from a forced shutdown condition on
  the Site Inspectors watch list to both NRC SALP-1 and INPO-1 ratings, company dual unit record
  breaking performance, and established world records for BWR single and dual unit continuous
  operations.

- Operated reactor, turbine, and auxiliary support systems to support the safe, reliable, economical, and
  environmentally sound production of power.

- Selected by operations management as one of three operators for extended assignments as Radwaste
  Control Operator, to pursue system, operational, and programmatic upgrades. Received awards for
  results produced in this area.

- Developed several computer programs to assist the operations unit with managing operator exposure and
  error free performance.

2001-2002 Giant Power & Light Co.
Radiological Engineer, Sizewell C

- Developed a remote valve decontamination device that saved the power company in excess of £450,000
  of critical path time during its first use.

- Performed a hydrogen water chemistry impact study to determine the impact of increased injection
  hydrogen rates on site exposure.

- Designed the containment and developed procedures used for the recovery of a damaged Americium-
  Beryllium neutron calibration source

Divides tenure at single employer into segments
by job and level reflecting advancement

Anthony Barbosa
Page 2

This is a running head on CV.

CONFIDENTIAL CV

1998-2000
Nuclear Associates   Various sites
Health Physics Supervisor/Lead Technician

- Windwhale Nuclear Generating Station, Suffolk (BWR)

- Paired with GE on full system decon (fuel installed) testing for EPRI

- Hinkley Fort, Somerset OH (PWR)

1997-1998
Careful Waste Management, Ltd   Hartlepool
Field Chemist

- Supervised packaging and shipping of hazardous materials

- OSHA 40-HR Hazmat trained

- On-call emergency supervisor/safety officer for field ops

1989-1997
Royal Navy   Faslane, Scotland
Engineering Watch Supervisor/Lead Engineering Lab Tech

- Managed 13-man engineering watch section in port/underway for Trident sub

- Supervised chemistry and radiological control department

- Article 108 rad con monitor

- Navy prototype staff instructor

EDUCATION

2003 Suffolk University
Master of Science in Nuclear Engineering

1999 University of East Anglia
Bachelor of Arts, Political Studies

INTERESTS

- Competitive offshore sailing, computers, bicycling, backpacking, scuba diving.

Personal interests convey image of competitiveness, technology priority, and healthy activities.

BUSINESS SPECIALIST
REVERSE CHRONOLOGICAL/PLAIN TEXT

This one-page CV is shown for technique; in real life, elaborate on skills, name software, explain skills claims. Back up your brags. Remember digital CVs can be longer than paper CVs.

Skills summary at top, skills summary at end: just what computers feed on.

```
ALBERTO LAFUENTE
12 Keats Close
Bristol BS99 7AU
0117 704-2694
e-mail: alf@newbiz.com
www.newbiz.com

NEW BUSINESS SPECIALIST
>>>>>>>>>>>>>>>>>>>>>>>>>>>>>>>>>>>>>>>>>>>>>>>>>>>>>>>>>>>>>>>>>

Client relationship management. Client planning. Product development.
Marketing materials. Capitalisation. Venture funding. Start-up
specialist.

EXPERIENCE

Sawyer Enterprises, Inc.  Bristol
Director of Marketing
2003 - present
Founding principal in this health-product corporation. Produced 300%
revenue increase in second year of operation from six-figure base.
Travelling for up to 75% of my time, including distributor contact
and training, site demos, trade shows.
• Sourced medical and technical services.
• Wrote company marketing plans.
• Served on executive team
• Brought in company's largest contract, £875,000.
• Bid with procurement contracts from government; 45% success

Contintentwide Bank            Bristol
New Business Account Executive
2001-2003
Responsible for soliciting large corporate accounts and loans;
enlarged base by £2.8 million. Hired and trained associates.

EDUCATION

Bristol University
Bachelor of Arts, History
2001
Continuing Education:
Marketing, Sales, Finance, Accounting
2002 - Present

HARD SKILLS
PC programs: word processing, spreadsheets (accounting and analysis).
Heavy Internet research skills. Technology savvy.

SOFT SKILLS
Communications: technical information to technical and non-technical
managers. Bilingual(English and Spanish).
```

INFORMATION TECHNOLOGY
REVERSE CHRONOLOGICAL/PLAIN TEXT

```
GEORGIA ESTRADA
107 Begonia Terrace
Reading, Berks RG6 7LT
Pager: 0617-999-0808
Email: gestrada@badgermail.com
```

Giving mobile phone number is a good idea: adds immediacy to contact.

```
JOB OBJECTIVE
++++++++++++++++++++++++++++++++++++++++++++++++++++++++++++++++
MICROSOFT WINDOWS OR NETWORK PROTOCOL DEVELOPMENT


SKILLS
++++++++++++++++++++++++++++++++++++++++++++++++++++++++++++++++
C, C++, CGI, CScript, DOS, HTML, HTTP, Java, Javascript, MFC, SQL,
SSI+, TCP/IP, UNIX, Lotus, Visual Basic, Visual C++, WebDBC,
Windows XP Professional, .NET Enterprise Server


EMPLOYMENT
++++++++++++++++++++++++++++++++++++++++++++++++++++++++++++++++
Clarion Systems                                      2005-Present
PROGRAMMER
Develop, maintain, and monitor product-building tools and
processes using Visual C++ and MFC on Win NT. Began as work
experience placement; promoted to regular status job.


Wonderwheels, Ltd.                                09/2004-01/2005
JUNIOR SOFTWARE ENGINEER
Work Placement: Team member responsible for design and development
of Windows XE real-time manufacturing application. Implement code
to improve application's performance. Enhance GUI features, assist
in test, and troubleshoot application.


RHI Labs, Ltd.                                    05/2004-08/2005
APPLICATION PROGRAMMER
Co-op job: Designed and developed two project tracking programs,
using MS SQL, Javascript, and HTML. Member of team to maintain,
enhance, and create NTSQL server applications. Tested programs,
gathered user requirements, and created help documentation and
released applications.


Thames Valley University Computer Sci. Dept.         2002-2006
PROGRAMMING ASSISTANT/TEACHING ASSISTANT
Assisted undergraduate students in C & C++ programming. Provided
technical support and acted as lab assistant. Projects: Java Poker
Game, War Gamescore, Inventory Database Manager, Assembler, and
Linker.


EDUCATION
++++++++++++++++++++++++++++++++++++++++++++++++++++++++++++++++
Thames Valley University
Reading
BACHELOR OF ARTS COMPUTER SCIENCE - May 2005
Attended on 4-year partial scholarship with work placement
```

Chapter 18

A Sampling of Special Needs CVs

*H*aving to fight to advance your career isn't unusual – neither are the employment war wounds on your CV. Many people looking for work have a few special issues that should be stamped "handle with care".

New graduates and women re-entering the job market need jobs but lack extensive paid experience. Career changers, including ex-military personnel, face the challenge of transferring skills and learning entire new job languages. Seasoned aces may have "too much" experience and must defend themselves against being labelled overqualified. People who have gaps in their records, who were demoted down the power chain, or who were exposed to too many temporary jobs must manage their CVs to sell skills rather than experience.

The following model CV samples generally match the templates in Chapter 9. In some instances, the sample section headings may not match the templates exactly. The templates contain the whole range of heading options, so you can pick and choose the best way to market your unique needs and interests.

GAP IN HISTORY
TARGETED

Paula G. Cramer

27 Redwing Ave.
Shepherd's Bush, London, W12, 0208 123-4567

OBJECTIVE: KELLEY-KENNEDY PRINTING COMPANY PRODUCTION MANAGER
to use 12 plus years of print production management experience and graphic arts knowledge

QUALIFICATIONS SUMMARY
• Handle all print project phases from design through prepress to final
• Budget management – competent, careful
• Education (college degree plus seminars) in management backs up experience-based skills

SKILLS SUMMARY

Desktop Publishing	Staff Management
Colour Separation Technology	Vendor Contract Negotiations
WP Suite, Lotus 123, MS Office XP, QuarkXPress,	Purchasing
PageMaker, Internet, All Word-Processing Software	Blueline Approvals

ACCOMPLISHMENTS AND EXPERIENCE

> Good treatment of two gaps – the first one was nearly three years, the other was six months. You have to read carefully to find the gaps because they are buried in the copy.

Lewisburg Marketing, Acton
PRODUCTION MANAGER AND PRINT BUYER (Direct Mail):
Managed direct mail print production from design development through mail date for 40+
concurrent projects, meeting deadlines for 2.5 million per week, 12/96-3/00
> • Directed prepress, design review, proofing, blueline approval, layout, print and
>   finishing schedules. Insured compliance with Royal Mail requirements.
> • Purchased for all job components and effectively managed £5 million annual budget;
>   set pricing and contracts for copywriters, designers, and printer negotiations.

The Maupin Company, Hammersmith
PRODUCTION COORDINATOR AND PLANNER
Planned and executed print production needs for clients, co-ordinated efforts of Account Executive,
Designers, and Production Staff, 4/95-6/96
> • Managed estimates, purchasing, job production layout, and projects submission to graphic
>   design, camera and stripping, providing proof-reading, scheduling, and blueline approvals,
>   working closely with press room manager to meet delivery deadlines.

PRIOR EXPERIENCE

Investment Litho Company, Hammersmith
GENERAL ASSISTANT
Worked part-time throughout college. Learned printing business from master printers, 6/88-6/92

EDUCATION   Goldsmiths College, London- B.A. in Business and Marketing, 1991
                 Open University 12 seminars, management

STUDENT
HYBRID

This resume puts all contact data on the same line although general scanning rules call for separate lines; newer systems will read one line, but put a minimum of six spaces between address, telephone, and e-mail.

Alexander Davidson

36 Old Church Road, Enfield, EN2 6FJ, Middlesex 0208 435-5555
E-Mail: alexd.ddd@mddx.ac.uk

Hard-sell language omits Chinese proficiency and is designed to counteract employer's potential assumption that Davidson (in UK as a student) will return to Asian nation. Otherwise, bilingualism should appear in objective.

Objective   Career-related summer position in Electrical Engineering;

Education   **Middlesex University**, White Hart Lane, London N17
Degree: Masters of Science in Electrical Engineering: December 2005
Degree: Bachelor of Science in Electrical Engineering
Honours Degree (BSc Hons)   Graduation: May 2004

Software Skills

MathCAD, MathLab, Pspice, Microcap, Fortran, Altera Logic Design System, programming M68HC11 microcontroller using Assembly language, C Language and other software utilities (word processing, spreadsheets).

Relevant Courses

Includes keywords in skills and courses section

- Systems, Signals and Noise
- Data Communications
- Fibre Optics Communciation
- Digital Image Processing

- Random Signal Theory 1 and 2
- Transform Theory and Application
- Digital Spectral Analysis
- Communication Network Design

Work Experience

Autumn 2000-present   **Tutoring Lab Supervisor**   Middlesex University
- Tutor students in Engineering, Mathematics, and Science courses

Summers 2000-2004   **Assistant Engineer**   Rilerad Projects Engineering, Hong Kong
- Collected data from engineers, produced progress report
- Assisted bidding team, preparing documents and breakdown quotations

March 1995-June 2000   **Administrator**   National Service Hong Kong Armed Forces
- Scheduled military training and vocational upgrading courses
- Improved mobilisation system to increase Reserve Corps processing rate during mobilisation exercise

Activities   Vice President, Institute of Electrical and Electronic Engineers (IEEE), student chapter
Secretary of National Society of Professional Engineers (NSPE), student chapter
Society of Physics Students
Intercultural Club

Fluent in Japanese

This is not a StandOut CV. Where are the achievements? How could this CV be kicked up a couple of notches?

REANNA DUMON

123 Tottenham Court Road, London, W1J 2HP
0207 456-7891
E-mail: rdumo@aol.com

Qualifications Highlights:

Seeking **physical therapist position** using eight years' physical therapy and nursing experience in Switzerland, UK, and Canada. Fluent in French, English, and Spanish. Trauma life-support, ECG, paediatrics, obstetrics, emergency and general nursing, internal medicine.

> Includes KeyWords in summary.

Education:

- Laval University, Quebec, Canada, Physical Therapy Certificate, 2003-2005
- Ste-Foy College, Ste-Foy, Quebec, Canada, D.E.C. in Technical Nursing (equivalent to Registered Nurse in UK), 1992-1995
- Garneau College, Ste-Foy, Quebec, Canada, D.E.C. in Physical Therapy, 1988-1990

Experience:

Royal London Hospital, 2000-20XX
Designed 25-page physical therapy clinic manual distributed to injured patients regarding methods of therapy and preventative procedures to eliminate further injury.
- Nurse: Clinical work: physical therapy, paediatric, obstetrical, and long-term follow-ups, child vaccination, laboratory procedures, home visiting, physical exams, medical evacuations, multidisciplinary case discussions.
  Community Health: school vaccination programs.
  Administration: patient transfers, medical visits, arranging meetings.

> Includes KeyWords in job descriptions.

Ungava Hospital, Nunavik, Canada, 1998-2000
- Co-ordinated physical therapy schedule and program for 16 patients.
- Paediatrics, obstetrics, general medicine nurse. Monitored staff of 30 paediatric nurses; managed 57 patients.
- Co-ordinated schedule for 37 nurses in general medicine unit, maximising hospital efficiency in patient care and personal organisational skills.

> Gives results.

Canntonnal Hospital of Fribourg, Fribourg, Switzerland, 1997-1998
- Nurse, Department of Internal Medicine. Managed 26 patients, 8 with PT needs.
- Trained 11 interns on internal medicine procedures, enhancing leadership, management, and interpersonal skills to implement teamwork ideal of hospital.

Bassee-Nord Health Centre, Quebec, Canada, 1995-1997
- Performed daily physical therapy sessions with 13 paediatric patients.
- Head Nurse - emergency care, general medicine and paediatrics nurse.
- Promoted to Head nurse in emergency-care unit within first eight months.
- Supervised 23 nursing interns and co-ordinated medicine schedules for 35 patients.

> Because physical therapy, not nursing, is goal, Dumon leads with physical therapy experience, although nursing experience is dominant. Dumon moves in and out of the two professions —PT and nursing.

SEASONED ACE
ACCOMPLISHMENT

Angus Blane

42 Plains Road
Broughton
Edinburgh
EH0 42B
0131 555-6932
E-Mail: ablane@icscotland.com

Senior creative/marketing executive

Experienced in major account management, new product and strategic concept development, advertising and promotion; spearheaded revenue growth from £13 million to £120 million in 5 years.

Omits section headings for more direct impact.

- Increased another company from £30 million to sales price of £125 million
- Revitalised company by effecting £10 million sales increase

Effective leader skilled in building, training and motivating highly profitable creative teams, and directing major projects to completion on time with strong cost control. Track record of developing and maintaining corporate relationships.

Creative/Marketing Success Highlights

"Advertises" marketing achievements.

Marketing Theme	Client
TANNIK'S CAPITALIST TOOL	TANNIK'S MAGAZINE
CALL THEM WITH CLARITY	RTO TELEPHONES
FLY US	ABROAD AIRLINES
OIL NO MORE	OIL GLEANERS LTD
LET OUR MACHINES WORK, YOU THINK	MATTISON PRODUCTS
FEEL SENSITIVE	CRIMSON SKIN PRODUCTS
EVERY BIT CRYSTAL QUALITY	CRYSTAL DISKETTES
MOIST AND FLAVOURFUL FOOD	NEW-TASTE DOG FOOD

Awards

Clio, Scottish Institute of Graphic Arts, Rissoli Award, Best Read Ad-Rosser Reeves, Communications Arts Award, Outdoor Billboard Design Award, and Andy Award, International Film Festival Silver Medal, Venice Festival of Advertising nomination for billboard advertising

Can change to computer friendly by switching "Creative Marketing Success Highlights" with "Professional Experience". That's the order in which computers expect to find data. But for human viewing, current presentation is different and effective.

(1 of 2)

Angus Blane

Developed all TVS advertising for 2 years. Directed turn-around of Morning brand cereal division. Other creative assignments in advertising, direct marketing, and new product development launches for:

Generative Appliances	Lowlands Bottling Co.
International Athletics Association	New Foods
Single Malts Association	Crystal

Sells industry reputation before employment history.

Professional Experience

Vice President ,   Wilton Marketing & Communications, Edinburgh,
Creative Director   1996-Present

Vice President,   McConnell and McCarthy, Glasgow
Associate Creative Director 1993-1996

Vice President,   Mark Jenkins Advertising, Edinburgh
Associate Creative Director 1986-1993

Angus Blane shows he's a pro by using advertising skills on his CV – in this model, Blane makes a virtue of open white space, citing only a few standout achievements.

(2 of 2)

SEASONED ACE
ACCOMPLISHMENT

Dana Brigham
123 Teal Way, Streatham, London, SW16 A87
e-mail: dbrigham@infonet.com Tel: 0208 123 6789

> Different typeface than body for more attention.

Urban Planner: 15 years' experience in urban planning with substantial management experience in public and private sectors. Experienced in preparing and managing general plan revisions, zoning code administration, redevelopment plans, environmental projects.

Qualifications and Accomplishments:

- Planner for Ken Livingstone's Congestion Charge project.

- Managed new housing developments on the riverfront of Bermondsey, including environmental analysis of plans' impacts and successfully contesting a court challenge.

> Gives results.

- Supervised land use and transport connections around the Dome for over four years, preparing staff reports to public bodies and private shareholders.

- Supervised 37 planners in public sector for Isle of Dogs.

> Brigham departs from template by combining qualifications and accomplishments.

- Assisted in establishing new residential area of Palm Docks.

- Directed task force in designing and implementing new green space and environmental standards for Palm Docks, developing builder sensitivity to community goals.

- Organised Hillside Development Panel for 1995 Central London Planning Association

- Managed preparation of New Docklands Plan; co-ordinated with 56 planners, presented to large groups.

Employment:
DEPARTMENT OF PLANNING, LONDON ASSEMBLY 2003-Present
Special Projects Planner, Planning and Community Development Department.

> Maximises white space.

LOCKEN AND CO., Bermondsey, London, 2000-2003
Director of Planning Department.

PALM DOCK DEVELOPMENT CORPORATION , Palm Dock, London, 1996-2000
Senior Project Manager, Planning and Research Section.

ISLE OF DOGS PLANNING DEPARTMENT, London, 1994-1996
Senior project manager of preparing environmental impact reports.

WOLHBAHN & SONS, Canary Wharf, London, 1992-1994
Senior Planning Consultant providing advisory services to local municipalities.

WESTMINSTER COUNCIL, 1988-1992
Supervising Associate Planner, Zoning Division, Planning Department.

Education:
Bachelor of Arts, Political Science, Brunel University, Bristol, 1987
Master of Science, Public Administration, Birkbeck College, London, 1990

Professional Affiliations:
British Planning Association, British Institute of Certified Planners

SEASONED ACE
ACCOMPLISHMENT

ANDREW WALLACE
P.O. BOX 123 CROYDON, SURREY, CR9 A12
0208. 456.1997
awall@aol.com

**Human Resource position using recruitment, appraisal,
and benefit skills accumulated over 10 years**

Older human resource
pro wishes to re-enter
private sector after
government stint; limits
work history to 10 years.

QUALIFICATIONS:

→ Directed human resource systems for two mid-sized corporations
→ Worked inside Equal Opportunities Commission structure; bullet-proof employee
   management
→ Expert in recruiting, benefits, evaluations, training, and outplacement
→ Use computer – or manual – applicant/employee tracking systems
→ Can manage contingent workforce

ACCOMPLISHMENTS:

→ Investigated and negotiated resolutions of 400 allegations of employment discrimination. Led
   investigation teams and instructed on negotiation procedures to maximise resolution success.

→ Performed EOC consultation, trained more than 60 employer and university organisations in
   human resource skills to establish increasingly effective management-staff working
   relationship.

→ Received 12 annual merit-based promotions; managed staff of 15 recruiters.

RECENT PROFESSIONAL EXPERIENCE:

→ 11/01 to 12/04 – **Employment Opportunities Commission,** London
→ 9/00 to 6/04 – **ACAS,** London – Chief Negotiator
→ 11/00 to 11/01 – **Swanky Interiors,** Notting Hill, London – Human Resources Director
→ 6/94 to 9/00 – **Lucrative Corporation,** Leadenhall, London – Human Resources Manager

EDUCATION:

→ **London University** – Master of Sciences, Human Resource Administration
→ **Mariner College** – Bachelor of Arts, Management of Human Resources
→ **DeMontfort College of Law** – Continuing coursework towards Doctorate

PROFESSIONAL ASSOCIATIONS:

→ Institute of Personnel Management
→ Society for Human Resource Management
→ CBI Training & Development Symposium
→ Kiwanis International

NEW GRADUATE
REVERSE CHRONOLOGICAL & TARGETED/COMPUTER FRIENDLY

DALE JOHNSON
12 Harpingdon Way, Hounslow, TW3 9PT
0208 567-8910   E-mail: dalej@nnn.gov

Objective: PARLIAMENTARY LOBBYIST
DOCTORATE INTERNATIONAL LEGAL STUDIES
Oxford University, 20XX

MASTER OF ARTS, POLITICAL SCIENCE
Brasenose College, Oxford, 20XX
Concentration in Government Planning & International Negotiation
Teaching Assistant in International Negotiation

BACHELOR OF ARTS, POLITICS AND SOCIOLOGY
University of Portsmouth, 20XX

> Johnson's research on the target showed they wanted an energetic, young person with his degrees. Objective and education centered for formal look and to highlight degrees that employer favours.

Bar Admission: Passed entrance examinations. Admissions pending.

WORK EXPERIENCE

> Summary omitted: saved for cover letter.

2002-2005   **Department of Trade and Industry**
Assisted in analysing Upper and Lower House bills. Reconstructed 25 legislative provisions that complicated international trade obligations. Corresponded with corporations, trade associations, EU agencies. Developed working dexterity with international negotiations.

2001   **CBI**
Assisted lawyers in drawing up Guidelines for Fair Advertising.
Worked in conjunction with ASA and DTI. Accumulated strong background in advertising ethics proceedings.

2000 **Charles Swabb**
Assisted 19 account executives in management activities, including investor research, telemarketing, mass mailings, computerised clerical operations, and communications. Tremendous experience with inter-company and public communications.

1997-2000 **Reese, Riley & Thorne**
Assisted library staff and lawyers with all library functions, including organisation and research. Modernised 14 computers. Compiled legal information for 32 lawsuits from cases and articles, acquiring early experience with legal negotiations.

MISCELLANEOUS

• Proficient with all applications, including LEXIS/NEXIS/WESTLAW databases.
• Hobbies include dinghy racing and golf.

> Personal interest included; Johnson's research shows target company's RezReaders value interest in sports.

NEW GRADUATE
LINEAR

Herman Ling

123 Northrop Avenue, Staines, TW18 6NA
0208 566-6789   E-Mail: hling@jkuafu.co.uk

Objective Marketing position in Agribusiness or Chemicals

Qualifications Focus: Plant pathology. MBA/Master's in Plant Pathology/Undergraduate degree in agriculture. Two years' international marketing experience. Bilingual – Chinese and English. Computer literate.

Communications
Skills
- Computer: MS Word, Excel, PowerPoint, WordPerfect, Lotus 123, Freelance, Harvard Graphics, PSI-Plot, SAS JUMP, QBasic programming, and main frame
- Language: Chinese (Mandarin and several dialects)

> Gives details on bilingual and computer claims in summary.

Experience

8/01-7/04 Graduate Research Assistant
University of Cambridge, Department of Plant Pathology
- Designed and implemented experiments in greenhouse, growth chamber, and field
- Developed weather-based advisory for improving control of plant disease with reduced fungicide

7/99-8/01 Account Manager, Department of Marketing and Sales
Detect Bio-Pharmacy Group, Beijing, People's Republic of China
- Developed channel strategies for entering Chinese marketplace
- Managed and developed sales accounts
- Developed promotion plan for marketing new medicine
- Participated in joint venture for manufacturing ingredients

> Prior experience in China. This experience is for UK job for a job in China, would emphasise Chinese connections.

9/96-6/99 Social Co-ordinator, Department Student Association
Co-editor, Department Student Journal
Beijing Agricultural University, Beijing, People's Republic of China

Education
Master of Business Administration, 2001
University of Milton Keynes

Master of Science, Plant Pathology 2000
University of Cambridge

Bachelor of Science, Plant Protection, 1999
Beijing Agricultural University, Beijing, People's Republic of China

Publications
Ling, Herman, Grant, P., and Milton, F. 2000 "Effects of precipitation and temperature on garden crop infection". *Plant Disease.*

Ling, Herman, and Kilkenny, E. 2000 "Comparison of weather-dependent crops based on soil concentration". *Plant Disease.*

Activities
British Phytopathological Society

> Despite advanced degrees, placed experience first to show market orientation.

RE-ENTRY HOMEMAKER
REVERSE CHRONOLOGICAL

Faith Marks
167 Wordsworth Road
Cricklewood
0208 779-1434, E-mail: fmarks@cts.com

> Space between text and line.

Objective
Social Studies Teacher
Teaching is my life. Comfortable with computers, communicate on a daily basis and research via e-mail and the Internet. Computer focus promises that children taught will not be left behind in a competitive era.

> Objective mixed with summary: concentration on e-mail & Internet shows stay-at-home is up-to-date.

Education
Bachelor of Science in Secondary Education
Goldsmiths College 2002

Qualified Teacher Status (QTS), Goldsmiths College
Economics, Geography, and World History

Teaching Experience

> Fast-learning, willingness to put self-interest aside for team good.

Substitute Teacher, Townville Elementary School   Autumn 2002
- Became expert at instant lesson plan preparation. Never refused last-minute assignments
- Worked with diverse student groups, expanding range of teaching capabilities. Not intimidated by challenge of middle-school behavioural problems
- Used considerable experience with children, ages five - twelve. Created exciting and motivational lesson plans.

Student Teacher, Townville Middle School, 10 weeks   Spring 2002
                    Grant Middle School, 6 weeks
- Taught History, Geography, and Government; developed multi-faceted daily lesson plans for each course
- Perfected computer fluency. Strengthened supervisory roles, delegation ability, organisational skills, and motivational techniques. Worked full-time while parenting
- Instructed extracurricular activities, including softball and computer club

Additional Experience
Advised graduate students, worked as student financial aid liaison. Analysed student financial information and matched to available funding.

SEASONED ACE
LINEAR

Stephen Ralston
77 Ridge Road, Coventry, West Midlands
Tel: 024 555-9876 E-mail: sralst@aol.com

> Alternative heading
> for Objective.

Profile: Property Management professional seeks to use high-quality history in supervisory position. More than 15 years' solid experience A to Z in property management.

> Ampersand okay –
> familiar phrase.

Qualifications :
- Skilled in profit & loss, reductions, distribution, and financial administration
- Restructure marketing plans strategically, advancing returns in excess of 20%
- Record of enthusiastic achievement of corporate objectives
- Managed multi-family properties in Birmingham, Coventry, and Wolverhampton

> Quantifies
> achievements.

Education and Training:
- **Bachelor of Arts in Education,** University of Wolverhampton
- **College of Certified Property Managers,** Apartment Management, Real Estate Finances and Management

> Keywords
> throughout.

Professional Certifications:
- Certified Apartment Property Supervisor
- Wolverhampton Real Estate License

> White space and
> bullets improve
> readability.

Professional Experience:

2000-Present **Senior Asset Manager** Greengrove Point Properties

- Manage marketing and operations programs for over 2,000 units
- Recruit, train, and hire over 100 employees, maximising $2M in capital improvements
- Consult on fair housing issues, minimising legal consultation costs by $2,000

> Quantifies and
> gives results of
> achievements.

1999-2000 **Regional Manager** Builder Companies of Birmingham

- Facilitated marketing programs for 10-12 properties throughout Birmingham
- Superintended successful lease-up and operation of 23-story luxury hi-rise property in Coventry
- Directed $2 million renovation of 125 year old property on outskirts of Solihull

1997-1999 **District Manager** Birmingham Property Management

- Created marketing and operations programs for two properties in West Midlands
- Facilitated $2 million renovation with lease-up three months ahead of schedule
- Maintained 98% occupancy in New Construction lease

> Ampersand okay –
> company name.

1992-1997 **Area Manager** Benedict, Young, Dalton, & McMillan

Assistant Manager on 1672 unit property in Birmingham area.
- Led company nationally for two years in leasing, averaging over 120 new leases per month
- Portfolio consisted of 2,000 units and over 100 employees
- Directed monthly regional sales meetings, initiated energy savings program that accomplished $150,000 work done to 14 properties, with profit exceeding $12,000

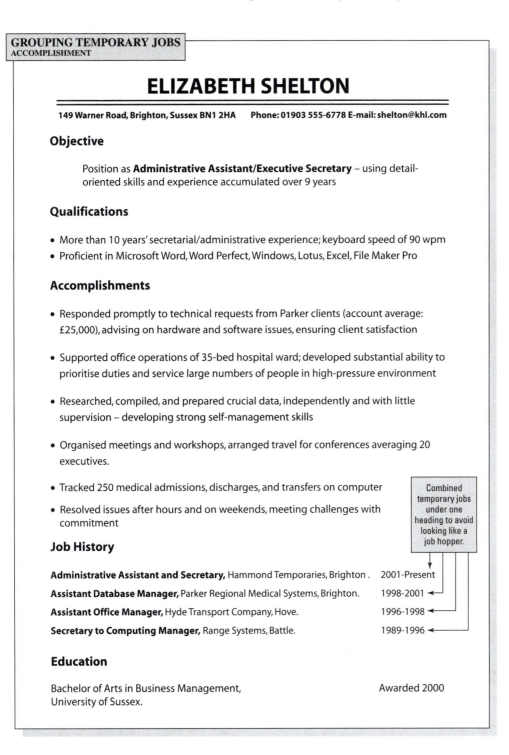

GROUPING TEMPORARY JOBS
ACCOMPLISHMENT

ELIZABETH SHELTON

149 Warner Road, Brighton, Sussex BN1 2HA   Phone: 01903 555-6778 E-mail: shelton@khl.com

Objective

Position as **Administrative Assistant/Executive Secretary** – using detail-oriented skills and experience accumulated over 9 years

Qualifications

- More than 10 years' secretarial/administrative experience; keyboard speed of 90 wpm
- Proficient in Microsoft Word, Word Perfect, Windows, Lotus, Excel, File Maker Pro

Accomplishments

- Responded promptly to technical requests from Parker clients (account average: £25,000), advising on hardware and software issues, ensuring client satisfaction

- Supported office operations of 35-bed hospital ward; developed substantial ability to prioritise duties and service large numbers of people in high-pressure environment

- Researched, compiled, and prepared crucial data, independently and with little supervision – developing strong self-management skills

- Organised meetings and workshops, arranged travel for conferences averaging 20 executives.

- Tracked 250 medical admissions, discharges, and transfers on computer

- Resolved issues after hours and on weekends, meeting challenges with commitment

Combined temporary jobs under one heading to avoid looking like a job hopper.

Job History

Administrative Assistant and Secretary, Hammond Temporaries, Brighton .   2001-Present

Assistant Database Manager, Parker Regional Medical Systems, Brighton.   1998-2001

Assistant Office Manager, Hyde Transport Company, Hove.   1996-1998

Secretary to Computing Manager, Range Systems, Battle.   1989-1996

Education

Bachelor of Arts in Business Management,   Awarded 2000
University of Sussex.

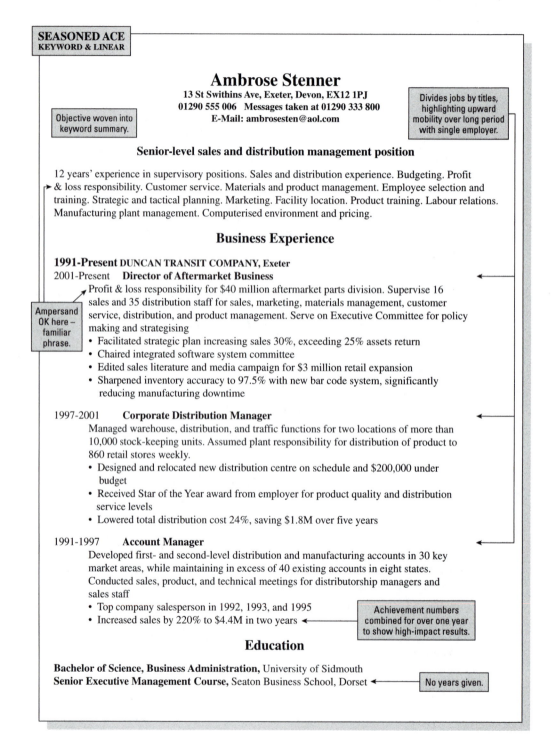

SEASONED ACE
KEYWORD & LINEAR

Ambrose Stenner

13 St Swithins Ave, Exeter, Devon, EX12 1PJ
01290 555 006   Messages taken at 01290 333 800
E-Mail: ambrosesten@aol.com

Objective woven into keyword summary.

Divides jobs by titles, highlighting upward mobility over long period with single employer.

Senior-level sales and distribution management position

12 years' experience in supervisory positions. Sales and distribution experience. Budgeting. Profit & loss responsibility. Customer service. Materials and product management. Employee selection and training. Strategic and tactical planning. Marketing. Facility location. Product training. Labour relations. Manufacturing plant management. Computerised environment and pricing.

Business Experience

1991-Present DUNCAN TRANSIT COMPANY, Exeter
2001-Present   **Director of Aftermarket Business**

Ampersand OK here – familiar phrase.

Profit & loss responsibility for $40 million aftermarket parts division. Supervise 16 sales and 35 distribution staff for sales, marketing, materials management, customer service, distribution, and product management. Serve on Executive Committee for policy making and strategising
- Facilitated strategic plan increasing sales 30%, exceeding 25% assets return
- Chaired integrated software system committee
- Edited sales literature and media campaign for $3 million retail expansion
- Sharpened inventory accuracy to 97.5% with new bar code system, significantly reducing manufacturing downtime

1997-2001   **Corporate Distribution Manager**
Managed warehouse, distribution, and traffic functions for two locations of more than 10,000 stock-keeping units. Assumed plant responsibility for distribution of product to 860 retail stores weekly.
- Designed and relocated new distribution centre on schedule and $200,000 under budget
- Received Star of the Year award from employer for product quality and distribution service levels
- Lowered total distribution cost 24%, saving $1.8M over five years

1991-1997   **Account Manager**
Developed first- and second-level distribution and manufacturing accounts in 30 key market areas, while maintaining in excess of 40 existing accounts in eight states. Conducted sales, product, and technical meetings for distributorship managers and sales staff
- Top company salesperson in 1992, 1993, and 1995
- Increased sales by 220% to $4.4M in two years

Achievement numbers combined for over one year to show high-impact results.

Education

Bachelor of Science, Business Administration, University of Sidmouth
Senior Executive Management Course, Seaton Business School, Dorset

No years given.

Part VI
The Part of Tens

"Being a pretty boy, being able to peel grapes, a good talker with flying experience would have made the perfect cabin steward but it would have saved us <u>both</u> a lot of time if you'd sent in a photograph, Mr Joseph."

In this part . . .

You see why the famous *For Dummies* Part of Tens is treasured for putting information quickly and simply on your table. Find out what really ticks off recruiters, simple ways to upgrade your CVs, how to back up your claims, and how to choose a professional CV writer (not that you'll need one). Plus, you get a detailed checklist you can use to score your own StandOut CVs.

Chapter 19

Ten (x3) Ways to Prove Your Claims

. . . .

In This Chapter

▶ Ten number statements to prove your accomplishments

▶ Ten percentage statements to document your claims

▶ Ten pound sterling statements to back your results

. . . .

So you have excellent communications skills, or you're a good networker, or you can make a computer slam dance with ease. At least, that's what you assert. How can we (potential employers) believe you?

Employers are more likely to believe your claims of skills and accomplishments when you back them up with specifics. A good start on backing up your statements is *quantifying* them with numbers, percentages, pounds, and pennies.

Decide for yourself. Compare the following statements labelled A with the statements labelled B. Which is the strongest, most attention grabbing, most convincing?

> A. Easy Ways to Be More Popular
>
> B. 50 Easy Ways to Be More Popular
>
> A. Towels on Sale
>
> B. Towels 40% Off
>
> A. Designed internal company insurance plan to replace outside plan at great savings.
>
> B. Designed £30 million self-insured health plan, saving estimated £5 million per year over previous external plan.

Obviously, the B statements win hands down! The take-home message is *quantify, quantify, quantify*. Look at the following statements in the three categories of numbers, percentages, and pounds. Fill in the blanks as an exercise to remind yourself to quantify your accomplishments and results.

Say It with Numbers

1. _____ (#) years of extensive experience in _____ and _____.

2. Won _____(#) awards for _____ _____.

3. Trained/Supervised _____ (#) full-time and _____(#) part-time employees.

4. Recommended by _____ _____ (a number of notable people) as a _____(something good that they said about you) for excellent _____(an accomplishment or skill).

5. Supervised a staff of _____ (#).

6. Recruited _____ (#) staff members in _____(period of time), increasing overall production.

7. Sold _____ (# of products) in _____ (period of time), ranking _____ (1st, 2nd, 3rd) in sales in a company of _____ (#) employees.

8. Exceeded goals in _____ (#) years/months/days, establishing my employer as _____ (number — 1st, 2nd, 3rd) in industry.

9. Missed only _____ (#) days of work out of _____ (#) total.

10. Assisted _____ (#) (executives, supervisors, technical directors, others).

Say It with Percentages

1. Excellent_____(your top proficiency) skills, which resulted in ____ (%) increase/decrease in _____ (sales, revenues, profits, clients, expenses, costs, charges).

2. Recognised as a leader in company, using strong skills to effect a/an ____ (%) increase in team/coworker production.

3. Streamlined _____ (industry procedure), decreasing hours spent on task by ____ (%).

4. Used extensive _____ (several skills) to increase customer/ member base by ____ (%).

5. Financed __ (%) of tuition/education/own business.

6. Graduated within the top ____ (%) of class.

7. Responsible for an estimated __ (%) of employer's success in _____ (functional area/market).

8. Resolved customer relations issues, increasing customer satisfaction by ____ (%).

9. Eliminated _____ (an industry problem), increasing productivity by ____ (%).

10. Upgraded _____ (an industry tool), resulting in ____ (%) increase in effectiveness.

Say It with Sterling – Counting Pounds and Pennies

1. Supervised entire _____ (a department) staff, decreasing middle-management costs by ____ (£).

2. Purchased computer upgrade for office, saving the company ____ (£) in paid hours.

3. Eliminated the need for _____ (one or several positions in company), decreasing payroll by __ (£).

4. Averaged ____ (£) in sales per month.

5. Collected ____ (£) in memberships and donations.

6. Supervised the opening/construction of new location, completing task at ____ (£) under projected budget.

7. Designed entire _____ programme, which earned ____ (£) in company revenues.

8. Implemented new _____ system, saving ____ (£) daily/weekly /monthly/annually.

9. Reduced cost of _____ (substantial service) by developing and implementing a new _____ system at the bargain price of ____ (£).

10. Restructured _____ (organisation/system/product) to result in a savings of ____ (£).

Chapter 20

Ten Pet Peeves of Recruiters

Check out what recruiters say when they think no "civilians" (job seekers) are reading. Both third party (independent) recruiters and inside corporate recruiters share their thoughts freely on various Internet forums.

Here are ten categories of transgressions that various e-recruiters cite as making them grumpy. Some categories contain comments from different recruiters. We report them anonymously to protect their privacy. My comments conclude each category.

CV-Free Pitches

I bristle at applicants who e-mail me a general question, "Do you have any technical positions open?" instead of a CV.

Comment: Spare yourself a non-answer for a non-CV. Attach a CV to your question.

Major Mismatches

I find it extremely annoying when people send CVs without reading our job posting. If we advertise for a pizza chef, a bike mechanic is just as likely to self-nominate himself for the job, leaving us to figure it out. We don't have time for goose chasing.

Our management positions require a background in a certain industry plus experience. We get responses from people with one year of experience and no management background. We get CVs that claim their experience is ideal or that they read the position and found it to fit their skills exactly, when in reality they have none of the experience detailed in the job posting.

We advertised for a telecommunications consultant with call centre experience and received a CV of someone with experience in movie production and no experience in anything we look for. I am sure applicants would have a more positive outcome if they applied for positions that are relevant to their experience, although I doubt this will ever change.

Comment: Some job seekers, particularly in technical fields, operate on the lottery theory and scatter CVs everywhere. A number of job seekers adhere to the 80 percent strategy (if you fit 80 percent of the job's requirements, give it a go) or believe that if you can manage one thing, you can manage anything.

Others seek ways to apply viable transferable skills to new environments and, failing to make a strong enough case, are rejected because some recruiters are too inexperienced, overworked, or insular to recognise the legitimacy of transitioning skills.

Still other job seekers just don't get it and waste everyone's time in applying for jobs for which they're dramatically unqualified.

E-Stalking

One applicant e-mailed his CV and a few days later sent another, saying he was waiting for a response. I replied that we would contact him if we were interested. A few days later, and once a week for a few months, he sent e-mails that only said, "Still waiting." Creepy.

I would like to tell job seekers to send only one CV. If someone is "open" to all appropriate positions, just say so!

Comment: Checking back periodically works best if you send new information of interest to the recruiter. You may scan and send a relevant news article with a brief "In case you missed this" note, adding that you continue to look forward to the right timing for an interview.

Saying that you're available for any appropriate position carries the risk that you'll be seen as too much of a generalist and expert at nothing, or you'll be seen as desperate. If you do it, define the field – "appropriate in the accounting field" or "appropriate in the retail financial field", for example.

Censor before sending your complaint

This is the true story of what can happen when you give into feelings of stress, frustration, irritation, and anger – and call then it like you see it. The following is an actual e-mail letter to a major defence contractor that employs tens of thousands of people:

To Whom It May Concern:

In response to the job openings posted at your Web site, I have applied for numerous jobs (probably over 100 different positions) by sending my CV to you along with e-mails during the last 4 to 5 weeks. I am extremely disappointed by the way my online job applications have been handled by [company name withheld].

If this is common practice in your company, sooner or later, people will find out how irresponsible and unprofessional you are and as a result, you will lose a lot of talented people.

Please take this matter very seriously. I think that your CEO or COO should know what's going on within the company. Sincerely, [job seeker's name withheld].

The recruiter who handled the complaint replies:

"This person was interviewed at a job fair and told that if he qualified for any positions, we would notify him. He then submitted 111 actual CVs for more than 40 different career positions. I have never met anyone who could qualify for that many positions. This individual doesn't get it. We now have removed him from all job searches in our company."

Staffing and technical systems consultant Jim Lemke says that stuffing the recruitment box with your CVs may become moot:

"Many of the major applicant tracking system vendors have released software that companies can use to require answers to online screening questions before permitting job seekers to attach a CV.

"If the questions are answered correctly (according to the company's standards), the recruiter or hiring manager is notified by e-mail that a new qualified CV is available for review. If the applicant doesn't pass the litmus test for qualification, the applicant's CV stays in the company's database and is searched on for future openings.

"This online screening technology does not stop the persistent applicant from sending additional CVs or e-mail or making phone calls. The trick is not to become a pest," Lemke explains.

For a more detailed explanation of the online screening process, head to Chapter 1.

Caps and Taps and Typos

My sore spot is receiving e-mails with no use of capitalisation whatsoever, or with some words mysteriously capitalised and those that should be (proper names, beginning of a sentence) are not capitalised.

For heaven's sake, use a spell checker. A neat CV will always be my preference over one that is not.

Comment: Every single book or article on CV writing I've ever seen recommends impeccable work. It would be a crying shame to put together a StandOut, well-researched CV only to have it discarded because of misspellings and typos throughout the text.

Too Much Information

I give bad marks to people who think that sending their CV multiple times will increase their chance of getting a call for an interview. It won't.

I dislike it when the applicant puts several addresses in the "To" e-mail box and mass mails the CV. This unprofessional shortcut looks like no care is taken in applying to each individual position.

Comment: Another practice to avoid is sending a hard copy of your e-mailed CV by post. Carry hard copies to an interview, but don't mail or fax an additional copy because doing so is unnecessary. Not only is it disrespectful to mass mail your CV addressed to multiple names, but it's no-one's business but your own where you're applying for work.

Date Grate

What annoys me is when job seekers send CVs and don't specify start and end dates for jobs. As if this won't be at the top of my list to ask in an interview and a reference check – if they get to the interview process at all.

Two old dodges don't fly with me: (1) Trying to hide a CV gap by listing employment dates at the end of the summaries rather than in the left-hand margin and (2) substituting the number of years at a company for the real dates.

Comment: Reporters are taught to put the most important facts at the lead of a story. Using the same theory of first things first, you would list your experience in this order: title of position, name and location of employer, and dates of employment.

Dates of employment don't have to be placed in the left margin. The right margin is perfectly acceptable and even preferred by some CV experts.

Guess Who

It's a pain when I get incomplete CVs and cover letters without contact information. We have offices in several countries and a hotmail.com address doesn't suffice.

A pet peeve of mine is receiving CVs without the current employer listed – "confidential" CVs. I can understand this treatment for Web job site postings but when sending a CV to a specific employer, the current employer should be identified.

Comment: As for the first comment, you can add to the "hotmail.com" (or other free mailbox established for a job search) a post office box and a dedicated telephone answering machine. That combination protects your privacy, but make it easy for a recruiter to contact you.

As for the second comment, you can use a generic description of your current position and skills, noting that you'll reveal the current employer's name in a job interview. We urge caution in fully revealing your identity and personal workplace information on the Internet (see Chapter 2).

File Style

I can't imagine why, but some people have to be told to submit a CV as a normal attachment in a common program (Word, WordPerfect, Notepad, and so forth). I have received two-page Word documents as zip files! I have the software to handle zips, but many people do not.

Comment: Zip files are for documents the size of Derbyshire, not CVs. No one wants to bother unzipping.

Useless and Uninformative

I grow peevish when forced to read through fluff that does not relate to a workforce position. It doesn't matter to anyone in my office that you were the local beauty queen. It doesn't matter to anyone in my office when you are 35, out of college, and have held several jobs, that you attended a prestigious prep school. It doesn't matter to anyone in my office that your wife is the vice president of a well-known company.

Another thing that bugs me is the use of fancy graphics and poems on CVs.

Comment: Stick to information related to your ability to do the job for which you are applying. Your CV should be able to sing your praises without resorting to verse.

Probable Prevarication

I hate wasting my time on CVs from people who claim to have attended a school they never saw the inside of and to have worked for a company that they didn't.

Comment: Lying about a point of fact easily proved or disproved is riskier than ever in today's era of fact-checking background investigations (see Chapter 1).

Chapter 21

Ten Simple Ways to Improve Your CV

So you've finished your CV, and disappointment could etch lines across your brow. No way does your CV show what you've got. When you desperately need the jolt of a double espresso, your CV seems to have as much punch as milky tea.

Possibly your CV needs a factory recall, and you should start again from scratch. Or, with luck, you may be able to power it up with just a kiss of makeover secrets like those we describe in this chapter.

Use Bulleted Style for Easy Reading

As the accomplishment and linear formats in Chapter 9 show, the use of one- or two-liners opens up your CV with white space, making it more appealing to read. Professional advertising copywriters know that big blocks of text suffocate readers. Let your words breathe!

Discover Art of Lost Articles

Although using articles – *a, an,* and *the* – in your CV isn't *wrong,* try deleting them for a crisper and snappier end result. Recruiters and employers expect to read CVs in compact phrases, not fully developed sentences.

The first person *I* is another word that your CV doesn't need. Look at the following examples:

With Articles

I report to the plant manager of the largest manufacturer of silicone-based waxes and polishes.

I worked as the only administrative person on a large construction site.

Without Articles

Report to plant manager of largest manufacturer of silicone-based waxes and polishes.

Worked as only administrative person on large construction site.

Sell, Don't Tell

Forget sticking to the old naming-your-previous-responsibilities routine. Merely listing, "Responsible for XYZ" doesn't assure the recruiter that you met your responsibility or that the result of your efforts was worth the money someone paid you.

By contrast, read over your CV and make sure you have answered that pesky "So what?" question, which is lying in ambush for each bit of information you mention. Try to imagine what's running through a recruiter's mind when you relate that you were responsible for XYZ: *So what? Who cares? What's in it for me?* Anticipate those questions and answer them before a recruiter actually has a chance to ask them.

Frame your CV in results, not responsibilities. As famous salesman Elmer Wheeler said, "Sell the sizzle, not the steak". Here are some examples of how to do just that:

- ✔ Perform preventive maintenance on 14 machines on daily basis; reduced repair costs 8 percent over previous year.

- ✔ Monitor quality control, identify problems, find solutions; lab insurance rates, related to mistakes, lowered this year by 3 percent.

- ✔ Organise daily work distribution for effective teamwork of 12 lab workers; absorb and solve workload issues from previous shift.

The 5 Percenters

Recruiters are wild about snaring the cream of the crop. If you're in the top 5 percent of any significant group (graduation, sales, attendance record, performance ratings) make sure that fact appears prominently on your CV.

Verbs, Nouns, and Writing

Old wisdom: Use lots of action verbs to perk up reading interest in CVs (see StandOut Words in Chapter 11). Later wisdom: Cash in the action verbs for nouns, the keywords that ward off anonymity in sleeping CV databases. New wisdom: With the return of the handsome CV, fully formatted for online attachments, use both verbs and nouns.

Use the nouns to construct a keyword profile at the top of your CV (see Chapter 9). Use the action verbs in the body of your CV to liven up your achievements.

Just don't mix noun and verb phrases in the same CV section. The following example explains.

Highlights:

- Founded start-up, achieving positive cash flow and real profits in the first year. [verb]

- President of point-of-sale products. [noun]

- Proven ability for representation of high technology products. [noun]

- Consistently achieved highest profit in 45-year-old company history. [verb]

Change the noun statements to be consistent with the verb statements:

- Founded point-of-sale vending company, generating positive cash flow and real profits in the first year.

- Proved ability to represent high technology products.

Writing instructors call this agreeable notion *parallel construction*.

Strip Out Sad Stories

If your career history looks like the fall of the Roman Empire, don't try to explain a long stretch of disasters on a CV. Save your explanations for an interview. Make the CV as adversity-free as you legitimately can.

An exception is when you have suffered multiple layoffs or a company closing within a short period of time. You don't want recruiters to think you are a job hopper. Instead, add brief notes at the end of comments for each employer that cut short your tenure – (Company ceased operation.) (Company downsized 70%.) (Company moved manufacturing abroad.).

And never apologise on your CV for any weakness that you may observe in your professional self. Shortcomings don't belong on your CV. Eliminate any negative information on your CV that can dull a recruiter's interest in meeting with you.

Reach Out with Strength

Select the qualifications and past job activities that speak to the kind of job you want and the skills you want to use. Highlight these. If, for instance, you want to transition from military training to civilian training, remain riveted on your training skills without diluting your message by mentioning your ability to use several simple computer programs. If you've muddled your CV's message with minor skills or skills you no longer want to use, get rid of them. Stay on message.

Object to a Wimpy Objective

Imagine an actor striding onto a stage, stopping, then standing there like a log addressing the audience: "I came to find out what you can do for me".

Not exactly a curtain raiser – any more than beginning your CV with simply awful objective statements like: "Seeking a chance for advancement", or "where my skills will be utilised".

Trash the trite "To obtain a responsible (does someone want an irresponsible?) job with challenging and rewarding (does anyone want dull and unrewarding?) duties".

Be an editor! Draw a line through limp wording that leaves everyone wondering if you're a washout. Your statement can be simple, yet effective: "Management position in finance where more than 10 years' experience will strengthen the bottom line".

My Fair CV

Pick up the phone and call the HR department where you want to work and are about to submit your CV. Ask, "Before I send you my CV online, I want to get the facts. Do you accept MS Word attachments, store them as formatted documents, and route them to line managers as images?" If the answer is *yes*, wrap fish in that ugly ASCII plain text CV and throw it away, revelling in the fact that you'll get to send the attractive version of your CV. If the answer is *no,* well, good try in this era of transition. After all, ugly is still better than unreadable.

Ditch the Cat

If you've included references to your spouse, significant other, domestic partner, or even a family pet on your CV, free your CV from certain shunning by deleting them. These non-workplace references won't help a recruiter see how you're perfect for the job, and, in many cases, they work against you.

From the annals of recruiters' funniest CVs:

- A song-and-dance recital about how a man's wife and he are Manchester United fans and want to move closer to the city so that he can go to home games
- A medical history of how a man's spouse is wracked with headaches, backaches, and sinus congestion – although it doesn't affect his ability to give all of himself to the job
- A chatty background account by a woman who got a cat for her husband and considered it a good trade.

Chapter 22

Solutions to the Top Ten CV Problems

. . . .

In This Chapter

▶ Fixing the outward appearance of your CV

▶ Resurrecting a CV deadened with job duties

▶ Checking your CV for errors

▶ Tapping into professional skills

. . . .

Does your job search seem to be marching and marching and marching but never getting anywhere? Find a few quiet moments to look back over your CV to see if it's the problem. Maybe it is and maybe it isn't. In either case, you're too close to the issue to see where your self-marketing tool needs improvement. Use these lightly written but heavy-hitting possibilities to stay focused.

Smoothing Out Tattered Pages

Does your paper CV look as though it's been in someone's backpack on a rock band's road tour? Does it seem less than professional in appearance, with hand-written updates – or, heaven forbid, does it sport a coffee stain or ink smudge? Does your CV subliminally suggest that your work may be as careless as your paper introduction?

The solution: When your document starts to look like a fourth former's homework, go the whole nine yards and freshen it up completely: Experiment with a different typeface. Print it on bright-white paper. Use a little bold type or a bulleted format to call attention to your accomplishments. Break up paragraphs. Try a linear format (see Chapter 9). Wrap your CV in white space.

Letting Go of the Big Squeeze

Does your CV look like rush hour on the Tokyo metro with all your information squeezed onto one chock-full page? Does it seem as difficult to read as the small print on a dodgy landlord's contract? Does your CV help drum up trade for the local optician?

The solution: Forget what you learned in fifth form, that "all CVs should be limited to one page". By cramming everything onto one page, you probably leave out impressive achievements. The litmus test about what to include is to ask yourself, "Does this fact support my qualifications for the job I'm chasing? Will it help me get an interview?" If so, don't leave it on the cutting room floor.

Cleaning Up Musty, Dusty Buzzwords

Does your CV hark back to language of yesteryear – like "affirmative action plan", when today's buzzword is "diversity?" Does it mention that you are a "go-getter" rather than "action-oriented?" Does your CV speak of "paradigm" and "proactive" instead of "new principle" and "action motivated?"

The solution: Thumb through appropriate trade publications, newspapers, and general business magazines. Notice the words that describe experiences you want to put on your CV. If you're not sure what a business word means, try looking it up on Word Spy (`www.logophilia.com/wordspy`). Word Spy notes that some CVs are "buzzword-compliant", which means littered with jargon and buzzwords.

Making your CV buzzword-compliant is effective only when the phrasing is up-to-date. Contemporary jargon identifies you as being an insider, not an outsider. (Chapter 11 identifies some StandOut Words.)

Looking Too Old in a Youth Culture

Does your CV look as though the person it describes fought in the Boer war? Does it seem weary because 20 years later you're still showing your first job after graduation? Does your CV exhibit middle-aged creep because it's padded with irrelevant experiences that bear little relationship to the job you want?

The solution: Condense your background that's older than 10 to 15 years. Consolidate other irrelevant experience under an "Other Experience" heading.

Should you omit graduation years? Opinions vary. One school says revealing graduation dates is akin to prehistoric carbon dating, and, therefore, you should leave them off. Another school says that's "fool's-paradise thinking", meaning that leaving off dates red flags your age and makes recruiters assume you're an old crumbly – even older and "crumblier" than you really are. See Chapter 4 for more ideas on how to put a spring into your CV's step.

Seeming Excessively Vague

Does your CV obscure your qualifications? Does it cloud the clues to the kind of work you want to do? Does your CV go too far in trying to keep your options open and, as a result, suggest you're willing to take any kind of job?

The solution: Offer an objective or profile of qualifications that defines your area of expertise. Expecting a recruiter to sift through your CV hoping to discover whether your qualifications match a job's requirements is expecting too much. Chapter 10 says more on objectives and summaries.

Reorganising Slovenly Structure

Does your CV look way too complicated? Does it consume too much time to figure out? Does your CV wander all over the shop, forcing the reader to take a wild guess as to where your interests and abilities lie?

The solution: Improve the organisation of your CV. Even if you've had four jobs in four different career fields, search for a common theme – a focus. Once you find the theme, make sure that every item in your CV supports that theme. A lack of focus is one of the biggest blunders a job seeker can commit. Check out Chapter 12 for tips on focusing.

Including Missing Achievements

Does your CV read like your inner mountain climber never learned to yodel? Does it present a fleshless skeleton that puts a reader to sleep faster than Valium? Is your CV as dull as a page from a tax manual?

The solution: Stop talking responsibilities and start talking results. Measure your results – numbers, percentages, pounds, and pennies – that show how you successfully reached high points in your work efforts, how you made a difference at each company. (Use the worksheets in Chapter 19.) If you don't list your results with your job duties, the employer may miss the fact that you are the perfect candidate for the job. Use a measurement, make an impact.

Adding Essential Keywords

Does your CV seem just fine with lots of action verbs, but it consistently disappoints you by producing too few, if any, invitations to drop by for an interview? Perhaps the problem is a dearth of keywords.

The solution: Fill your CV with all the keywords that count toward the job you seek. Otherwise, your CV will remain sleeping in a database until Mars is colonised. For lots of help on keywords, turn to Chapter 11.

Checking for the Unrepentant Typo

Does your CV consistently come through with typos and grammatical mistakes? Does it look as though you forgot to proof-read it? Does your CV reflect the imperfect you?

The solution: Even the sharpest eyes miss mistakes (as we well know), so ask a friend to double-check your CV after you proof-read for errors in four steps:

1. **Check the punctuation, grammar, and spelling.**

   Using your computers spell- and grammar checker is a good start, but don't stop there. Spell- and grammar checkers won't find words that aren't there, ones inadvertently left out.

   A full stop often looks like a comma, a *he* like a *she,* and an extra space is often overlooked; a computer doesn't catch these types of errors. Furthermore, checkers approve spellings that represent the wrong word. *As far as the spell checker is concerned, for example,* a force to be reckoned with *and* a farce to be reckoned with *are both equally good.* You may not agree.

2. **Slow down.**

   Use a ruler to read the entire document aloud, line by line. Speed kills StandOut CVs.

3. **Read backward, from the bottom up.**

   Start at the lower right-hand corner, reading backward from the bottom to the top, word by word. You may be a little cross-eyed when you're finished, but because you're not reading for content, you're likely to spot word warts and other blemishes.

4. **Read for content.**

   Do one more read-through, this time for clarity. To illustrate how words can trip over themselves, have a smile at these signs from around the country:

   - **In a laundrette:** "Automatic washing machines. Please remove all your clothes when the light goes out".

   - **In a dry cleaner's:** "Anyone leaving their garments here for more than 30 days will be disposed of".

   - **In a conference room:** "For anyone who has children and doesn't know it, there is a day care centre on the first floor".

   - **In a rural pasture:** "Quicksand. Any person passing this point will be drowned. By order of the District Council".

   - **In a safari park:** "Elephants Please Stay In Your Car".

Understanding That the Problem May Not Be the CV

Does your CV continue to fail in your job search? Does it seem that no matter how often you revise it – or have experts revise it – it fails to excite interest? Does your CV seem to be an insurmountable problem?

The solution: The factors keeping you from employment may have nothing to do with your CV. A variety of obstacles – from an excess of better-qualified applicants and hiring freezes to interview errors – may be holding you back.

Do you feel like you're wasting your time, fixing your CV and not getting the results you want? If you sense you're chasing your own tail, then it's time to seek a professional opinion. Free advice is available at the Department for Work and Pension's JobCentre Plus. You can find out where your nearest JobCentre Plus is from your local library or on the Web at www.jobcentre plus.gov.uk.

Chapter 23

Ten Tips for Choosing Professional CV Help

In This Chapter

▶ Selecting a personal CV pro

▶ Evaluating online CV builders

*T*o use a professional CV writer or not? That is the question.

"No!" answers one recruiter, "I don't recommend professional services. Write your own. Interviewers have certain expectations from the CV. When a professional writer creates an overblown image that you can't live up to, the interview will crash because the interviewer feels she's been fooled. That wastes everyone's time, including yours."

Yes! Another career adviser says: "Seldom would I recommend that job seekers write their own CVs, regardless of their intelligence or writing ability. They lack objectivity. They often spin their wheels focusing on the wrong things, either over- or under-reacting to their experiences."

These two opinions differ because effectively packaging yourself on paper is not a naturally acquired ability, but a skill you set out to learn.

We come down on the side of the second adviser's opinion – use a pro to write your CV, if you want. You should, however, organise your own material to present to the professional writer just as you organise your taxes to hand over to an accountant. The reason is simple: Organising your information primes your mind for job interviews.

In today's volatile job market where job-change is a growth industry, you, you need a StandOut CV. When you need help producing such a document, talented CV writers are your friends.

Using a CV Pro

In an age of personalisation – personal financial advisers, personal trainers, personal shoppers, personal career coaches – why not a personal CV pro? Prime candidates for CV services are first-time CV writers, people with a chequered history, and people who haven't thought about CVs in years. Follow these tips to choose a personal CV pro wisely.

CV firm or clerical service

Many *clerical services* (CV typing services) do a nice job of word processing your CV for less than £100. A clerical service is a good option if that's all you need.

Most people need more, and clerical services are in a different business than *professional CV firms*. Clerical services sell clerical processes. CV firms sell expertise in fluently articulating what you want to do and the evidence that proves you can do it.

A CV pro knows a great deal about the business of marketing you to employers, has the latest trends and buzzwords on tap, and coaches you around potholes in your history. A CV pro knows how to do online as well as paper CVs.

Signs of reliability

After you've decided to use a CV professional, how can you find a good one? By doing the following:

- ✔ Get a referral from a satisfied customer.
- ✔ Ask for a referral from a local career centre consultant, recruiter, employment agency consultant, or outplacement consultant.

If you're being laid off, inquire within your corporate human resource department. These people often know who does the best work.

The fact that a CV firm has been in business for a long time and has done thousands of CVs is no guarantee of competence – but it's a sign that some customers must like what they do and have spread the word. The acceptance of major credit cards is another indicator of stability. The more established services will often also be members of their professional body – the Recruitment and Employment Confederation (REC). Check with the local

Trading Standards Authority (you can find its address at www.trading
standards.net) for the number of unresolved complaints; if the number
is more than a couple, move on. Merely asking the firm for its interview success rate wastes time – how can the rate be proven?

Free initial consultation

Request a free, brief, get-acquainted meeting. A telephone encounter serves
the purpose, but you may prefer a face-to-face session. Speak not to the boss
or a sales representative, but to the writer. The same firm can have good and
poor writers. Ask the writer what general strategy will be used to deal with
your specific problems. If you don't hear a responsible answer, keep looking.

A responsible answer does not imply discussion of the specifics of how your
CV will be handled. Much like browsing in a shop to look at the merchandise
and then ordering from a discount catalogue, people browse professional CV
services to pick writers' brains and then write their own CVs. CV pros caught
on to this move and developed laryngitis. Moreover, it is irresponsible for a
CV pro to go into detail about how your CV will be handled until more is
known about you. You want to know the general approach – the kinds of
strategies discussed in this book.

Another tip-off is the technology issue. Ask prospective CV writers these
questions:

- ✔ Do you know how to prepare and send CVs by e-mail?
- ✔ Do you know how to add lots of keywords to make CVs searchable?

Positive responses suggest the professional is on the leading edge of technology and, by inference, on the leading edge of the employment industry.

Dependence on forms

Most CV pros ask you to fill out a lengthy, detailed form – much like the one
new patients fill out in a doctor's office. (You can substitute the worksheets
in Chapter 13.) The form is a good start, but it's far from enough. Eliminate
the firms that don't offer dialogue with the writer. The CV pro should interview you to discover your unique experience and strengths. You and the CV
pro are colleagues, sharing a task.

The problem with form dependency is that you may merely get back your
own language prettied up in a flashy format. That's not what you want a CV
pro to do for you.

The cost issue

Prices vary by location, but expect to pay over £200 for a professional service. Never pay by the page – longer isn't better. Find out the rate for branching out from a core CV to create a CV targeted specifically for an individual employer or occupation. Perhaps you'll want to target in several directions, requiring several CVs – can you bargain for a bulk discount? Also find out the charge for minor alterations and the charge for an update two years from now. And ask what extra copies will cost.

Speaking of copies, don't be persuaded by an offer of, say, 100 copies for a discount price. Even if it seems like a bargain, you may want to make changes long before your stock is gone.

Beware of a CV professional who gives lifetime free updating – it's unrealistic to expect quality work when the professional isn't being paid.

Some college and university career services may also be prepared to help former students and pupils. Most of these services offer some form of CV writing assistance free or at a low cost.

Samples

Ask the CV pro to show you samples of his CVs. Look not only at content, but also at production values. Choose a CV pro who has invested in state-of-the-art technology: a good computer and a laser printer. The CV pro doesn't need showy graphics programs or 30 typefaces with 300 fonts. Nor does the CV pro need a high-end copier – copy shops are plentiful. You judge the quality of the content, layout, word processing, paper, and printing.

Taking aim

For maximum impact, you want to target each CV you send out to a specific employer or career field. You can do this either by customising your CV or by using a core CV in tandem with a targeted cover letter.

Make sure your CV pro understands this concept. You need a CV that has "you" written all over it – *your* theme, *your* focus, and *your* measurable achievements – all matched to a career field you want. Skip over those who sell the same template CV over and over.

Avoid CV pros who offer assembly-line presentations, virtually indistinguishable from thousands of others created by the service. Ignore CV pros who plug your information into a fill-in-the-blanks standard form, garnished with prefab statements. Definitely ignore those who try to camouflage the sameness of their work by printing out CVs on A3-sized parchment paper and folding them into a pretentious brief. Employers use these CVs to light their cigars.

Also, be careful of the pro who caters to you instead of to your target audience. A heavyweight CV pro warned me that some CV services cater to their customers, not their customers' customers – with fancy brochures, excessive colour, and whimsical paper.

About certification

There is no professional association for CV writers per se, nor any kind of certification by which you can pick out the qualified from the unqualified. Members of the Recruitment and Employment Confederation are bound to a code of practice, however, which you can find at the association's web site (www.rec.uk.com). Some companies that are not members of REC have chosen to adhere to the standards of practice laid down by the Guidance Council, also known as the National Advisory Council for Careers and Educational Guidance (www.guidancecouncil.com).

Because there is no formal certification you should remember that just because a company isn't an REC member doesn't mean that there's anything wrong with it. The answer is to look at work samples, not certification.

Using Online CV Builders

On the theory that you get what you pay for, you may be wondering how good are the CV builders offered online at virtually all substantial Web sites? Not great, but not bad.

The online CV builders can be very useful with one Big If: *If you remember to think for yourself and not assume the technology will bring to light your most marketable qualities.*

The automated CV builders are designed to benefit the recruiting side of the employment industry, not the job seeking side. So if you use a free CV builder as your chief template offline as well as online, be alert to the need to make amendments. For example, if the template calls for a section on references, delete it. If you prefer to use a skills summary, lose the job objective section if it calls for much more than a position title.

A Poor CV Is No Bargain

Appreciate the hidden costs of a poor CV: A hack job can cost you good job interviews. When the finished product is in your hands, you should be able to say:

- ✔ This is a StandOut CV – it makes me look great! It looks great!
- ✔ This CV doesn't leave out any skills that are targeted to the jobs I'm after.
- ✔ I like reading my CV; it won't put the recruiter to sleep.

Chapter 24

Ten Areas to Check Before Sending Your CV

In This Chapter

▶ Developing a StandOut CV

▶ Making sure your StandOut CV stands out

▶ Eliminating errors in your StandOut CV

*B*efore going public with your CV, make sure it's a StandOut. One way to do this is to evaluate your CV in important areas – things like style and format, language, and so on.

This chapter can help you take a critical look at your CV. Just tick the boxes in front of each item only when your CV meets StandOut standards. When you can honestly check off each item, your CV is ready to go.

Format and Style

❏ You select the best format for your situation. For example, you use reverse chronological if you're looking for a job within the same field; you use functional if you're changing fields. (Chapter 9 explains CV formats.)

❏ If you select a CV alternative, such as a targeted letter, portfolio, or special report, you go all out to make it a hard-hitting, effective document. See Chapters 4 and 16 for details on alternative CVs.

Focus and Fit

❑ You consider the overall impression of your CV. You present yourself as focused – not desperate to accept just any job.

❑ Your CV has a theme. It says what you want to do and proves you have the qualifications to do the work.

❑ Your CV is aimed at the employer you want, or at minimum, at the specific occupation or career field in which you seek employment.

Achievements and Skills

❑ Your skills relate to the skills needed for the job. You cite at least one achievement for each skill.

❑ When you answer a job ad, you make an effort to match skill offered for skill required.

❑ You quantify by using numbers, percentages, or pound and penny amounts for each achievement. You quantify any statement you can. (For ideas on how to quantify your accomplishments, head to Chapter 19.)

❑ You highlight results, not just responsibilities.

Language and Expressions

❑ You use adequate keywords (nouns) to make your CV searchable. You use StandOut words (action verbs) to put vitality in your CV.

❑ You eliminate words that don't directly support your bid for the job you want, as well as such meaningless words and phrases as "CV" or "References available".

❑ You use industry jargon where appropriate, but you translate acronyms, technical jargon, or military lingo into easy-to-understand English.

Contents and Omissions

❑ You begin with either a skills profile or a job objective.

❑ You follow your skills profile or objective with your experience.

❑ You only begin with your education if you're a new graduate with virtually no experience, or if your target job is related to education and training.

❑ You don't list personal information that isn't related to the job you seek, such as marital status, number of children, or height.

❑ Your content supports your objective.

Length and Common Sense

❑ You limit your CV to one or two pages if you're lightly experienced, or two or three pages if you're substantially experienced. These page counts are only guidelines; your CV can be longer if necessary to put your qualifications in the best light. Additionally, your CV can exceed three pages if it's a professional CV.

❑ You don't jam pack a jumble of text on one page because you know it discourages reading.

Appearance: Attached and Paper CVs

❑ Your e-CV in a fully formatted Word document (or equivalent) looks much like a fully formatted paper CV. You use an open layout with white space, minimum one-inch margins, headings in bold typeface or capital letters, bullets, and other low-key graphic elements that make your CV look professional.

❑ Your paper CV is printed on white or eggshell paper, both for a business impression and because it may be scanned into a database.

Appearance: Plain Text CVs

❑ The e-CV that you send to online job sites (Monster, WorkThing, and so on) and to recruiters whose older technology doesn't accept attachments is dispatched in plain text (ASCII) with no graphic frills.

❑ You do not send a *cover note* (very brief cover letters) with your CV to job sites – unless your CV does not match a specific job for which you're applying. In contacting recruiters with older technology, you compose a unified e-mail message that contains a cover note, which is immediately followed by your ASCII CV.

Note an important exception in this era of transition: In responding to a job posting or initiating contact through a company Web site, notice whether the site's applicant portal has a button by the Browse text box. If you see a Browse button, you can assume that your MS Word CV can be attached and that everyone can look at the document on the site. If the site doesn't have a browse button, the company applicant portal probably can't accept attachments. In that case, follow the instructions on the applicant portal. These instructions are likely to tell you to cut and paste your CV or to e-mail it as ASCII text.

❏ You take the correct submission action based on your alertness to the technology.

Sticky Points and Spin

❏ You thoughtfully handle all problem areas, such as grouping irrelevant jobs, as well as long ago, part-time, and temporary jobs.

❏ You account for all the gaps in the timeframe of your CV.

❏ You scour your CV for possible hidden negatives and eliminate them as described in Chapter 12.

Proof-reading and More Proof-reading

❏ Your CV contains no typos, no grammar disasters – no errors of any kind. You not only use your computer's spell-checker, but you also double-check (and triple-check) it.

❏ You also ask others to carefully read it. Typos are hot buttons to many employers – two hiccups and you're history!

Index

FOR DUMMIES®

The easy way to get more done and have more fun

UK EDITIONS

The easiest way to rent out your property for profit

Renting Out Your Property FOR DUMMIES®

Melanie Bien
Robert Griswold

A Reference for the Rest of Us!®

0-7645-7016-1

A state-of-the-art guide for British diabetics

Diabetes FOR DUMMIES®

Dr Sarah Jarvis, GP
Alan L. Rubin, M.D.

A Reference for the Rest of Us!®

0-7645-7019-6

An easy book for a tough game

Rugby Union FOR DUMMIES®

Nick Cain
Greg Growden

A Reference for the Rest of Us!®

0-7645-7020-X

An insider's guide to Formula One™

Formula One Racing FOR DUMMIES®

Jonathan Noble
Mark Hughes

A Reference for the Rest of Us!®

0-7645-7015-3

Britain's past brought right up to date

British History FOR DUMMIES®

Sean Lang

A Reference for the Rest of Us!®

0-7645-7021-8
Due November 2003

The easiest way to pass the ECDL™ 4 exam

ECDL 4 FOR DUMMIES®

Rob Young

A Reference for the Rest of Us!®

0-7645-7022-6
Due February 2004

The easy guide for UK investors

Investing FOR DUMMIES®

Tony Levene

A Reference for the Rest of Us!®

0-7645-7023-4
Due March 2004

Available at bookstores nationwide and online at
www.wileyeurope.com or call 0800 243407 to order direct

WILEY

FOR DUMMIES®

The easy way to get more done and have more fun

COMPUTING & TECHNOLOGY

0-7645-0893-8

0-7645-0838-5

0-7645-1651-5

0-7645-0261-1

0-7645-1664-7

0-7645-0894-6

Also available:

Dreamweaver® MX For Dummies®
0-7645-1630-2

Microsoft Office 2000 For Windows For Dummies®
0-7645-0452-5

Windows XP All-in-One Desk Reference For Dummies®
0-7645-1548-9

Office XP For Dummies®
0-7645-0830-X

Excel 2000 For Windows For Dummies®
0-7645-0446-0

Macromedia® Flash™ MX For Dummies®
0-7645-0895-4

PHP and MySQL™ For Dummies®
0-7645-1650-7

Word 2000 for Windows For Dummies®
0-7645-0448-7

Access 2000 For Windows For Dummies®
0-7645-0444-4

Creating Web Pages All-in-One Desk Reference For Dummies®
0-7645-1542-X

Networking For Dummies®, 6th Edition
0-7645-1677-9

HTML 4 For Dummies®, 4th Edition
0-7645-1995-6

Creating Web Pages For Dummies®, 6th Edition
0-7645-1643-4

Upgrading and Fixing PCs 1 Dummies®, 6th Edition
0-7645-1665-5

Photoshop® Elements 2 Fo Dummies®
0-7645-1675-2

Networking For Dummies® 5th Edition
0-7645-0772-9

Red Hat Linux 7.3 For Dummies®
0-7645-1545-4

Microsoft Windows Me Fo Dummies®, Millennium Edition
0-7645-0735-4

Troubleshooting Your PC Fe Dummies®
0-7645-1669-8

Macs® For Dummies®, 7th Edition
0-7645-0703-6

Linux For Dummies, 4th Edition
0-7645-1660-4

VBA For Dummies®, 3rd Edition
0-7645-0856-3

C# For Dummies®
0-7645-0814-8

Web Design For Dummies®
0-7645-0823-7

PMP Certification For Dummies®
0-7645-2451-8

Excel 2002 For Dummies®
0-7645-0822-9

Dreamweaver® 4 For Dummies®
0-7645-0801-6

Available at bookstores nationwide and online at
www.wileyeurope.com or call 0800 243407 to order direct

WILEY

FOR DUMMIES

The easy way to get more done and have more fun

GENERAL INTEREST & HOBBIES

Guitar FOR DUMMIES
0-7645-5106-X

Spanish FOR DUMMIES
0-7645-5194-9

French FOR DUMMIES
0-7645-5193-0

Italian FOR DUMMIES
0-7645-5196-5

Psychology FOR DUMMIES
0-7645-5434-4

Managing FOR DUMMIES
0-7645-1771-6

Also available:

Japanese For Dummies®
0-7645-5429-8

Architecture For Dummies®
0-7645-5396-8

Rock Guitar For Dummies®
0-7645-5356-9

Anatomy and Physiology For Dummies®
0-7645-5422-0

German For Dummies®
0-7645-5195-7

Weight Training For Dummies®, 2nd Edition
0-7645-5168-X

Project Management For Dummies®
0-7645-5283-X

Piano For Dummies®
0-7645-5105-1

Latin For Dummies®
0-7645-5431-X

Songwriting For Dummies®
0-7645-5404-2

Marketing For Dummies®
1-5688-4699-1

Parenting For Dummies®
2nd Edition
0-7645-5418-2

Fitness For Dummies®
2nd Edition
0-7645-5167-1

Religion For Dummies®
0-7645-5264-3

Selling For Dummies®
2nd Edition
0-7645-5363-1

Improving Your Memory For Dummies®
0-7645-5435-2

Islam For Dummies®
0-7645-5503-0

Golf For Dummies®
2nd Edition
0-7645-5146-9

Stock Investing For Dummies®
0-7645-5411-5

The Complete MBA For Dummies®
0-7645-5204-X

Astronomy For Dummies®
0-7645-5155-8

Customer Service For Dummies®, 2nd Edition
0-7645-5209-0

Mythology For Dummies®
0-7645-5432-8

Pilates For Dummies®
0-7645-5397-6

Managing Teams For Dummies®
0-7645-5408-5

Screenwriting For Dummies®
0-7645-5486-7

Drawing For Dummies®
0-7645-5476-X

Controlling Cholesterol For Dummies®
0-7645-5440-9

Martial Arts For Dummies®
0-7645-5358-5

Diabetes For Dummies®
0-7645-5154-X

Wine For Dummies®
2nd Edition
0-7645-5114-0

Yoga For Dummies®
0-7645-5117-5

Drums For Dummies®
0-7645-5357-7

Available at bookstores nationwide and online at
www.wileyeurope.com or call 0800 243407 to order direct

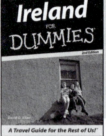

FOR DUMMIES®

The easy way to get more done and have more fun

TRAVEL

  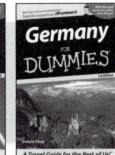

Walt Disney World & Orlando
For Dummies
0-7645-3875-6

Germany For Dummies
0-7645-5478-6

Ireland For Dummies
0-7645-5455-7

Spain For Dummies
0-7645-5495-6

New York City For Dummies
0-7645-5451-4

Scotland For Dummies
0-7645-5477-8

 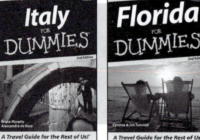

Paris For Dummies
0-7645-5494-8

Italy For Dummies
0-7645-5453-0

Florida For Dummies
0-7645-1979-4

Also available:

Alaska For Dummies®
1st Edition
0-7645-1761-9

Hawaii For Dummies®
2nd Edition
0-7645-5438-7

Arizona For Dummies®
2nd Edition
0-7645-5484-0

California For Dummies®
2nd Edition
0-7645-5449-2

Boston For Dummies®
2nd Edition
0-7645-5491-3

New Orleans For Dummies®
2nd Edition
0-7645-5454-9

Las Vegas For Dummies®
2nd Edition
0-7645-5448-4

Los Angeles and Disneyland
For Dummies® 1st Edition
0-7645-6611-3

America's National Parks For
Dummies® 2nd Edition
0-7645-5493-X

San Francisco For Dummies®
2nd Edition
0-7645-5450-6

Europe For Dummies®
2nd Edition
0-7645-5456-5

Mexico's Beach Resorts For
Dummies® 1st Edition
0-7645-6262-2

Honeymoon Vacations For
Dummies® 1st Edition
0-7645-6313-0

Bahamas For Dummies®
2nd Edition
0-7645-5442-5

Caribbean For Dummies®
2nd Edition
0-7645-5445-X

France For Dummies®
2nd Edition
0-7645-2542-5

Maui For Dummies®
0-7645-5479-4

Chicago For Dummies®
2nd Edition
0-7645-2541-7

Vancouver & Victoria For
Dummies® 2nd Edition
0-7645-3874-8

Available at bookstores nationwide and online at
www.wileyeurope.com or call 0800 243407 to order direct

WILEY